RELIGION AND ITS
NEW TESTAMENT
EXPRESSION

RELIGION AND ITS NEW TESTAMENT EXPRESSION

By

H. BULCOCK

M.A., B.D.

Lectures Delivered to the
Liverpool Board of Biblical Studies

New York
THE MACMILLAN COMPANY
1929

MADE AND PRINTED IN GREAT BRITAIN BY
UNWIN BROTHERS LIMITED, LONDON AND WOKING

FOREWORD

THESE studies are chiefly intended for the general thoughtful reader; technicalities have been avoided as much as possible, and an attempt has been made to present the subjects as simply as their nature will allow. Some of the matter has appeared in *The Congregational Review* and *The Holborn Review*, and a fuller treatment of Chapters XV and XVI is given in a previous study, *The Passing and the Permanent in Saint Paul*. The book has been written with the consciousness of various religious problems felt by the modern mind, and the author has felt the need of approaching many of his themes from perhaps unfamiliar angles. He trusts, however, that his work may be found, in the broad sense, evangelical and helpful to faith.

CONTENTS

PART I

CHAPTER I

The Scriptures are an expression rather than an ultimate source of Religion. The values of a study of historical religion. A method of interpreting ancient faith. The question of infallibility. The Church. The Scriptures. The words of Christ. The ultimate authority in life, Nature, experience. Theology as a Science of Religion, and Revelation as Religious Discovery. Religious changes not due to uncertainty but to wider certainty. The values of Jesus Christ in accordance with these principles.

CHAPTER II

The claim that the basis of Faith lies in certain characteristic intuitions raises the problem of the nature of intuition. Two types of instincts: Vitalistic, "Lapsed intelligence." Relation to religious feeling. The claim for a sexual origin of religious consciousness. Fear and Religion. Dr. McDougall's theory of compounded elements. Criticisms. Primitive Spiritualism and Religion. Religion is the outcome of a fundamental Mysticism. Cosmic and Religious Consciousness.

CHAPTER III

The "matter of intuition" in philosophy. Descartes's *cogito ergo sum*. Locke's denial of Innate Ideas is not a denial of intuition. Kant shows the insufficiency of current theistic arguments to prove God. Jacobi's claim for an intuition of God. Hegel's criticism of Jacobi does not imply a denial of intuition, but a denial of its sufficiency for an adequate appreciation of the Absolute. The idea of the Absolute derived from cosmic consciousness. Max Müller's claim for a direct perception of the Infinite. The intuition of the Infinite is parallel to perceptions of the finites.

CHAPTER IV

The fundamental paradox of existence. Being and Becoming. The One and the Many. Eternity and Time. The idea of Analysis. The approximation in Becoming to Being. Mysticism is the method proper to the mode of Being; finite perception proper to the mode of Becoming. True Mysticism is cosmic consciousness. Its religious significance. Features of the revelation of Mysticism: (*a*) The essential unity of life; (*b*) optimism; (*c*) communion with deity; (*d*) social solidarity; (*e*) ethical harmonies; (*f*) newness of life; (*g*) sense of immortality.

CHAPTER V

CHAPTER VI

CHAPTER VII

PART II

CHAPTER VIII

set New Testament thought in historical perspective. Rejection of "Christ-myth" theory, but grave historical problems of Gospels remain. Evidences of elaboration, doctrinal, miraculous, ecclesiastical, apocalyptic. We must treat the Scriptures as we would any other ancient writing, and read them in the light of universal experience. The clearness of the spiritual teaching of Jesus.

CHAPTER IX

Dependence upon Mark for the general framework of events. The question of Mark's eye-witness. His mentality. Plain, non-mystical, prosaic in his thinking, attracted by externals, inadequate spiritual appreciation of Jesus. Non-critical as a historian. His rough artistry. Love of miracle and apocalypse. Matthew's Gospel a "compromise" work for the Jewish and Gentile sections of the Antioch Church. The author of our present "Matthew's Gospel" not an eye-witness. Luke's Gospel an attempt to improve on Mark's. But Luke is not an eye-witness. He uses Mark, and there are no "we" sections in the Third Gospel. The Fourth Gospel sets in a framework, largely Marcan, a spiritual and mystic tradition. Although this is elaborated in view of the history and experiences of the Early Church, its origin may have been in mystic sayings of the historical Jesus to which Mark was not sensitive. The impression from the work of uneven spiritual genius, as if two minds were being expressed, the one that of a spiritual mystic, the other that of a sacramentalist and theologian. This suggests that the author is dealing with a tradition which he himself would not have created. Does this mystic tradition go back to the historical Jesus?

CHAPTER X

The inquiry confined to those aspects which bear upon the questions of New Testament perspective and development and the nature and limits of Christ's claims. The Infancy stories. The Baptism and Temptation. Miracles of Healing. Spiritual significance of the miraculous. The Messianic claim. Wrede. Burkitt. Schmiedel. The suggestion that the Messianic claim arose gradually out of the transformation of the current ideas of the Messianic Kingdom. The date of the dawning of the Messianic consciousness in the mind of Jesus. The historical causes of Christ's death. The Resurrection tradition. The question of its relation to later New Testament speculation and to living faith.

CHAPTER XI

Jesus came "to open out the choked-up wells of human intuition." His credential and authority in His spiritual appeal to men of all ages and classes. His world-appeal lies in His fidelity to the universal and eternal elements in religion. The features of religious Mysticism in the authentic teaching of Jesus. The inwardness of morality and faith. The honouring of life—natural sacramentalism. Stress on communion with the Father. Significant features of the Lord's Prayer. Optimism and Providence. Eternal and immortal life.

CHAPTER XII

CHAPTER XIII

CHAPTER XIV

CHAPTER XV

Church need not imply a specific *Kyrios* doctrine in the Hellenistic sense. Simple beliefs of the Primitive Community. Adoptionist view of Christ. Apocalyptic stress. The expectation of an Enochian Son of Man could only be satisfied by a Second Coming. Twofold idea of salvation: (*a*) moral, (*b*) apocalyptic. Undefined propitiatory values in the death of Jesus. The Resurrection a credential Messianic miracle but not part of a mystic operation, as with Paul. Non-mystical views of Baptism and the Church Meal. The Parousial hope, central in this period, though illusive and dangerous, was significant of man's fundamental intuition of the Eternal Goodness.

CHAPTER XVI

Features of a further development. Christ as apocalyptic Enochian Son of Man finds a Hellenistic translation. He becomes the mediating Logos and functions as a Mystery *Kyrios*. Mystic views of Baptism and the Church Meal. A Mystery "gnosis" in Christianity. Sacramentalism. The Two Worlds. Date of this development. Birth of Paulinism as a distinctive system at Ephesus. Factors—the need of defining and relating vague ideas brought together by the Messianic apologetic. Germs of Hellenistic thought from Paul's early days. The Galatian controversy. Sympathetic relations with the Asiarchs. Suggested influence of Apollos on Paul's thought. Alexandrianism. The Logos. "Wisdom" in Jewish literature. Philo's double idea of Mediatorship. The Mysteries and their Christian parallels. Communion with the Divine in Christian experience. The theologies of Redemption, though theosophic in form, testify to the fundamental consciousness of the Love of God. Other characteristics of Mysticism found in Paulinism.

CHAPTER XVII

Is Christ the "focus" of a unified cosmos or a Mediator of a divided universe? Origin of the idea of Mediatorship and its fundamental defects. (*a*) The World Soul. The "Fiery Wisdom" of Heraclitus. The soul an aspect of substance, although this view is to be distinguished from the doctrine of "soul" as mere "attunement." Tendency to regard the World Soul as something added to dead matter. Strife and Love (Empedocles) and Nous (Anaxagoras) are additions to substance. (*b*) The Two Worlds. The Socratic and Platonic doctrine. Its difficulties. Suggested source in the paradox of Being and Becoming. The two worlds are two aspects of the one world. Plato's mediating World Soul between the two worlds (Timaeus). Philo's use of Plato's myth. The mediating Logos. Aristotle's wavering challenge to separability. Stoicism. The Gnostic Demiurge. The doctrine of Emanations (Plotinus) and its difficulties.

CHAPTER XVIII

Christological problems arising out of the Johannine idea of the Two Worlds and the mediating Logos. The Paraclete. Similarity to the idea of Emanations. Philonic precedent. The Logos in the

CHAPTER XIX

PART I

CHAPTER I

THE SOURCE OF RELIGIOUS KNOWLEDGE

I

It may seem a certain inversion of the generally accepted order to begin with the universal elements of religion, and from them to work back to their New Testament expression. We have accustomed ourselves to think of the Scriptures as the authority for our religious knowledge, bearing the seeds which, when developed, may become universal religion, whereas in our study we are suggesting a wider, primary source of religious knowledge, from which our Scriptures are the outcome. But this point of view seems forced upon us by a profounder knowledge of our Scriptures and by a deeper appreciation of the seat of authority in religion. In the early days of Biblical criticism Henry Drummond, the Scotch evangelist, without any abatement of his evangelical ardour, met the problems of faith raised by the new methods of Scriptural interpretation by claiming that "Religion does not come out of the Bible; the Bible comes out of Religion." Walt Whitman indicated the same truth by saying—

We consider Bibles and religion divine. I do not say that they are not divine;
I say that they have all grown out of you, and may grow out of you still.

Our claim, then, is that all Scriptures and Faiths have really their foundation in the intuitions and experiences of the human soul, and must be explained and confirmed by a return to the region of personality. God has first written His Name on the fleshly tablets of men's hearts, and man has copied it as he could on the external tables of stone. In broken terms of the thought and knowledge of his own day he has borne witness to his sense of worship, God-consciousness, duty and hope. Later generations have tended to look upon this outward projection of faith as the external fount of religion, rather than the expression of a religion which had its real source in the ever-flowing wells of divine intuition in human souls. In degenerate periods of religion men have been so much concerned with the imperfectly carved tables of stone that they have undervalued the eternal revelation of the heart from which faith arose, and from which it can still spring. Even, also, as vital religion arose from the soul, so it can be confirmed in the soul. Essential religion will ever be a matter of experience, but not of reliance on unconfirmable statement.

II

The study of historical religion is still required to give a sufficiently wide base for our knowledge of the will of God, which is partly revealed in age-long experience of social order and moral law. We must avoid the perils of subjectivism and limited experience. We need the guidance and suggestion of the great souls of the race in order to discover our own souls and their revelation. Again, there is inspirational value in regarding the noble lives of the past; nor can we cut off our present faith from the stages which led up to it without violence to that sentiment and association which play no small part in faith and its potency. We should be infinitely poorer if we were ignorant of the beginnings of historical Christianity, and especially of the life of our Lord, even though His influence might in large measure have been felt by us, transmitted through a succession of Christian personalities, without the origin of their influence being actually known by us. The history of Christ in the flesh is precious to us, but even in His case we find the religious significance of the Gospels in those events which have relation to eternal principles and processes, and are illustrative of moral and spiritual law continually in operation, rather than in traditions of abnormalities, which isolate Him from the continuous moral and spiritual revelation and action of God. The past has its value for us only in as far as it becomes intelligible in the present and "tallies" with it. The faith of history is helpful only in proportion as it corresponds with the faith of experience and enables us to read the spiritual signs of our own times.

III

This view of the psychological origin of doctrines suggests a method of interpreting the ancient forms of faith so as to yield an eternal spiritual meaning and value. Behind the local and temporary forms of historic faith can be traced fundamental spiritual intuitions of abiding worth. The fact that the ancient forms of faith have been found inspirational indicates that in some degree they have expressed eternal truths and at some point have touched living experience. Our task is to trace, as we can, that vital origin of eternal truth, the primary experience finding answer in later experiences of men's souls. The expectation of the Second Advent, regarded as a literal event in history, has been disappointing and misleading, but it remains significant if regarded as a "projection" of man's unconquerable hope that the creation moves to a divine event, and that, despite present woes and mystery, the universe is ultimately sound. The doctrines of Salvation, set as they are in first-century forms, provided by Leviticism and Gnosticism, may be unconvincing for us, and yet they bear witness to a sense of the love of God which "will not let us go," and to a spiritual experience of transformation through the life, spirit and teaching of Jesus of Nazareth. There is significance in all forms of worship, sacrifice and hope which have found expression in the world, however crude and foolish some of these may now seem to be. The forms may change and fail, and a superficial, sceptical world may mock at all this; but wiser men will find meaning in all the broken faiths, the discredited theories, the passing religions, the discarded gods, the outgrown creeds. There is truth even in the unscientific guesses made to explain reality, for they bear witness to a reality to be explained. Many of our doctrinal forms may not be scientifically exact, philosophically sound, nor intellectually satisfying, but the reality of spiritual hopes, cravings and experiences lies behind them, and we may come nearer to truth by believing, rather than rejecting, even imperfect doctrines which have made their spiritual appeal and answered something in the human heart from generation to generation.

We need to distinguish between two kinds of doctrines. With a doctrine of *inference*, all will depend upon the preciseness, accuracy and soundness of everything which enters into the argument; with doctrines of *intuition* the case is different. The process here is not that of arguing out truth from data, but the witness to a datum by suggestion and symbol. The difference is similar to that between scientific philosophy and impressionist poetry. At the same time, there are dangers in symbolic doctrine, if its nature is not recognised as symbolic. Symbolic theology may come to be a hindrance to closer and more scientific expressions of truth; it may create unnecessary misunderstandings with schools using other mental symbols of faith; or in the failure of a particular symbolic form of theology, faith itself may seem to be discredited. There is constant need, therefore, of seeking the inwardness of our doctrines and of the reference of faith to the fundamental intuitions and experiences of the human soul, in which we believe all forms of vital doctrine have had their origin, and where the spiritual confirmation of their inner truth may ever be found. Adopting the method of interpretation suggested, seeking the kernel of experience beneath the forms of historic doctrine, we may work back from a mass of theological conceptions, perhaps bewildering

and unappealing, which in the passage of time and the
changes of thought may be coming to hamper rather than
help religion, to a few simple and supporting master-truths
found in the Holy of Holies of the human soul.

IV. THE SEAT OF AUTHORITY IN RELIGION

Although we may realise that all Scriptures have really
their foundation in universal religious consciousness, in the
intuitions and experiences of the human soul, and must
be explained and confirmed by a return to that region of
personality, yet there is a sense in which we may still speak
of the Scriptures, and even of the Church, as "authorities"
in religion, just as we speak of eminent scientists as "authorities" in science, or of universities as "authorities" in general
knowledge. But we must make clear in our own minds the
two senses in which the word "authority" can be used.
(a) *The "Authority" of Nature.*—We may use the term Authority
as indicating the ultimate foundations of knowledge, the
basis of belief lying in the very foundations of reality, the
elementary experience around which theories are formed,
the starting-point of speculation, that which in the constitution of things compels us to think in one way rather than in
another, and from time to time determines and corrects all
our theorisings and speculations. This is the "matter of
intuition," the "authority" in Nature and life which becomes
known to us in observation and experience. We may desig-
nate this as the Authority of Nature. (b) *The Authority of
Interpretation.*—But we are compelled to express this Authority
of Nature in intellectual terms, just as we come to state the
phenomena of Nature in terms of scientific knowledge.
Physical phenomena must find expression in the sciences of
physics, chemistry and the like, and the conception of
"Authority" in a further sense begins to form—the Authority
of Interpretation. Interpretation, theorising, speculation,
have a varying quality; they are true to the facts of Nature in

different degrees, and change from time to time as the facts of Nature become more fully known and understood. All this is in contrast to the absolute fixity of law and Nature itself. Further, with this variety of interpretation, certain geniuses and experts and institutions will stand out as "authorities," and their judgments, decisions and guidings will be in some measure respected and accepted by ordinary men. In a world where all men cannot be geniuses and experts, and much must be taken on the word of those who are, the need of such "authorities" is obvious. Nevertheless, we must also realise the limitations of such authorities. They are not absolutely infallible, and their pronouncements are necessarily modified by the slow growth of knowledge. Their value and their continued influence and recognition among men depend upon their fidelity to Nature, correspondence with reality, and their adequacy to cover the facts of experience. We will refuse in the long run to respect universities the teachings of which are felt to be obsolete, works of learning which fail to take account of new discoveries, "authorities" whose pronouncements are found discredited by failure to explain the facts of existence. The fundamental "authority" lies in Nature itself, and from this all other authorities, in the secondary sense, must derive all the real authority they possess.

V

Another conception of "authority" has emerged historically, which seems, however, to be without intellectual soundness or justification. That is the idea of an external authority, of the nature of "interpretation," but imparted miraculously and possessing the qualities of finality and infallibility. We have such claims for Church and Scriptures. But when these claims are examined, we are driven back to the criterion of the Authority of Nature. If in abstract theory an infallible Church can be postulated, we are forced to ask what substantiates the claim. If against an infallible Romanism an infallible Mohammedanism makes a counter-claim, who shall fairly settle the rival infallibilities, and on what grounds? We stand in need of some further criterion than that of the self-claim of a Church or Faith. The test must be that of the Authority of Nature, Life, Experience. If it be claimed that "the Church is infallible," we must ask what constitutes the "Church." Why should Rome or High Churchism have advantage, say, over Quakerism? The resort to Apostolic Succession and Apostolic Authority is only a restating of the claim, but not an escape from the funda-mental problem. There may be suggestive value in the pronouncements of a Church, inasmuch as these may be the expression of a collective judgment, but such judgment is clearly neither infallible nor ultimate. The variation and diversity of judgment give rise to further questions: *Why* should the judgment of one branch of the Church be deemed superior to that of another? Or why should we select a certain period of the Church, the first, the fourth, the sixteenth, or the twentieth century, and claim that the pronouncements of the Church in such a period have an authority superior to those of the Church in some other age? They may have, but if so, why? We are forced back to a more ultimate court of appeal—the Authority of Nature.

VI

If we appeal from the Church to the Scriptures, we have not escaped our difficulties. It becomes more and more clear with a scientific reading of the Scriptures that we cannot treat them as an infallible law book or compendium of doc-trines. The Bible exhibits a process of growth; it speaks with many voices; it reveals many levels of development; there are spiritual hills and valleys. No Christian claims that the Old Testament is on quite the same level as the New. There are writings of gold and "epistles of straw," to use Luther's famous phrase. But *why* should we say so? Why pick out certain sections and claim for them a higher authority than that of others, or a greater religious value? What is the principle of discrimination? Where lies that further court of appeal to which we are all constantly referring in our interpretations and valuations of Scripture?

VII

Is this to be found in the words of Christ? Have we not realised in our experiences of soul and our observations of living that He has the words of eternal life? But this very statement presupposes the existence of another criterion—namely, something in life itself, something in the soul itself. We accept Christ as our Guide and Teacher, because what He says rings true to experience and to our deepest moods. Deep answers to deep. We have acknowledged the existence of a further court of authority, by which we test even the words of Christ Himself. He holds us because He has interpreted that more ultimate authority so closely and faithfully in His teaching.

By realising this fact we save ourselves from several problems which arise from what we now know of the nature of the Gospels. (*a*) If we were merely making a mechanical authority of the words of Christ, if we were making His words in their literality ultimate in themselves rather than throwing us back on the authority which lies in experience, human nature and human life itself, how should we face the fact that even in the first three Gospels there are sections which look like interpolations; for example, passages found in the apocalyptic chapter of Mark, which we should very much hesitate to attribute, at any rate, in their literal New Testament form, to a soul with so keen a spiritual insight as that of Jesus? Or there are sayings which are obviously not merely reported, but partially, and sometimes wrongly, interpreted as well. The "sign of Jonah" in the more probable contexts is the simple preaching which brought about repentance, set in contrast to miracles and signs, such as the Pharisees were seeking from Jesus. Our Lord was evidently trying to show men that the credential of true prophetic teaching was in its own spiritual and ethical appeal. But in another context the "sign of Jonah" is presented, apparently still in the words of Jesus, in relation to the miracle of the Resurrection! Or what must be said of the problem of the Fourth Gospel? The writer seems to have paraphrased, expanded and interpreted in his own free style the *logia* of Jesus, and yet to have set all this within the formula "Jesus saith." Once more it is evident that Jesus often said things with a touch of exaggeration in order to strike the imagination of His popular audiences. His very literary style forbids us taking every saying literally. He seems to have presented many of His thoughts cryptically in order to make men think out His meaning. "We must read the Sermon on the Mount with common sense." But this is an appeal beyond the mere words to something else!

VIII

These are hints at problems which are serious and acute if we regard the words of Christ as ultimate in themselves and without reference to further criteria lying in Nature, life and experience. But if we acknowledge these further criteria of Nature in the broad sense as ultimate, all these other "authorities" of Church and Scripture and the words of Christ fall into their rightful and necessary place. They help us in varying degrees to find the ultimate authority of reality lying in Nature and in the soul. We may refer again to the analogy of science. The authority for the science of electricity is in Nature itself. Its laws are revealed in natural phenomena directly perceived or perceivable by ordinary persons. Certain individuals may be more skilled than others in noting and relating these phenomena; they may point out to others where law is revealing itself, and suggest experiments which others may confirm. These more discerning folk—"authorities" in science—really send us back to Nature itself. Copernicus, Newton, Franklin, Darwin owe whatever authority they possess to the confirmable correspondence between their teaching and Nature itself. So in religion. The Church, the Scriptures, the masters of the spiritual life, the thinkers who have set forth philosophies of religion, may help us to discern the deep things of faith and the right rules of action. The Church is an authority for us inasmuch as it offers the help of collective judgments and the experiences of centuries. It is a shallow mind which will disregard the suggestiveness of the accumulated spiritual wealth of the historic Church. There is a similar value in the Scriptures. They do not mechanically command, but they suggest. They also carry with them the credential of the fact that for thousands of years they have helped men and women to find their souls and live out their best lives. But the ultimate criterion, the final seat of authority, is in that Life in which God has written His law and manifested His nature.

IX

Theology, then, becomes a Science of Religion, and Revelation is another name for Religious Discovery. This realisation need not disturb our faith. Knowledge gained by religious discovery is no less a gift from God than if a miracle book had been dropped from the skies, for both the data and the faculty of man to appreciate the significance of the data come from God. Nor do we abolish the supernatural, for we interpret this not as the unnatural, but as the natural needing God for its ultimate basis and explanation. Supernatural Religion is not inconsistent with Natural Theology.

Further, if it should be objected that even judgments based on the feelings of the heart and the observations of human life are far from being unanimous among men, we can answer that we are here working with methods which have given us that other knowledge of life which we feel to be in general reliable. We do not claim finality and infallibility for our scientific knowledge, but we feel that we are never out of touch with realities, and that we are employing methods which will in the long run correct our errors. It is no small gain if we can find for religious knowledge a basis as satisfactory and reliable as that which we have for general scientific knowledge. The fact of change in our theories, scientific and religious, rightly regarded, does not signify precariousness and uncertainty of knowledge. The very reason why we give up an old theory in science in favour of a new is that we have new facts which we need to explain. It is *a widening certainty* which leads to change and gives to thought its very appearance of uncertainty. We know something, or we should have no grounds for changing our knowledge. So faith changes its forms, not because religion is uncertain, but because of growing knowledge based on wider and clearer certitude. The alternative, cherished by infallibilists and obscurantists, is the fixity of stagnation, a dead faith which has ceased to live and grow.

We recognise, then, a wide field of revelation—the history of the world, spelling out the moral laws of God; the implications of science and philosophy; spiritual biographies; personal experience; cosmic intuitions traceable under a score of religious systems; universal instincts of faith; the soul's yearning for larger life; the unconquerable sense of immortality; the mystic's intuition of the Infinite and of Eternal Goodness; the instinct for prayer; the appreciation of the good and worthy and true when it emerges; the spiritual sense of Communion with the Over-Soul; the consciousness of sin. Religion has its deep roots in human personality, life and experience. Essential Christianity is a matter of experience. Christianity has always been greatest and most appealing when it has interpreted itself in terms of confirmable life; it has been most uncertain and unconvincing, most liable to abuses and priestly exploitations, when it has gone beyond the strict limits of human experience. We accept the guiding teachings of Jesus of Nazareth, and preach Him as Lord and Master in full accordance with these principles laid down. He has led men to discover their souls and to find the springs of living water flowing from their own personalities. We seek for His words the confirmations of Christian living. And when men have gone deep in their souls and made trial of the heart to reveal the infinite and eternal things of God, they have found themselves at the feet of Christ, hailing Him as the Life, the Truth, the Way.

CHAPTER II

THE NATURE OF RELIGIOUS CONSCIOUSNESS

I

WE suggest, then, that the basis of faith must be sought in life and experience, and chiefly in certain characteristic intuitions. Religion in its historic forms has arisen from a religious consciousness, and still arises from this experience. But here we encounter certain radical questions: What is the value of this consciousness? Can we account for it in ways which challenge its validity as a distinctive and fundamental experience? Has so-called "religious consciousness" been derived in some way from other forms of consciousness? We have grown somewhat sceptical of "intuitions" and suspicious of their apparent feature of "immediacy," because ideas which seem to come to us with compelling force and without any mediate intellectual process of which we are aware, and which therefore seem primary, fundamental and infallible, may turn out to have considerable intellectual histories, either in the race-mind or even in the mind of the individual who experiences such "intuitions." The mind seems to do much of its work subliminally. Hints given from waking life develop "behind the veil." It is a common experience to find an uprush of ideas coming to us, as it were, ready-made, and possibly with emotional accompaniments which stamp them for the non-critical, as divine "revelation." But such "revelations" turn out to have some relation with previous thoughts and feelings. Somewhere the stream can be traced before it began its subterranean course. "It is not necessary," says Dr. Rufus Jones (*Encyclopaedia of Religion and Ethics*, vol. 9, p. 84), "to conclude that 'oracular communications' or mysterious information or ideas with

novelty of content come into the world through the secret
door of mystical openings. 'Ideas' and 'communications'
and 'information' prove always when they are examined to
have a historical background." We must also consider the
possibility of telepathy operating subliminally and disguising
for the receiving subject the essentially mediate nature of
such revelation. The revealed idea may have its origin, not
in infallible heavens, but in another finite mind, and be
transmitted telepathically to the mind of the receiver; or
traditions imparted to us at an early age may come to us
later with an apparent "immediacy" and compelling force,
and yet these traditions are only hardened human opinions
which owe their strength for us to accidental circumstances
of early training or sentimental associations.

II

We must consider also whether religious consciousness can
be explained as due to perversion or wrong interpretation of
feelings which have their real origin in "non-religious"
instincts. "Instincts" may apparently be of two classes:
(a) One is attracted to Bergson's suggestion that instinct is
a form alternative to intellect, expressing a vitalism wider
than either. The brain is not the creator of mental life, but
rather transmits for special purposes, and consequently limits
to certain narrowed forms, a larger mental life lying, as
it were, in the background. True instinct is not intelligence
grown automatic—it is another course which the vitalistic
activity has taken. Each expression has its own characteristics.
Intellect gives us the relations of things, hesitates, acts
imperfectly, but has a wider field. Instinct has greater initial
skill, but works with a more limited range. We do not find
the perfecting of the two moods in a single type, although we
find them existing side by side. Where intellect develops,
instinct weakens. McDougall (*Body and Mind*, p. 373)
suggests that with the growth of local organs and nerve

centres, the vital principle tends to exhibit the phenomenon of intellectual consciousness. In the absence of the locally developed organism the vital principle works as "instinct" in a more distributed form. Possibly the general urgings of religion towards worship or communion may be regarded as instinctive in this sense.

(b) But certain urgings which we call "instincts" seem to be akin in their nature to "habit" and to have been developed from race-needs and race-experiences. It is more than doubtful whether this explains all forms of instinct, and the theory involves the acceptance of a widely challenged Lamarckian basis. This theory of "lapsed intelligence" suggests that actions originally intelligent form into habits and grow automatic. We may compare learning to walk or to play the piano, in our individual life. In the course of generations these processes become ingrained in the race-constitution and are regarded as "instincts." Thus Schneider (*Der menschliche Wille*) explains our instinctive fear in the dark as due to the dangers which beset our forefathers living in an age of insecurity when wild animals and robbers were abroad at night. Children's games may have their origin in primitive human customs, or the mutilation of insects or the search for eggs may, it is suggested, be old food-hunting habits persisting in children's "instincts." Domesticated animals seem to show new instincts after some generations, e.g. shepherd dogs run round rather than at a flock of sheep, although it is hard to eliminate imitation as a factor in such cases.

The whole theory, as we have said, rests upon the Lamarckian view that acquired characteristics can be transmitted. This view has received the strong challenge of the Neo-Darwinians led by Weismann, who have denied that such a process can take place "chiefly because it seems impossible that individual experiences should impress themselves on the structure of the germ-plasm." But it has been suggested by McDougall and others that the structure of the germ-plasm may not be the only link between the generations. If we can conceive a psychical as well as a physical factor in the process of transmission, the objection against the Lamarckian principle loses weight, and we are free to accept a theory of the partial transmission of the effects of experience from one generation to another. "Such modification," says McDougall (*Body and Mind*, p. 378), "would be least in respect to characters which have long been established in the race and are least susceptible to modification in the individual by psycho-physical activities (especially bodily characteristics and the fundamental forms of psychical activities). It would be greatest in respect to more recently acquired mental characteristics which are the peculiar property of man, and it is just these characters (mathematical, musical, artistic, and the capacity for sustained intellectual and mental effort) which seem to exhibit the clearest indications of the effects of experience and psychical effort, cumulative from generation to generation." It must be stressed that we are not claiming that this theory of "lapsed intelligence" gives a complete explanation of instinct, but it may be held (providing that we take the Lamarckian view) side by side with Bergson's vitalistic explanation noted above, to explain similar though not identical phenomena; and this second class of "instinctive" impulses may cover certain "religious" sympathies and proclivities which may be of an acquired character, originating in social circumstances which in the race's evolution have passed away, while the race-habits of thought and impulse to which they gave rise continue to persist. For example, from the old habits of mind connected with magic religions we may inherit tendencies inclining us to superstitions in faith which are quite out of harmony with the general rationalising spirit of our own times. We may inherit feelings connected with certain forms of guilt, or the need of an intercessor, or conceptions of monarchical deity, or miracles or sacramental action, which do not belong to our age and yet make a vague appeal to large bodies of people.

The well-marked tendency to mediaeval thoughts and practices in religion may largely be due to a race inheritance from a bygone generation embedded in our present religious consciousness. But these are not primary elements in religion, nor does this process explain a good many features that seem central and fundamental in religious consciousness—for example, the cosmic consciousness involved in religion, the sense of the Eternal and Infinite.

III

Again, the religious consciousness has been traced to a sexual origin. Shroeder, for example, argues that "all religion in its beginning is a mere misrepresentation of sex-ecstasy, and the religion of to-day is only the essentially unchanged evolutionary product of psycho-sexual perversion" (quoted by Selbie, *The Psychology of Religion*, p. 11). A sexual instinct, unsatisfied in its procreative function, gives rise to the idea of a God to be loved. Love to God is a perversion of a "mating-love." Religious awakening is often at the age of the awakening of the sex-consciousness. There are abundant sex-associations with the more primitive religious cults. Psycho-synthesists (the psycho-analysts who, after pulling the psyche to pieces, seek to recompose it) claim that the treatment of undesirable sexual impulses is to divert or sublimate them into religious forms.

On all this one may comment that the association of sexuality with primitive cults would seem more reasonably attributable to "assimilative magic." The earth must be fertilised by some associated act of fertilisation. Simultaneous quickenings of personality at an adolescent age do not imply that the religious awakening is due to a sexual one. The claim for "sublimation" is a doubtful one. The curing of sexual impulse by the introduction of creative or religious interests seems capable of explanation as the filling of the mind with a strong competing interest and claim on the attention, in accordance with common mental law. Selbie (p. 13) comments: "The fact that religion is capable of sublimating primitive instincts like those of fear or sex shows clearly enough that it is not all compacted of them, but is something *sui generis*, and therefore able to use them for its own high ends." And the conclusion of W. James (*Varieties of Religious Experience*, p. 12, note) is convincing: "The plain truth is that to interpret religion one must in the end look at the immediate content of the religious consciousness. The moment one does this one sees how wholly disconnected it is in the main from the content of the sexual consciousness. Everything about the two things differs—objects, moods, faculties concerned and acts impelled to. Any general assimilation is simply impossible. What we find most often is complete hostility and contrast."

IV

Epicurus, Lucretius, Hume, Strauss and others attribute the rise of religion to fear. Men were conscious of possible harm from the unknown forces of Nature, and on human analogy it was conceived that there was a power in Nature to be feared and propitiated. This might explain a devil to be hated, but hardly a God to be loved and to be associated with ideas of comfort and deliverance. "From the age of the Chaldean tablets, the Vedic hymns, the Egyptian Book of the Dead, a *friendly* deity has appeared in religion." Further, man continues to believe in God and to love Him when he has ceased to fear Him. We may "mock Him when we do not fear," but to mock is not necessarily to deny the existence of deity. The higher religions aim at "a perfect love which casteth out fear." Or, again, the elementary and central idea of Sacrifice, according to Robertson Smith and others, is not to placate an outraged or terrible God, but to effect a communion between the worshipper and the worshipped— a characteristic feature of religion.

V

The unsatisfactoriness of the theory that a sense of fear created the idea of God has led to a modified form—the conception that fear created a god of fear and gratitude a god of bounty, and that in the evolution of the race, by fusion and syncretism, the gods combined to form a really "religious" god. Religious emotion, Dr. McDougall claims, is compounded of admiration (itself compounded of wonder and submission), plus awe (compounded of admiration and fear), plus reverence (which is made up of fear, wonder, submission and gratitude, and even the last-named is compounded of tender emotion and submission). "The history of religion seems to show us the general genesis of this highly complex emotion: primary religion seems to have kept separate the superhuman objects of its component emotions —the terrible, awe-inspiring powers on the one hand, the kindly beneficent powers on the other. And it was not until religious doctrine had undergone a long evolution that by a process of syncretism and fusion it conceived the conception of Deity, whose attributes were capable of evoking all the sentiments of this complex emotion of reverence" (*Social Psychology*, p. 135). The theory would require a fusion of ideas of supernatural powers not regarded in the first instance in a religious way, but rather as a crude scientific explanation of certain experiences. Man becomes afraid of certain aspects of Nature, and makes a Nature god of terror, on the human analogy of the tyrannous chief; or he conceives Nature in certain beneficent aspects, and so makes a Nature god of bounty to whom he is grateful; in neither case, however, would a genuine religious sentiment appear. But presently there comes about a fusion of the god causing fear and the god inspiring gratitude, etc., and the amalgam deity, with attributes collected from many sides and many experiences, is able to inspire an amalgam sentiment, made up of

c

fear, gratitude, admiration, wonder, but now having a distinctive quality of its own, described as "religious," and accompanied with a corresponding power of evoking religious worship.

Various reflections are suggested by this theory: (1) We have the problem of the combination of objects prior to that of the emotions called forth by them. We cannot, of course, treat fear, admiration, wonder and the like as entities which can be compounded like chemical substances; we cannot divorce the constituent emotion from an object. Fear is fear of *something*; admiration is admiration of *something*; we cannot separate the feeling from that which called it forth. If the religious sentiment were an amalgam of these constituent feelings, there must be, as McDougall points out, a mental object, capable of producing a number of emotions which blend and create an entirely new emotion. But how came about the amalgam of objects themselves? What was the principle of combination, the link of cohesion? Was that itself "religious" in nature? In which case an obvious reflection presents itself: Did the "gods" amalgamate because they were "gods"? The worshipped objects, it is presumed, combined by syncretism and fusion, but why, prior to this, were they worshipped? The theory requires the combination of objects to form a god without any prior postulation of the idea of God or worship.

(2) The idea of the evolution of religion, as a historical process, from low forms of fetishism and magic to spiritual faith, is not without challenge from the side of anthropomorphic study. Andrew Lang in his *Making of Religion* finds a good deal of evidence on which to base a theory that from the earliest stages of culture up to Christianity there has been held the belief in a spiritual Supreme Being. He confesses that he does not know how the belief was attained (we suggest that its origin was in mystical or cosmic consciousness), but he will not accept the idea that the lofty notion arose from the lower circle of fetishism and the like, which

he regards as an amalgam of degeneration rather than an origin. Religion and fetishism, he claims, arose from two distinct mental areas.

(3) It would seem that the complex notion of God should produce all these sentiments of fear, reverence, admiration, etc., *simultaneously* if this entirely new compound of religious sentiment should be formed. But, as a matter of fact, there are alternations of sentiment, as we contemplate different aspects of God. Sometimes we have the emotions of fear, sometimes of gratitude, but if we had a true compound this alternation of mood and the varying of proportions in the amalgam might be expected to dissolve the religious senti- ment as a distinctive compound. Again, we *recognise* this element of fear, or the element of gratitude, whereas we should expect that in a true compound the religious sentiment would transform its component parts and exhibit new stable characteristics, distinguishable from those of the constituents.

(4) The theory requires us to deny a religious quality to the early stages of the process leading up to religion, and makes the claim that religion arose from the combination of crude scientific postulates. But there seems to be a radical difference in nature between science and religion. Science has its basis *without*, in the objects which it examines. It is a mirror of external nature; it deals with the world of nature, analysed and classified. But religion has its seat *within*, and the external world only stimulates an inward power and faculty. Would external nature have produced "gods" if there had not been that element within man's soul to be wakened and stimulated? From the earliest stages of religion it would seem that such a distinct faculty was at work, developing from within, with the external world stimulating but not originating the sense.

(5) Once more, the theory does not explain the character- istic feature of communion, or craving for union with the Divine, which has marked the occurrence of religion in all ages. In science we contemplate and marvel; in art we admire

and may seek to imitate and create, but in religion we experience a sense of affinity, a sense of participation, an instinct for finding our place within the larger whole. This particular feature seems to mark off the religious experience and emotion as *sui generis*, primary and underived. We can conceive such an experience of union causing awe and a tinge of fear, joy, ecstasy, and a sense of dependence, but it does not appear to be the outcome or product of these feelings in any way, or to be the result of logical inference or argumentation based on scientific facts. There is, as Réville points out, something which marks off religion proper from science and philosophy: "These are subjects exclusively of the intellect, and although religion may be the subject of a science and a philosophy, it differs from both in its roots. It rests essentially on the awakening, or the calling into activity, of a sentiment *sui generis*, which impels the intellect to image the object of it under forms corresponding to its degree of knowledge, but which springs spontaneously in the soul. This internal fact of the religious sentiment by no means implies that the forms with which it is furnished by the intellect answer exactly to the reality of the object. We can very well feel the effects of beings and forces of which we are only able to form vague or false ideas" (*History of Religion*, pp. 66, 67).

VI

The theory that religion arose from primitive spiritualism does not quite satisfy the facts. Andrew Lang lays down the hypothesis (*The Making of Religion*, pp. 301 ff.) that "there are two sources of religion, (*a*) the belief, how attained we know not, in a powerful, moral, eternal, omniscient Father and Judge of men; and (*b*) the belief (probably developed out of experiences normal and abnormal) in somewhat of a man which may survive the grave. The second belief is not logically needed as given material of the first, in its apparently earliest form. It may be, for all we know, the later of the two beliefs chronologically. But this belief, too, was necessary for religion, first by supplying the formula by which advancing intellects could conceive of the Mighty Being involved in the former creed; and next, as elevating man's conception of his own nature." But the problem of the former and leading element of religion remains. We believe that this is accounted for by the experience of a specific intuition of the Infinite and Eternal. At the root of Faith lies a Cosmic Consciousness. Religion is the outcome of a Mysticism fundamental in the human mind and personality.

CHAPTER III

INTUITION AND FAITH

I

WE have realised that much which we loosely call "intuition" may be nothing more than the results of discursive reasoning, in one way or another disguised—subliminal intensification of hints given by the conscious mind, or the results of old experiences forgotten by the individual, or possibly inherited from an ancient race-consciousness. But the denial of these complex conceptions as genuine intuitions obviously does not involve the denial of some fundamental intuitional elements in our knowledge. In the common perception of finite things we become directly and inevitably aware of that something which by its nature coerces us to regard it in one way rather than another, or exhibits features which we cannot alter by our desire or will. By desire or imagination we cannot cut steel as we cut butter, or melt a stone as we melt wax. There is that in the nature of things which by its inherent "necessity" makes our knowledge possible.

There is, of course, the difficulty of conceiving what pure intuition can be, because intellectual processes of comparison, the noting of resemblances and differences, enter into our simplest perceptions, as Bergson reminds us. But there must be a point where there is mere awareness of something which can be compared and brought into relation with other things. There is the "matter of intuition" (however we may regard this metaphysically), possessing certain features and qualities not derivable from the intellectual processes of understanding. Our question is, *whether corresponding to these intuitively realised data of finite experiences there is an intuitively realised datum of the Infinite:* whether there is a mode of per-

ception or a fundamental consciousness which lies at the
root of religion. Can men see not only with their eyes but
with their souls, and perceive not only the objects of "sense"
but apprehend intuitively the Infinite and Eternal?

II

We may come to the answer of our question by a brief
consideration of the history of philosophical intuition.
Philosophy has, of course, recognised this class of intuitively
gained foundations of knowledge, but the history of philosophy also reveals differences of opinion as to the area of the
intuitive field, helps us to recognise the problems of intuition
and to recognise the tests which we need to save us from too
easy an acceptance of that which apparently lies beyond
analysis. We need to bear in mind the charge which Höffding
(*History of Philosophy*, vol. i, p. 45) brings against Reid's
Intuitional School: "Its great mistake is its belief that one
can directly read eternal truths in the simplest perceptions,
and it believes, too, in as many original instincts as there are
unintelligible phenomena—a very convenient way of explanation." Höffding's comment is a caution rather than a denial
in regard to intuition, a warning lest we close up our
inquiries too soon, or make an ultimate authority of the
unintelligible, or mistake a stubborn problem for an un-
resolvable intuition.

DESCARTES, allowing scepticism to go back as far as it will,
conceives that it breaks against the intuitive certainty of
self-consciousness. *Cogito ergo sum.* "The man who calls
this a syllogism," comments Hegel (*Logic*, § 64), "must
know little more about a syllogism, save that the word
ergo occurs in it. Where shall we look for the middle term?
It was as a self-evident or immediate truth that the *Cogito
ergo sum*, the maxim on which the whole history of modern
philosophy was built, was first stated by its author."

LOCKE's argument in his *Essay against Innate Ideas* is by

no means a denial of intuitive knowledge. "The first book," says his expositor, A. C. Fraser, "is to be read as an energetic protest against anything in human knowledge being supposed to be independent of rational criticism. Such a view 'eased the lazy of pains of search, and stopped the inquiry of the doubtful concerning all once styled "innate." No knowledge should have a claim for protection against a free criticism of its reasonableness.' " But Locke is forced in certain passages to acknowledge an intuitive element in knowledge. "He would follow Hooker," remarks Fraser again, "in saying: 'To make nothing evident of itself unto man's understanding were to take away the possibility of knowing anything. . . .' Herein is that saying of Theophrastus true—that 'they who seek a reason for all things do utterly overthrow reason.' " Locke, after all, seems to allow intuitively perceived elements, very simple and primary in nature. They do not constitute knowledge until brought "under relation," established by the elaborative activity of the understanding. But, within limits, Locke emphatically recognises an intuitive field of primary consciousness, and he claims, like Descartes, that such elementary awareness implies being. "As for our own existence, we perceive it so plainly and so certainly that it neither needs nor is capable of proof."

III

KANT, struck with the bankruptcy of empiricism in the hands of Hume, attempted, like Reid, to restore the place of intuitionalism in cognition, but showed a greater power of analysis than Reid for the task. He emphasised the *formal* intuitions which help us to construct knowledge. He claims a place for constitutive notions and "regulative ideas." Both in the inner and outer series of our experience there are "given" elements. From the standpoint of the empirical "ego" the material of the non-ego, or the "matter of intui-

tion," is given. The ego may supply moulds for the content
of experience, it may constitute this into forms of time and
space, but one is compelled to ask why some objects should
appear to the "empirical ego" as greater or smaller than
other objects, or why the *diversity* of shape and weight and
colour. (This is not a statement of Kant, but a reflection
suggested by it.) Kant is not concerned with the question
whether this "substratum of sensibility" exists in or out of
the mind, for his problem is to discover what faculties we
possess besides "mere perception." It is sufficient for him to
distinguish between an inner and outer series in experience,
although he is sometimes led to speak of "the thing-in-itself"
as if it were an unknown, out-of-consciousness objective.
But he lays it down as a principle that without "given"
elements Reason is empty; on the other hand, without formal
constitutive Reason, Empiricism would be blind.

The question arises: Does Kant encourage the idea of an
intuition of God? In his *Pure Reason* Kant shows that the
popular arguments for God become contradictory in the
antinomies. The arguments valid for the phenomenal world
break down when carried beyond their province of concrete
experience. There is a "regulative idea" which guides our
thoughts in the direction of unity, but it can never reach
that unity and finality as a definite object, reality or fact.
The "regulative idea" only applies within experience. By
logic God can neither be proved nor disproved. Kant seems
here to be encountering the world-paradox of Being and
Becoming, the One and the Many, Infinite and Finites, and
realising that the laws of thought which operate in the
world of finites cannot be applied to the Infinite. The One
embracing the Many cannot be treated as One among the
Many.

But in his *Practical Reason* Kant comes nearer to the idea
of an intuitional basis for religion. Moral freedom is undeni-
able, and on this moral intuition Kant bases inferred belief
in God and immortality. Man must be immortal to gain a

perfect moral satisfaction denied in this present life, and God becomes necessary to preserve and safeguard this moral scheme. This seems like "grammar to explain speech"! Kant is suggestive in claiming that God cannot be placed as an Infinite Object among other finite objects, and that if He exists, His being must be approached in some way other than that which applies for the finite world. We shall presently inquire how far the idea of "cosmic consciousness" represents such a special method of perception—the method of "Faith" for the knowledge of the universe regarded in an ultra time-and-space aspect. And one asks the further question: If Kant can build so much on the intuition of duty and moral freedom, is it a great step to the intuition of God Himself?

IV

This was the step taken by JACOBI, who conceived that not only do we become immediately conscious of finites regarded as distinctive objects, but we also become aware of the Infinite as a distinctive reality by some kind of mystic insight. The attempt to approach infinity by means of the intellect (an instrument which he felt was only capable of dealing with the finites of the time-and-space world) would only result in putting the Infinite into misleading finite and conditioned forms. The intellect from its very nature could produce nothing other than a finite and anthropomorphic God. Had not Kant shown that the use of the principles and categories legitimate for finite things proved contradictory when applied to the Infinite and Eternal? The antinomies suggested that the intellect had its limitations, and, applied beyond its province, led to contradictions and absurdities. Thus it appeared to Jacobi that the Infinite must remain unknown, or that it must be apprehended by some other method. Since we are in some way aware of the Infinite, Jacobi claimed the competency of direct intuition to give us knowledge of that Supreme Fact which was beyond the range of intellectual methods.

It is true that HEGEL vigorously attacked Jacobi, but this was not on the ground that we have no intuition of the Absolute, but on the ground that an intuition which leaves the idea of God abstract and unrelated to the general body of concrete experiences and reasoned thought is insufficient. Hegel significantly acknowledges that we have certain immediate intuitions, and among them this very intuition of the existence of the Absolute, and that the existence of God, the Eternal and Infinite, is involved in our very thought of it. Philosophy does acknowledge immediate intuitions. It must begin somewhere and with something. The quarrel between Hegel and Jacobi is not here but in the apparent suggestion of the latter that the intuitive knowledge of God is self-sufficient in its isolation from the general body of mental life; that "God lies outside of the mechanical interconnection to which knowledge is said to be confined" (*Logic*, p. 122). Hegel's attack is upon "the distinctive doctrine that immediate knowledge alone, to the total exclusion of mediation, can possess a content which is true." He challenges a "watertight compartment" theory of knowledge. All must be related. Hegel makes a good case for the necessary complementary knowledge of the Infinite in the finites: for the filling in of the bare category of Being with all the wealth of the familiar concrete experiences of the finite world and with the implications of our finite thoughts. Even philosophical intuition is in a sense intellectual. It is a perceptive work of the mind, even if it must be distinguished from the reasoning work of the mind. Intuition must be interpreted and in some way conceptualised before it can take any place at all in the thought world. It must be brought "under relation." Intuitional knowledge is, after all, knowledge, and it cannot enter the chamber of Mind without some reckoning with the doorkeeper of Understanding and without offering some promise of interrelation with the other occupants. Intuition cannot afford to adopt the standoffish and superior and exclusive attitude towards the general world. To say that God *is*, is to say very little. We want to know what God is—that is to say, the relation of this Absolute Fact to the other facts of our experience. An Absolute which stood by itself would be valueless—indeed, unintelligible. Or how could there be a true Absolute with a world of finite, concrete phenomena lying outside it? The finites must be read in the light of the Infinite, and the Infinite in the light of the finites. For Hegel the finites were the Infinite under a certain analytic aspect, and the Infinite could be approached through them and be understood by the implications and unfoldings of the general finite and concrete universe. But the case for an immediate intuition of the Absolute has not broken down with Hegel. The intuition rather marks out a territory to be explored, or it is the consciousness of a fact complementary to the universe of perceived finite facts, and to be brought into some kind of relation with the latter.

V. The Idea of the Absolute derived from Cosmic Consciousness

How did men come to speak of the Infinite, the Absolute, the Eternal, the One? By some means or other the mind of man has become aware of two aspects of reality—the particular, the finite, the sectional, the temporal; and on the other hand the Complete, the Infinite, the Eternal, the One. We can understand men speaking of the Many. The Manifold of finite experience has come to consciousness through the sense-data of perception. But how have we become aware of the other aspect? Is it due to some formal unifying operation of mind, a "regulative idea," a way in which the mind works? Or is there an all-embracing Reality which evades us only because it is omnipresent and from its nature cannot be placed among other objects? Does the One, the Eternal and

Infinite, actually exist? Or have we some special form of consciousness by means of which we perceive the Infinite, in which case the "regulative idea," instead of being a mere guide for finiteness, contradicting itself when used to demonstrate the infinite and eternal, becomes in relation to the Infinite what the objective idea is to the finites? Only on such a supposition that we actually perceive the Infinite, in Cosmic Consciousness, would we be able to keep consistently to Kant's principle of confining knowledge to that which comes from the mind working with perceptive experience ("without perception understanding would have nothing to understand"), and on the other hand do justice to those religious and moral intuitions which are recognised in the *Critique of Practical Reason*.

VI

It was largely the demand for concreteness which set Hegel on his suggestive and fascinating search for the Absolute along dialectic lines. But it is, of course, evident that the world did not come to the sense of the One along the lines of Hegelian dialectic. This process may support and enrich the idea of the One, but it can hardly explain its presence in our minds. We cannot explain our sense of the One by merely aggregating or compounding the Many or by discovering the converging applications of the diverse. For (*a*) by this method, how should we know that we had reached the One or that there was a One to be reached? (*b*) Historically, the sense of the One seems to have been realised before intellectually demonstrated. Men have spoken of the One from the earliest days of thought, but the dialectic demonstration is not yet convincingly worked out even for philosophers. The sense of the One would be the culminating discovery of all thought, the farthest removed from the sense of the Many—indeed, the last fact in human knowledge to be discovered. Hegel, of course, never claimed that man arrived at the idea of the One from dialectic discovery. He accepts the Infinite as an intuition, and only tries to find out its significance and to enrich its meaning by dialectic. And to him the One was concrete, for all concrete things were aspects of it.

It is interesting to note Professor James's remark (*Varieties of Religious Experience*, p. 389): "What reader of Hegel can doubt that that sense of a perfected being, with all the otherness soaked up into itself, which dominates his whole philosophy, must have come from the prominence in his consciousness of mystic moods? The notion is thoroughly characteristic of the mystical level, and the *Aufgabe* of making it articulate was surely set to Hegel's intellect by mystical feeling."

There can be what has been called a "false Infinite," argued from our consciousness that groups form, and still larger groups; therefore there must be a supreme group, an infinite which is but the name for the hypothetical largest unity of all possible experience. But why should we conceive a culmination to the process of expansion? We come back to some positive sense of the Infinite—the "real" Infinite, not gained by inference, but by some intuition or sympathy or by a species of perception.

VII

Max Müller, in his Hibbert Lectures, claims that this sense of the Infinite actually arises from direct perception. "Behind, beyond, beneath and within the finite the infinite is always present to our senses. It presses upon us; it grows upon us from every side. The finite by itself without the infinite is simply inconceivable—as inconceivable as the infinite without the finite. As Reason deals with the finite materials supplied by the senses, Faith, or whatever else we like to call it, deals with the infinite which underlies the finite. . . . Exactly where man's eyesight breaks down, there presses upon him, whether he likes it or not, the perception of the unlimited or infinite. It may be said that this is not perception in the ordinary sense of the word. No more it is, but still less is it mere reasoning. In perceiving the infinite, we neither measure nor count, nor compare, nor name. We do not know what it is, but we know that it is, and we know it because we actually feel it and are brought into contact with it" (*Origin and Growth of Religion*, p. 38). . . . "The infinite, instead of being a late abstraction, is really implied in the earliest manifestation of our sensuous knowledge. If the infinite had not been from the very first present in our sensuous perceptions, such a word as infinite would be sound and nothing else" (p. 45). . . . "With every finite perception there is a concomitant perception, or a concomitant sentiment or presentiment of the infinite. . . . I maintain that we as sentient beings are in constant touch with the infinite, and that this constant contact is the only legitimate basis on which the infinite can and does exist for us afterwards. The infinite is an *aistheton*, though not a *phainomenon*; it is felt, though not yet represented. I maintain that here, as elsewhere, no legitimate concept is possible without a previous percept" (p. 38).

VIII

We may look upon a picture in two ways: (*a*) as a whole, an *ensemble*, as Whitman would say, and (*b*) as a multitude of detail in form and colour, which detail might be noted in comparative, though probably not in absolute, isolation. Both aspects come to us in experience; they are the same object, though the aspects are essentially different. We do not say that the one is appearance and the other reality, for one is as real as the other. The one does not annul the other; the impressions are complementary. The impression of the whole canvas, indeed, depends on the varied forms and colours making up the picture; on the other hand, our impressions of each detail may not be quite independent of the complexion of the whole. So we might conceive the infinite and the finites of the universe, affecting us in similar complementary manner. The former will not affect us directly through the time and space forms, but rather through impression, sentiment, "regulative idea" (giving this more than a formal significance), or cosmic consciousness.

There seems, then, to be a double "finite-infinite" feature in human consciousness, even of a normal kind. Descartes found in the finite quality of his self-consciousness the grounds for arguing out the existence of a perfect God. It was rather a case of analysing consciousness and of distinguishing the twofold quality of its intuition than of argumentation in any proper sense. We cannot speak of the finite without implying the infinite. We may give more attention to one feature than to the other, but it would seem that we could exclude neither. Possibly the ordinary man who experiences this "finite-infinite" consciousness so stresses the world of phenomenal and finite parts and sections that in the main he excludes the other aspect, although its implications are interwoven with all his finite thought. But there are other moods in which the sense of the finite is more vividly realised, and may come to predominate over the sense of the finites without quite excluding the latter. This is the experience of Cosmic Consciousness, Faith, Mysticism. It is, we take it, the intuition of the whole, complementary to the intuition or perception of the parts. Even as there is an element of the "given," an intuitional basis, even in the perception of a common object, some starting-point for conception, in the case of finite things, so we may believe that there is an intuitional basis, giving the sense of the totality of existence, realised in Mysticism or Cosmic Consciousness, and that this is the real starting-point of all the fundamental conceptions of Religion.

CHAPTER IV

MYSTICISM AND ITS REVELATION

I. THE TWOFOLDNESS OF THE UNIVERSE

OUR line of thought involves us in the recognition of a curious fundamental paradox of existence which grows upon us the more it is thought about, and manifests itself in a variety of forms. The universe is at the same time One and Many, Infinite and a multitude of finites: a cosmos eternal and established yet incessantly changing. The world falls into two master-categories, never to be identified, never to be dissociated. As Evelyn Underhill says: "Over and over again, as Being and Becoming, as Eternity and Time, as Transcendence and Immanence, Reality and Appearance, the One and the Many—these dominant ideas, demands, imperious instincts of the man's self will appear—the warp and woof of his completed universe" (*Mysticism*, p. 49). The symbol deity of philosophy is Janus, the god of the two countenances. The fundamental problems of thought chiefly arise from this paradoxical twofoldness of the universe, and some of the larger conceptions of religion are only to be appreciated in the light of this philosophy of Being and Becoming, the Finites in the Infinite, the Many in the One. Some consideration of it seems a necessary preliminary to the study of Religion in general, and particularly to the study of Religious Mysticism.

II. BEING AND BECOMING

Even in the early Greek period of Philosophy the two aspects of Change and Permanence impressed those early thinkers and largely constituted their problems. The quest for the underlying *phusis*, or the recognition of law, or the Platonic search for the permanent in the realm of Ideas, bears witness to the sense of something abiding in the world of Change. The world was ever perishing, yet the world remained. Beneath the flux of the universe was some enduring basal substance, or some principle of permanence. Even HERACLITUS, preaching the Philosophy of Change, found a universal and eternal *phusis* in fire, and a controlling, unchangeable principle of Law. Ceaseless Change did not annihilate Being, and the permanence of Law could hardly be stated apart from Substance, whose regularity of behaviour was hypostatised under the idea of Law. For Law is not a separate entity, which, as it were, "polices" substance, and which can withdraw and enjoy its permanence, while substance, released from its guardianship, can flow away into decay and extinction. Law is the aspect of substance behaving with regularity from its own inherent nature, and thus the permanence of Law involves the ultimate permanence of substance. Similarly Change cannot be regarded as another entity which can appear apart from substance. Change is change of substance. The verb must have its noun. There cannot be change apart from that which changes. Becoming involves Being.

When, on the other hand, PARMENIDES, impressed with the aspect of Being, came to deny Becoming, and in his emphasis upon Permanence came to declare that Change was illusion, the position could not be tolerated. All human experience asserted the fact of change and motion. Life is at once Being and Becoming, static and kinetic, permanent yet changing. We must somehow conceive Change in Permanence, Becoming in Being. EMPEDOCLES made the suggestive distinction between change *of* the whole and change *within* the whole. It seems possible to claim that the permanent is that which never ceases to change. Physicists tell us that what seems to us the most solid and permanent substance is in reality masses of whirring energy-units.

The universe of Being must be conceived on the same pattern. The ceaseless change of substance is all within the closed circle of existence.

III. THE ONE AND THE MANY

In our experience of the universe we encounter numberless manifestations of form; on the other hand, we have the ineradicable intuition of unity. The Many are completed in the One; the finites are embraced within one perfect, completed and completing organic Infinite. We have symbol of this constitution in any organism. The one body has many limbs. The one tree has its multitude of branches, twigs and leaves. Thus the limb has, as it were, a double aspect. It is the limb, with its characteristic features and functions, marking it off from other limbs. It is at the same time part of the body with its one organic life. The body has a double aspect: it is a unity; it is at the same time a multitude of diverse forms. So also finite objects have a double aspect. They are finites; they are also parts of the Infinite. They have their own nature; they also contribute towards the nature of the all-embracing Infinite. It is what it is because they are what they are. The Infinite again has a double aspect. It has a unitary quality, a completeness which it possesses as the Infinite. It cannot be reduced to something less than itself and remain the Infinite. But the Infinite cannot exist apart from the finites which make it up. Abstract the Many from the One, and the One cannot maintain its existence. Take away boughs, branches, roots, leaves, twigs —and with them the tree is gone. It will be noted that the Infinite can be used in two senses—the *endless*, as in the case of a numerical series, or the *complete* or *perfect*, as in the case of a circle (Mackenzie, "Infinity," *Encyclopaedia of Religion and Ethics*). Our use of the term, applied to an organic whole, is akin to the latter sense. We regard the Infinite, not as the endless, but as the complete, to which philosophic intuition points, and which also seems to be realised through a kind of sympathy or cosmic sensing in the special experience of Mysticism. Infinity is neither a name for the indefinite nor a label for an endless series; it is rather an absolute or zero for existence.

IV. ETERNITY AND TIME

Here we have another form of the fundamental paradox of the universe. In common experience we become aware of successiveness, order, process in the unfolding of existence. But the existence thus revealed can hardly be thought of as having beginning or end. It transcends time though including it. We realise through time that which is beyond time. Time is the form in which timeless existence manifests itself. Eternity is the *simul totum* of time-experiences. Reality appears to us in a time-order, but to impose a time-order, with its beginnings and ends, upon reality as a whole would be to rob it of its reality, for we may define the real as the eternally existing. "There was never a time when it was not, nor a time when it will cease to be." We cannot assert real existence of that which arises from nothing and proceeds to nothing. Time and Eternity have different characteristics. What may be said of the one may not be said in all particulars, at any rate, of the other; but we cannot regard them as dissociated. We experience the reality of Eternity through the forms of Time; our conception of Time presupposes the reality of Eternity.

It is interesting to note the testimony of the mystics to what is apparently a direct sense of Eternity, even as they make their claim to a direct sense of the Infinite. Even as Space melts into Infinity, so Durational Time merges into Ageless Life. Dante in his mystic flight discovers that the planetary heavens, the sun and the moon, the time-measurers, are beneath his feet. He has reached a new existence where time is abolished. In God "everywhere and everywhen are focused in a point."

V

In order to conceive the nature of this general dualism we may employ the helpful idea of *Analysis*. J. B. Baillie, in a pamphlet on *Truth and History*—another of the forms which this fundamental dualism takes—says: "If we take the fact of Change, of Process, simply as it is presented to us, without attempting to view it in reference to an end, or what we should call a purpose, we shall find its significance, its content, to lie in this: that it is a mode or means of manifesting difference in that which undergoes the process." But there is an important feature to be recognised in this analysis. In regard to Time and Eternity there is a *progression* through Time to Timelessness. "The process of development in time is to be regarded as leading up to an end that is timeless, in such a fashion that each subsequent stage in the development is nearer to the nature of eternity than the antecedent stage . . . in a sense, the eternal has its place at the end of the time-series " (Mackenzie, "Infinity," *Encyclopaedia of Religion and Ethics*). We conceive that this principle may be applied to other forms of Being and Becoming. There is a progression of the finite towards the Infinite, an approximation in Becoming to Being. With our special theological interest, this principle is of particular value in relation to Morality and Personality. The highest Morality in the sphere of Becoming approximates to the strictly ineffable Morality of the Absolute Being. The highest Personality in the sphere of Becoming approximates to the Infinite Personality. The importance of this fact for our Christological ideas will be apparent.

VI

We must stress the fact that we are dealing with one existence with *aspects*, and not with *separated* worlds. Our formula must be, not the Many *and* the One, but the Many *in* the One. We must also guard ourselves against making the distinction as one of reality and unreality. There is a tendency—e.g. in Spinoza—to make the finite unreal, to make "aspect" suggest deprivation and imperfection, a falling short of reality, whereas in organism the smallest part must be as real as the whole. They are of correlative nature, and one gives meaning and significance to the other, whether we direct our thoughts to the smallest part or to the whole. Again, the Substance, the All of Spinoza's thought, is only gained by a negative process of denying all that is asserted of the finites, and thus instead of a comprehensive whole, giving significance and meaning to the parts, we have an abstract and unintelligible Absolute. Such tendencies of Spinoza's thought need the corrective of Hegelianism, which finds the reality of the whole without sacrifice of reality in the parts, and the meaning of the whole involved in the meaning of the parts. If the One embracing the Many is real, the Many that constitutes the One must be real. How can substance be made out of a collection of shadows? The relation of the whole and the parts is a complementary one, so that it is as true to say that the whole is an aspect of the parts as to say that the parts are an aspect of the whole.

Similarly, the particulars of Becoming must be as real as the fact of Being, which may be regarded as their end and summing up. The experiences of Time and Sense may be conceived as

> Machinery just meant
> To give thy soul its bent,
> Try thee and turn thee forth sufficiently impressed.

There may thus seem to be a sort of unreality about the transitory world of sense-experience. But we cannot be satisfied in dismissing as in some way unreal the factors which serve reality. There is reality in the part and in the process as truly as in the completed whole.

We believe that this supreme paradox throws light on certain other problems of faith. We suggest that as the Finites are to the Infinite, as the Many are to the One, as Time is to Eternity, as Becoming is to Being, so in like manner Morality, which is a phenomenon of finitude, is to Absolute Goodness: individual Personality is to the Personality of God: Humanity is to Divinity (see *The Idea of God*, pp. 71 ff.).

VII. Mysticism

By these several approaches we come to the phenomenon of Mysticism, and seek to interpret Religious Experience and Thought in the light of it. At the outset it is necessary to make an important distinction. The term Mysticism is sometimes used in a loose sense to cover the mysterious, the occult and theosophic, or such "revelations" as those claimed by St. Teresa, which made her confident of the assumption of the Virgin into heaven, or by St. Ignatius Loyola, which gave him inward sanction for the truth of the doctrine of the Trinity. But these "revelations" are individual, sometimes contradictory as well as diverse, and obviously have some relation to the subject's previous training and thought. Mysticism in this usage is a kind of intense emotion giving apparently supernatural sanction to elaborated beliefs coming from other sources. Such "mystic" colouring of impressions and judgments, really derived through ordinary intellectual inference, does not, of course, confer upon them the infallibility of truth and reality. The perils of Mysticism lie in accepting an emotionally-touched judgment as final, infallible, direct from God and beyond criticism.

But Mysticism in the sense in which we are using the term *indicates the faculty of man to realise the Infinite and Eternal*— a Cosmic Consciousness which is of an elementary and revelation-bearing character. It is an experience providing foundation-data upon which the intellect can build. It has significance for non-mystics as well as for mystics. It is a sense which apparently possesses the most striking mark of intuition—that of universal and persistent spontaneity. Thus William James writes: "The overcoming of all the usual barriers between the individual and the Absolute is the great mystic achievement. In mystic states we become one with the Absolute, and we become aware of our oneness. This is the everlasting and triumphant mystic tradition, hardly altered by differences of clime and creed. In Hinduism, in Neo-Platonism, in Sufism, in Christian Mysticism, in Whitman-ism, we have the same recurring note, so that there is about mystical utterances an eternal unanimity which ought to make a critic stop and think, and which brings it about that the mystic classics have, as has been said, neither birthday nor native land. Perpetually telling of the unity of man and God, their speech antedates language, nor do they grow old" (*Varieties of Religious Experience*, p. 149).

VIII

The definitions of Mysticism indicate its religious significance. "Mysticism," says Edward Caird, "is religion in its most concentrated and exclusive form—that attitude of mind in which all other relations are swallowed up in the relation of the soul to God" (*Evolution of Theology in the Greek Philosophers*, vol. ii, p. 210). "Mysticism," says Pfleiderer, "is the immediate feeling of the unity of the self with God. It is nothing, therefore, but the fundamental feeling of religion—the religious life at its heart and centre." On the one hand McTaggart defines Religion as "an emotion resting upon a connection between ourselves and the universe at large"; Dean Inge, on the other hand, speaks of Mysticism as "the attempt to realise in thought and feeling the immanence of the temporal in the eternal and of the eternal in the temporal"; or Rufus Jones defines it as "the historical doctrine of the relationship and the potential union of the human soul with the Ultimate. Mystical experience is direct experience of God."

We may note also that when the implications of Religion are worked out, Faith in its characteristic features appears to be based on the ideas of life as *a totality*. "God" is the Absolute Reality "in whom we live and move and have our being." Providence in its highest sense is the Law of the whole Cosmos. Religious optimism must be based on the sense that in the last resort the universe is sound. Immortality means more than survival beyond the grave: there might be ultimate perishing after a period of such survival. Religious Immortality is Eternal Life. In all these religious conceptions there is a universal and infinite reference; they would seem to have their origin and confirmation in some mode of consciousness other than, and complementary to, our consciousness of the finite world. This mode, we believe, is that of Mysticism, Cosmic Consciousness, Faith. Faith is not the inferring of the unseen from the things that are seen, similar to the scientific inference of a theory based on scientific facts: still less is it irrational or credulous acceptance of tradition; it is the direct and immediate sensing of certain unified aspects of existence. We become aware of the detailed finite aspects of existence by means of our common sense-perceptions; we also become aware of reality as a whole by a kind of parallel intuition, sympathy, mystic sensing. "The mystics," says Dean Inge in a picturesque phrase, are "men who see with their souls"—and what they see is the *whole* of things.

IX

In these forms of mystic or cosmic consciousness we appear to have genuine *data for knowledge*. Professor James says he cannot help ascribing metaphysical significance to his mystic experiences. Religion rests upon some intuitional phenomena which reason may investigate but cannot produce. "One may say truly, I think, that personal religious experience has its root and centre in mystical states of consciousness" (*Varieties of Religious Experience*, p. 379), and "even the personally non-religious might accept the conclusions of a Science of Religion based on such personal religious experience, much as blind persons now accept the facts of optics" (*ibid.*, p. 456).

We have, however, a difficulty *of ineffability*—the feature of the mystic consciousness which Professor James finds most characteristic of it—a feature which gives little promise of cognitive illumination, and hardly seems consistent with the metaphysical contribution which Professor James claims elsewhere for Mysticism. He remarks: "The subject of it immediately says that it defies expression, and no adequate report of its content can be given in words." On the other hand, these experiences have a certain positive quality, and they set in one intellectual direction rather than in another. They have not been without influence upon human life and thought, and something in them has been translatable into intellectual forms. The explanation of this ineffability is that Mysticism or Cosmic Consciousness is dealing with the Infinite, and the Infinite cannot be conveyed under the forms of the finite. How can we speak of the One *embracing* the Many as One *among* the Many? Cosmic Consciousness can only receive its revelation in broad, indeterminate impressions, and hint its content in symbols more or less inadequate. The language of faith is necessarily poetic and impressionist. This constitutes its difficulty for precise minds. The cosmic sense of the mystics has, we believe, created the figures of our theologies, our pictures of gods and God, our theological dramas put in terms of time and space. These, however, can only be regarded as symbols of truths which, in a sense, are beyond telling. They are "myths," as Plato used the word, suggesting rather than stating truths. Of necessity, the Infinite cannot be adequately described in terms of finitude. The God who walks the Garden of Eden, and personally investigates the situation at Babel, does not answer the cosmic requirements of omniscient and omnipresent Spirit. Nevertheless all these attempts to objectify and anthropomorphise God are witnesses to the soul's sense of a Reality of which human thought must take account.

X

It is not, however, impossible to indicate the general features of this Revelation which comes to us from these states of mystic consciousness. We find them underlying all our great Christian doctrines in one form or another. (1) The first is *the essential unity of all life*. "The mystic states," says William James, "point in definite philosophical directions, one of which is Monism." We become aware of the Absolute. This must not be taken as a doctrine of amorphous pantheism, in which all values, distinctions and parts are obliterated. When we take away branches, leaves, roots, there cannot remain a tree apart from these. The universe must be conceived as an organic and not an amorphous Oneness.

(2) The mystic or cosmic consciousness, again, sets in the direction of *Optimism*. To return to our figure of the picture, the great patches of black among the details fall into a larger harmony of black and white when we look upon the picture as a whole. The inferences from the world of finite phenomena are so mixed, and there is so much to suggest an ultimate evil rather than an ultimate good, that one doubts whether man could keep his conviction in the soundness of the universe if he had not this faculty of sensing the whole, of standing back from the picture and receiving the combined impression of its detailed and finite parts. But, despite the challenges of the dark things in life, there has been found a significant optimism, most pronounced among men of religious or mystic temperament. "A sunny confidence in

the ultimate triumph shines from the writings of most of the mystics" (Inge).

(3) A third feature of the cosmic consciousness is that of *Communion or Assimilation with Deity*. In the most intense experiences of the great mystics the individual seems almost swallowed up in the Over-Soul. "I am as great as God; He is as small as I," cries Angelus Silesius. Such experiences seem to have supplied the ideas underlying many ancient sacrificial customs and most of the practices of the Mysteries (see p. 67). This feature finds abundant expression in Christian hymns and other sacred literature. It is found conspicuously in Indian religions and practices. It is the theme of the Mohammedan Sufis. In its light we interpret our doctrines of Prayer and Sacramental Communion. It helps us to understand some of the central teachings of Paul and the Fourth Evangelist.

(4) Mysticism also gives a sense of *social solidarity*. Walt Whitman thus describes one of his mystic states:

Swiftly arose and spread about me the peace and knowledge that
    pass all the arguments of earth. . . .
I know that the spirit of God is a brother of my own,
And that all men ever born are also my brothers, and the women
    my sisters and lovers,
And that a kelson of the creation is love.

The mystic is aware, not only of his oneness with God, but also of his oneness with his brethren, or perhaps one ought to say he is conscious that life is a living organism in which all the parts, ultimately unified in God, are related to one another. A consciousness of this relationship is also one of the means of realising the unity of life in God. If we have communion with the brethren, we tend to have fellowship with the Father. There is, to use a phrase of the old mystics, "a discovery of God in His creatures."

(5) One element in our ethical sense seems born out of certain harmonies or discords between the individual sympathy and will and the Absolute and Divine Will, and seems

a corollary from our cosmic consciousness. We have the intuitive faculty whereby the soul knows itself to be in spiritual harmony with God. We are conscious of the meaning of spiritual health, of "being in tune with the Infinite," of the blending of our individual note with "Creation's chorus." This sense of spiritual harmony has an obverse in the sense of Sin. The faculty which gives us the consciousness of spiritual health gives us also the consciousness of spiritual discord with the whole—the consciousness on which our doctrine of Sin is based. Sin is faulty spiritual relationship with the Absolute; the individual will and sympathy are at discord with the Divine. The section fails to harmonise with the whole.

The courses of life leading to this experience of "being in tune with the Infinite," or prompted by such experience, may not be intellectually right nor socially healthy. Here we must recognise another set of harmonies. The thing which is objectively "good" is that which is harmonious with the whole universe of facts and forces, that which is in accordance with the law and the pattern of the cosmos. The perfect act is the right thing (that which is in objective harmony with the laws of Nature, in its broadest interpretation) done in the right spirit (which is intuitively realised by the soul, as being in harmony with the spirit of God).

(6) A further feature or group of features characteristic of Mysticism may be suggested by the phrase "newness of life." Dr. Bucke (*Cosmic Consciousness*, p. 2) says: "The prime characteristic of cosmic consciousness is a sense of the cosmos—that is, of the life and order of the universe. Along with this there occurs an intellectual enlightenment . . . a sense of moral elation, an indescribable feeling of joyousness, elevation and exaltation and a quickening of the moral sense. . . . With these may come what may be called the sense of immortality, a consciousness of eternal life—not a conviction that he *shall* have this, but that he has it already."

The former set of features is interesting as corrective of

a dangerous inference from cosmic optimism, shallowly interpreted. If "all be well," why strive and agonise in an attempt to alter things? There is a false tendency of Mysticism which leads to the heartless doctrine that "to the wise man public calamities are only stage tragedies, or even stage comedies" (Plotinus, *En.* 3. 2, 15), or to the "unholy indifference," which Vaughan in his *Hours with the Mystics* (p. 52) rightly despises. But against this apparently enervating tendency one can point to the instances of the energetic Spanish mystics, or of the Quakers, or of St. Paul, who was a mystic and the most convinced of cosmic optimists, yet at the same time the most active and progressive member of the Christian Church and the most desperate and militant of its fighters; or of many modern philanthropists and reformers in whom Mysticism, zeal and altruism have blended (cf. Inge's *Mysticism*, Intro., p. xi). It would seem that Mysticism has among its features an energising force, an *élan vital*, and that the contact with the Whole imparts to the true mystic some of the Life-Urge of the Whole, which in its nature is not static and placid, but kinetic and dynamic. The whole is living and pulsating with the energy of life, and the mystic, in harmony with the whole, shares this life and energy and becomes an instrument in its creative evolution.

(7) The mystic's *sense of eternal life* is important. It is obvious that the doctrine of immortality in the largest sense cannot be reached by mere examination of finite phenomena. It may be that Psychical Research can some day demonstrate convincingly that human personality survives after death, but this is something less than proving that men shall always survive. It is conceivable that the soul should survive for a period and yet ultimately perish. It would seem that fundamentally our belief in immortality must rest upon a consciousness which transcends the time-series. As Fischer remarks in the second chapter of his work on Kant: "Mortality seems a time conception. The timeless world would be immortal and eternal. The true notion of immortality

coincides with that of eternity. But since without sensuous perception there are no knowable objects, the immortality of the soul can never be theoretically demonstrated." It would seem that the cosmic sensing of the Infinite and Eternal makes its own impression upon us, and thus man maintains his unconquerable sense of immortality, however haltingly he may express it.

XI

Summing up: we conceive that true Mysticism or Cosmic Consciousness is a special but not abnormal form or mode of consciousness, by means of which we become aware of the wholeness of reality. It provides a complement to our knowledge of the finites, perceived through the common observation of the senses. Such an awareness of the cosmic reality gives us, not the form of objects, but a certain mental "complexion," settings of attitude, "regulative ideas," the general outcome of which is the persistent and ineradicable consciousness of the unity of all life, communion with the Infinite, optimism, a sense of the unseen, eternal life and immortality. The mystics through their vision supply the world with certain inspiring and sustaining elements which it is not the province of the observation of the finites to give. This revelation is not superior to nor more "supernatural" than that of finite perception. Nor must it be considered in any way as a complete substitute for it. It is only valid in its own field, which is different from, and complementary to, the observation of finite phenomena and the reasoning based thereon. Mysticism is the method proper to the mode of Being; common perception of finites is the method proper to the mode of Becoming. The two revelations are ultimately involved, and both are essential to the fullness of human knowledge and for the adequate appreciation of reality.

The vital religious beliefs of mankind appear to be based primarily on this cosmic mode of consciousness, and the recognition of these intuitions of Mysticism seems necessary for the appreciation of religious doctrine and for the understanding of its source and validity. In the following studies of the Idea of God, the Eternal Goodness and Immortality we shall seek to indicate the factor of cosmic consciousness, at the same time recognising the complementary function of the reason to find intellectual expression and justification as far as it can in the finite sphere.

CHAPTER V

THE IDEA OF GOD

I

We cannot hold that a ready-made dogma of God with certain definite human relations was miraculously imparted at the beginning of the history of the human race. Such complex ready-made revelation is not in accordance with the constitution of mind nor with its method of development in all other departments of knowledge. We do not have our sciences delivered to us in infallible books or graven on tables of stone. We have given to us the tools of an inquiring spirit, certain powers of observation, laws of logic, axioms of thought, on the one hand; and on the other the materials to be examined—a flash of lightning, a world of mountains, rivers, sand and rock, a starry sky with its peculiar phenomena; then we are left to construct our complex sciences of electricity, geology, astronomy and the rest. Similarly, we must look for the discovery of our religious knowledge in its complex breadth, not in primitive, ready-made revelation, but through the combination of mental faculties as tools, working on certain observations and experiences as materials.

But although we have no primitive revelation, there seems to be a distinctive and fundamental datum for the idea of God. In the unfolding of human personality man has become aware of *forms of consciousness of such nature and quality that they have provided a starting-point for speculations of God, demanded intellectual symbols of Him, and involved the tracing of intellectual relationships between God and man.*

E

II

Man makes two discoveries of self-consciousness. The first is that of apparent isolation. He gains the sense that he is apart from the rest of the universe. He has his individuality and privacy of consciousness.

> The baby, new to earth and sky,
> What time his tender palm is pressed
> Against the circle of the breast
> Has never thought that "This is I."
>
> But as he grows, he gathers much,
> And learns the use of "I" and "me,"
> And finds—"I am not what I see,"
> And "other than the things I touch."

The second great discovery of self-consciousness is, curiously enough, that after all we are *not* completely apart from others. We are not like peas in a sack; we are parts of an organism. *We feel that we have a vital relationship to the whole.* We are integral parts of the universe life, not merely in the region of social contact and relationship, but in a deeper sphere of personality. This seems to be the significance of the experience of "personal religion." The "natural man" regards himself as a self-contained entity without relationship to the whole. He is as a pea in the sack. But the developed man, or in religious terms the man of faith, the "twice-born," has realised that he belongs to a larger whole; he is part of an organism. This sense of relationship may affect him in various ways. In the first dawning of this consciousness he may be aware of a discord to which he was not previously sensitive. He may realise a sense of Sin. Or he may be disturbed by a new restlessness and yearning. There is truth in Pascal's thought: "To be seeking after God is already to have found Him." A sense of spiritual incompleteness bears witness to some degree of spiritual contact with God. The highest experience of the relationship, however, is when a man feels himself "at one with God." "Thou hast made us for Thine own self, and our hearts are restless till they rest in Thee."

III

We find the origin of the idea of God in such experiences of soul, *when in one way or another man feels that he is not complete in himself, but belongs to a larger whole. His soul is related to an Over-Soul.* Granted this consciousness, experience, intuition, and the idea of God in some form, as men can intellectually interpret the experience, will naturally follow. Around this primary and essential intuition other elements gather. There are inferences from men's scientific and philosophical knowledge, the intellectual arguments for the being of God, deductions from design, causation, moral phenomena, but it would seem that essentially and primarily the idea of God had its own distinctive psychological origin. There is, as Réville points out, something which marks off religion proper from science and philosophy (see p. 36). Even with primitive man God was something other than a crude scientific explanation of why things happened; there was the significant element of *worship* with a quality of its own. God was not merely to be contemplated, nor even to be feared as an outside power, but He was One to be realised in and through relationship with the worshipper. In the ancient Mystery Religions the element of mingling, communion, assimilation was expressed in a score of ways—by prayer, sacrifice, eating and drinking the sacred food, being drenched with the blood of the sacred animal, "putting on" the god in shape of mask or mark, assimilative mutilation, mystic marriages, and the like. Under all these practices can be traced an experience either of incompleteness or communion. "In glancing over a map of religions," says Réville again, "we are struck by their multiplicity and diversity. . . . All principles and forms produce at first sight the effect of a confused mingling of incongruous phenomena to which it seems rash to attribute any element in common." But on investigation a significant common feature appears—the consciousness of "a bond uniting the human mind and that Mysterious Mind, whose domination of the world and of itself it realises, and to which it delights in finding itself united" (*History of Religions*, p. 25).

IV

We begin, then, by regarding God *as that which corresponds to a mode of cosmic consciousness*. As such, we believe that we are dealing with a reality quite as definite as that of a material object or of a human body. As Lotze points out, when we speak of Matter or a Body it is only the naming of a certain set of experiences. "Matter" is no solid core or substance having a peculiar right to be regarded as real. What exactly it is we do not know. It may be a storm of electrons. It may be the resistance of other monadic centres—other "souls" pressing against our own. We give it the name Body or Matter, but this is only a convenient label to suggest an experience of consciousness. We become aware of another set of phenomena which we indicate by the words Mind or Soul. This has no bodily form, but we can be as certain of its real existence as if it had. We do not know the innermost nature of a "soul." But we know that Mind or Soul is as much a reality as is the Body, for it enters into experience and manifests itself in phenomena. Both Body and Soul are labels for a group of distinctive experiences. Exactly in the same way we become aware of God—an experience of consciousness of a particular kind and quality. We feel that we have here touched reality, different in nature from that of what we call the body, but as actual as that. It is different, too, from our experience of finite Minds and Souls. It is the Over-Soul. This must be as real as the other objects of our experience, and as inscrutable in its ultimate nature as they are. When we can tell the meaning of a piece of stone or of the "flower from the crannied wall," we may try to tell the ultimate meaning of God. And yet as we know something of stone and flower from the nature of our experience of them, so we may know something of God.

V. The Attributes of God

The old method of realising the nature of God by gathering together a number of Scriptural texts expressing His attributes has become quite unconvincing. We must seek some more fundamental principle of realising the nature and attributes of God. There are some things which we can say about Him from the very nature of our cosmic consciousness.

Firstly, He is *the Infinite, the Eternal, the Absolute.* "The Lord, our God, is one Lord." This may seem in itself a somewhat barren conception. But life and thought would become perplexing and disquieting unless we could thus conceive existence as monistic and unified. The consistency, rationality and security of the universe is bound up with the conception of the unity of God. Further, this conception of Monism is enriched by the specific experience of worship or communion. As individuals, we may realise a certain kind of union with this Absolute. A feature of God is *that He can be worshipped, and worship is communion.* We must not interpret this communion to mean that there is some kind of giving and taking between two finites, however small one may be and however great the other, as long as they remain finites. The nature of the process is that the finite finds its place in the Infinite. Schleiermacher suggests the significance of the experience in the description: "I lie at the bottom of the Infinite World. I am in that moment her soul. I feel all her infinite life as my own. This is the generative moment of all that is living in religion." On the other hand, we must retain the place of individuality in this communion. There is a certain fixity, character, privacy about each finite part, each individual soul; and to the part, feeling itself as a part, the whole is external, even as the tree is external to the leaf and the ocean to the bay. There will always be in the religious experience *a reaching out*, on the part of the individual, to That which is beyond the individual self. It will be as clear an element that the individual soul is not God as that it is eternally impossible to isolate the individual soul from Him in whom "we live and move and have our being." These two features of experience give worship its particular quality. Man will worship because at the same time God is *in* him and God is *beyond* him. Unless God was in him, and there existed this vital relationship between the whole and the part, he would realise no need for worship. But worship would not be worship unless there was such a difference between the part and the whole as to set up, as it were, a spiritual motion.

Von Hügel, commenting on Feuerbach's theory that God is the illusive external projection of man's own nature and idealism ("The Absolute, the God of man, is man's own nature. Consciousness of God is self-consciousness. Knowledge of God is self-knowledge, but ignorance of this identity is fundamental to the peculiar nature of religion"), remarks: "In Feuerbach's scheme it is precisely the illusion, the inversion, it alone which gives religion its entire special power. Precisely the same content, which in its 'true' place and character leaves one cold or but superficially moved, becomes when seen in its 'false' place and character the greatest, often the most terrible, fact of history." God is the Infinite Reality, at the same time, in and beyond us. In Him we live and move and have our being, and yet we "reach out, if haply we may find Him."

A further feature of the nature of God, arising from our cosmic sense, is that *this One is good*. Cosmic consciousness is optimistic. For the moment we may say nothing of morality in the strict sense—the love, mercy, pity, courage, in a word the character of God, for these are features of finite relationships, and for the present we are dealing with the Infinite. But we can attribute to the Infinite, from the quality of our cosmic consciousness, the one feature of soundness, or goodness, in a metaphysical, if not strictly a moral, sense.

VI

Our conception of God is still very vague and, indeed, uninspiring. But we can tremendously enrich our description of God's nature and attributes by remembering that *this is not an amorphous One*. All the features, the life, the traffic, the operations of the universe, of this and of all worlds, are gathered up in His life and being. God, so to speak, is the supreme aspect of it all, and is known through it all, although He Himself is different from any part of it, just as the tree is different from the trunk, the branch, the twig, and the leaf.

We must call to mind the doctrine of the twofold aspects of existence, God is not only *Being* but *Becoming*. He is what He is; He is eternally living out what He is. The long struggling life of finite creation, the long history of humanity, is, as it were, the Eternal and Infinite God analysed and manifesting His meaning. The *Erdgeist* in Goethe's song claims—

> In Being's flood, in Action's storm,
> I walk and work, above, beneath—
> Work and weave in endless motion
> Birth and death, an infinite ocean,
> A seizing and giving the fire of living.
> 'Tis thus at the roaring Loom of Time I ply
> And weave for God the garment thou see'st Him by.

We need to realise both aspects of God. He is, so to speak, the white light and all the spectrum colours which constitute white light, and one aspect gives meaning to the other. God Transcendent possesses a characteristic and final quality known to the mystic, yet hardly to be described by him. The Absolute may not even be analysed without losing some of the quality which belongs to it in virtue of its wholeness. The One cannot be reduced to less than the One without losing its distinctive character. It is impossible to state the whole in the terms of the part, or of the parts. "Empiricism," says Hegel (*Logic*, p. 79), "labours under a delusion if it supposes that while analysing the objects, it leaves them where they were"; or again: "The whole, though we see that it consists of parts, ceases to be a whole when it is divided." We "murder to dissect." For this sense of the Infinite and Absolute there can be no exact substitute or equivalent. The God of mystic worship, strictly conceived, stands alone—Eternal, Infinite, Undivided, Worshipful. Being cannot be reduced to description in the world of Becoming without losing a quality which must be felt rather than expressed. Therefore it may not be quite untrue to say: "Our fittest eloquence is our silence, when we confess without confession that Thy glory is inexplicable and beyond our reach"—a statement which Edward Caird (*Hegel*, p. 140) criticises, and which calls for criticism if it is carried beyond its legitimate limit, and taken to signify that this is the only statement of God desirable or possible. For God needs conceiving in a complementary fashion as having relations with the manifold world.

VII

The Eternal and Infinite Fact can only be suggested under forms obviously conditioned and finite, and therefore inadequate as precise statements. Men have conceived God anthropomorphically, and have found the difficulties of the conception when they have dwelt upon the finite features and traced the finite relations with other things involved in the anthropomorphic conception. To mention one instance, human form and omnipresence are conflicting notions. No

Zeus has descended from the skies and remained Zeus. But we may legitimately have *symbols* of that Transcendent Reality. Theology has its *eidolons*, valuable as symbols of Transcendent Reality as long as their true nature as symbol is realised and respected.

But we cannot remain content with a general and vague idea of the Absolute. We seek also the *analytic* expression of the Supreme. Man will not be satisfied in leaving the aspect of the Infinite isolated and out of relation with other elements of human knowledge. To reduce religion, with its characteristic sense of the Infinite, to a mere matter of finitude would be to rob religion of an essential element, but it is also true that a God who is merely transcendent leaves the finite barrenly secular. There may be and must be *Religion Analytic*, with a place found for God in the finite processes of human life and thought. The significance of the whole must be felt, not merely as a sentiment of the whole interfusing the parts, but in precise terms of the finite world. We must work out the immanence of God as well as hint, as we are able, the nature of His transcendence. We must see God, as it were, analysed in section and process—God Becoming.

VIII

Under what forms, in what conditions, then, would such a manifested God reveal Himself? "God is Love"—but Love cannot conceivably be shown in an amorphous Oneness. For the operation of Love there must be at least a second being, an other than self. For the manifestation of God, who is Love, there must be *a world of individuals*, all of whom in some sense through their interrelations are capable of manifesting Love, Mercy, Helpfulness. Moral manifestation, further, needs *contrasts*. God is goodness, but in a world where there exists nothing but goodness, goodness as a manifested thing would paradoxically disappear. There would be nothing against which goodness could measure or express itself. The manifestation of God would further require *a world of need*. The black facts of life have some explanation and justification inasmuch as they provide conditions wherein the highest spirit in the universe indwelling in humanity can show what it is. Through the claims of the weaker and needy the indwelling Divine Love can become manifest. Could we ever realise God if there was nothing for God to do? "How were pity understood, except by pain?" Manifestation also needs *a field for growth*. There must be an observable process from a less good to a more good. In the earlier stages of the process we should hardly recognise the presence of anything divine, but in the later stages will appear the truth underlying the words "Man was created in the image of God." And finally the manifestation of what God is needs *a moral scheme in which both freedom and limitation play a part*. There must be some power to choose and some opposition to give goodness and character their significance. Virtue only shows what it is through test and struggle.

These reflections suggest to us that the world as we find it—the world of individuals, of endeavours and limitations, of good and evil, of growth, and challenge and slow conquest, is none other than the revelation, the manifestation, the race-incarnation of God: the Becoming aspect of the Divine Fact of the universe, complementary to its transcendent Being. In the spectacle of evolving life are we not beholding the Eternal Reality manifesting its nature—a cosmic process showing what goodness, character, God mean? God is eternally what He is, but He is continually manifesting His nature, personality, life and will in the multiforms of the universe, in millions of personalities, in numberless interrelations and interplays of individual lives, and by a process of time, growth, succession of events, by struggles and strivings in a world of opposition and limitation.

This view is to be distinguished from that of Pantheism of the Hindu type by a consideration of *values*. God manifests

Himself in life, but not *equally* everywhere. He "sleeps in the stone, dreams in the animal, wakes in the man," and in human life itself there are worlds of degree between the lowest and highest members of the race. In Hinduism the argument runs, "God is all—therefore anything may serve as a god," but in Christian immanence (and the doctrine of immanence, as Professor Pringle Pattison points out, must form the basis of any sound conception of the universe) the principle of values had been respected. Christianity has realised a profound truth in its claim that in the face of Jesus Christ, the Highest and Holiest, we see the express image of the Father.

IX. Divine Personality

This, then, is our general point of view, and its statement involves us in a number of questions, the facing of which may help us to explain and elucidate the doctrine: How, for instance, shall we regard the problem of Divine Personality? Personality as we know it seems to imply the limitations imposed by relationships. Morality, which is the central feature of personality, requires, as we have suggested, a social order and an opposition, if it must be morality. At first sight the idea of an Absolute with personality and morality seems impossible. How can God, the One, the Absolute, the Omnipotent, without a second like unto Himself, or any alien or resisting principle, possess either morality or personality? On the other hand, if we make God the highest and mightiest of the finites, He is still finite and thus falls short of being God. But if we can conceive the One and the Many—the One embracing the Many, and the Many contributing their meaning to the One—we may regard the Absolute as gathering up into unity all the significance of finite personalities. What happens in man's relations one with another belongs also to the All-embracing Fact. "It would be a strange kind of All," says Sir Oliver Lodge, "that included mountains and trees, the forces of Nature and the visible, material universe only, and excluded the intelligence, the will, the emotions, the individuality or personality, of which we ourselves are immediately conscious." We do not, however, regard the Personality of God as isolated, but rather as the personalities of the finites under the infinite aspect—*sub specie aeternitatis*. Divine Personality, like Infinite and Eternal Being, cannot strictly be stated in terms of finite personality; we cannot treat the One embracing the Many as One among the Many. At the same time, personality as it appears in finite relations, morality as it works out between man and man, is a sectional expression of the real but ineffable personality and morality of the Absolute. The personality which we attribute to God is eternally being revealed in human process and cannot be isolated from it. Behind all the struggles of human personality lies a Supreme Personality who is involved in the whole process, inseparable from it, and yet transcending it, even as the Infinite transcends the finites which give it its content and from which it is eternally inseparable.

One does not think of the Divine Personality as human personalities *merged* in some way in a supreme Crowd-Unit or Group-Soul. Experience of a Group-Soul, as a matter of fact, only means the intensification of the individual soul, not an obliteration of it. When I fall in love, I do not lose my individuality, but find unsuspected possibilities in it. Our idea of Oneness must not imply absorption, or individual annihilation, or merge into an amorphous One. The tree does not become one by the leaf ceasing to be a leaf. The picture does not become one by rubbing out all the detail. Abolish the Many and the One disappears with them. Individuality must therefore be retained and respected in our conception. God is realised through an intensified self-realisation. He is not best expressed through colourless, self-effacing, hollow, mediumistic creatures, but in men of pronounced personality and developed individualism, in "independents," in men who dare to think and act from the fullness of a developed nature.

X. Sin

What must we say of the problem of human imperfection and sin? If we realise that there can be no morality, not even the morality of a God, without test, struggle, growth from lower to higher, we may realise the place of even imperfection and sin in the scheme of the universe. It would transgress the principle of values to identify the human sinner with God, but wherever even a sinner makes a struggle against sin, or even realises that his sin is sin—something mean, unlovely and unworthy of his best nature—there is the veritable manifestation of God Himself. There must be test, struggle, temptation, the possibilities of a fall, if goodness and character must have meaning. As Walt Whitman daringly suggests in his *Chanting the Square Deific*, the existence of Satan is involved in the very conception of God.

On the other hand, our line of thought does not abolish the gravity of sin. Even if man "learns to walk by falls," or if sin should be involved in a process of race-education, it has none the less a sinister character, an evil and tragic positiveness, or there would be no learning or education. The lesson would be emptied of all meaning. Factors in a real education must have a real quality, or the whole business of education becomes unreal and farcical. We dare not treat our lessons lightly, play with our tasks, or ignore our disciplines on the ground that the whole process is meant to be beneficial and to have a useful end. It may be true that we look upon sin as a relative evil to serve an ultimate good, but that ultimate good may not be served by evil unless it keeps its character of evil—real, serious, tragic. We cannot identify a term in the antithesis with the synthesis which it serves.

Indeed, our line of thought, so far from condoning or

weakening the meaning of sin, in one way, at any rate, intensifies its gravity, for the whole scheme of life finds its significance in moral ends. Nature is a great and, indeed, tragic struggle, and the end served by the thousand hardnesses of life must itself bear the seriousness and weight of the process. The grim realism of life means an equally serious end to be served by life—and, as far as we can judge that end, it is the manifestation of moral character—the sense of evil as evil, and the conquest of the soul over evil as evil. Drawn into that end is all the grimness, hardness, seriousness of experience, the intensity of struggle in the whole process of creation and life. So far from sin being trivial, light, unimportant, accidental, it bears the gravity of the whole travail of the universe.

XI. Apocalyptic Interference

This view of God also seems to deliver us from a certain apocalyptic confusion. God as *Being* is Infinite, Eternal, Omnipotent, in the sense of His perfection and completeness; God as *Becoming* is finite, limited, struggling, aspiring, courageous, activist—the God of H. G. Wells. The aspects are complementary, but their terms are not interchangeable. We must respect the universe paradox. Unfortunately this is what men commonly fail to do. They say that God is omnipotent, omniscient, unlimited. He can do what He wants, and therefore if we piously worship Him and honour Him and praise His wisdom and love, He will put the earth right in His own time. Missionary labours, the League of Nations, Copec and the like are feeble and futile attempts contrasted with the apocalyptic emergence and operations of the omnipotent Deity. But in this world of Becoming, in this activist sphere, is it too much to say that such an alternating "finite-Infinite" God does not exist? The Infinite God exists; God acting finitely exists, but a finite God who be-

comes Infinite at will, who accepts the laws of finite manifestation and escapes from them when He so desires, who
capriciously turns Himself, as it were, from tree to leaf and
from leaf to tree—such a Deity is inconceivable. He would
reduce everything to chaos and confusion. God is in life, not
mingling in the game as an outsider, with the privileges of
omnipotence, but "playing the game," steadily and consistently, in human endeavour and slow painful conquest. He
wears a human countenance, sees visions and dreams
dreams, strains and suffers, sweats and agonises. "Lo, God
is in this place, and we knew it not."

XII. AN INTERPRETATION OF THE TRINITY

This Being-Becoming, Many-in-One view of God helps us
to appreciate the truth of the doctrine of the Trinity. The
Trinity is a formula of organism. It acknowledges the One,
but it is no formless, amorphous One. It is One in Many and
Many in One. It reminds us that God has aspects. It is a
challenge to the exclusive idea of God as a static Being. It
rightly denies polytheism and the tritheism which orthodox
Trinitarians so often confuse with the doctrine to which they
are supposed to adhere. The paradox of the Trinity arises
from the paradox of Being and Becoming. The first *persona*
of the Trinity is God *Being*, the Infinite and Eternal; but
God also appears in the forms of *Becoming*. We see Him in the
historical Jesus; we know Him in the Spirit which works in
human affairs towards a "far-off divine event." God appears
in limited and finite forms. He is flesh, knows sorrow and
pain, and hangs upon a cross in agony of soul and body.
And thereby we know that God is Love and Pity, Courage
and Self-Sacrifice. With this point of view we can realise
the profound truth of the Incarnation. Jesus must be truly
human actually to manifest the Divine. A Christ who might
escape at any moment the limitations of the flesh could

never truly reveal Love, Mercy, Sympathy and Courage. If we touch His genuine humanity we destroy His revelation of the moral values of God, only to be manifested in limitation and with opposition. At the same time, the doctrine of values gives our Lord His distinctiveness and supremacy. God does not reveal Himself equally in all that appears in the universe. To gain the necessary approximation to His moral nature we must seek the highest expression of personality in the universe, and thus those who have seen Jesus Christ, full of grace and truth, have seen the Father.

CHAPTER VI

THE ETERNAL GOODNESS

I

No phenomenon is more striking, persistent and unconquerable than man's belief in an ultimate eternal goodness. Despite the sorrows and tragedies of life, man persists in believing that "God's in His Heaven—all's right with the world." Faith has never been blind to the dark sides of life, but it is characteristic of religion—at least of all developed religion—that it has always felt that in the balance of the universe Evil can never outweigh Good. Where Religion cannot trace the vindication of the Eternal Goodness in the world that is seen, it finds room for it in worlds unseen and unknown, although one must ask why we should set goodness rather than evil in that unknown. The Gnostic, acutely conscious of the pain and tragedy of creation, postulates his Demiurge but refuses to make him the Supreme God. Satan has always been an inferior. Salvation and Deliverance have ever been the keywords of even the gloomiest religions. Yet it would seem that, apart from some kind of spiritual intuition, some revelation of mystic or cosmic consciousness, we have no very secure grounds for such belief. Why do men look for a "far-off divine event"? Not merely because of evolution. The world may indeed be growing, unfolding, working out to something better, giving promise that "every winter shall change to spring." But Nature also seems to be working in circles. Every winter changes to spring, and every spring to summer, but then summer changes to autumn and autumn to winter. The boy grows to manhood, and the man, having had his day, passes to old age, and having developed from childhood returns to "second childishness

F

and mere oblivion." The tide comes in, reaches high-water mark, but the ebb invariably follows the flow. What guarantee is there that evolution itself means anything more than growth to a certain point, to be followed by reversion? It is, of course, equally possible that the whole process is one of continual ascent, or even that a circle of growth and decay may serve a higher end, just as the growth and decay of tissues serve the life of the body; but we need some data of experience other than those of physical observation to direct and justify the more hopeful view.

II

Have we not grounds for the belief in the ultimate Eternal Goodness, in the particular optimistic quality of mysticism or cosmic consciousness? William James, in addition to stating that optimism is one of the directions to which mystic consciousness points (*Varieties of Religious Experience*, p. 416), says elsewhere (p. 388): "Looking back upon my own experiences, they all converge towards a kind of insight to which I cannot help attributing some metaphysical significance. The keynote of it all is invariably a reconciliation. It is as though the opposites of the world, whose contradictoriness and conflict make all our differences and troubles, were melted into unity. Not only do they, as contrasted species, belong to one and the same genus, but one of the species, the nobler and better one, is itself the genus, and so soaks up and absorbs its opposite into itself." It is as though the mystic has the power of looking upon the universe-picture as a whole, and can feel that, however puzzling and black the section may be here and there, the whole is harmonious. St. Augustine, faced with the problem of evil and finding no intellectual answer, declares: "I entered into my inmost soul, and beheld even beyond my light and soul the Light unchangeable. He who knows the truth knows what that Light is, and he who knows it knows Eternity. Eternity, Thou art Love! And I beheld that Thou makest all things good, and that to Thee is nothing whatever evil" (*Confessions*, vii. 10).

But although it would seem that ultimately nothing but some form of perception which would "sense" the whole *simul totum* could give this belief in the ultimate goodness of the universe, man will naturally and wholesomely seek to find intellectual correspondence with this intuitively perceived truth and to meet certain specific challenges to such belief arising from the experiences of life. We proceed therefore to consider some problems of Providence and some lines of reconciliation between finite experience and this intuition of the eternal goodness of the whole.

III

Is God really omnipotent? A fear has repeatedly entered into the soul of man—a fear which much of our human experience has inspired and seemed to confirm. This is the fear that God is not all-powerful and that there is a cosmic risk and uncertainty. What guarantee is there that "Right the day must win"? May not God in the end be overthrown, His purposes be frustrated, and the universe tumble off into hopeless ruin? The picture-writing of the Scriptures suggests that already in one or two crises the rebellious world nearly got out of hand. Once the situation called for the desperate remedy of a flood which destroyed nearly all mankind. Even after this the rebellious principle reasserted itself once more, and God was driven to another extreme expedient of sending His only Son to do battle with the increasing power of evil. All this suggests man's fear that the position of God in the universe, the hold of God upon the world, is exceedingly precarious.

The possibility of cosmic disaster, in fact, might seem

forced upon us by the very nature of moral freedom and responsibility. Could man really choose between good and evil, could he be anything other than a puppet, unless God could be genuinely thwarted and the world be made precarious by the misuses of man's freedom and responsibility? As soon as God gave man a genuine moral freedom, did He not thereby give up His omnipotence, with all the tremendous risk of consequence involved?

Further, it may be urged that there could be no reality of earnestness in the human struggle if things were sure to come out right in the end. Would not life become an empty pageant? To this it may be replied that the penalties of transgression would constitute a deterrent, and the desire to avoid them would give sufficient seriousness to human effort, apart from the question of the final destiny of the race and the cosmos. But there is a deeper answer. Over against the contention that if the world be subject to a Divine Determinism our moral strength and resolution would be sapped, it may be urged that if there should not be an absolutely sure Divine order of the universe, there would be at once a collapse of all moral striving. Who would have heart to endure and battle for the true and just if he did not feel that behind the universe there were sure and unalterable laws and an unfailing rationality and right, throughout the whole scheme of our living and striving?

The moral scheme requires both Freedom and Determinism. We can reject neither without falling into untruth and without the surrender of elements vital to living. To different aspects of truth both Augustine and Pelagius, Calvin and Arminius, with their opposite emphases, were witness. Spinoza, laying stress on the unity and wholeness of the universe, was led to doctrines of Necessity and Determinism, which are the grounds of his condemnation by moralists; on the other hand, the latter's scheme of the world would most certainly collapse, and fail to provide adequate moral stimulus and foundation, were there not also profound truth in Spinoza's ultimate Determinism. We must find some way of holding both sides of the truth.

IV

We return to our conception of the twofoldness of existence—Change within Permanence, Becoming within Being. What seems to us a solid piece of stone is constant activity, ceaseless change, yet governed by the laws of the stone's constitution. Or, again, the animal behaves with a striking variety of action, but it is all within certain limitations involved in its nature. So also we must regard the moral action of man. He is free within limits—the limits of his own moral nature. It is as much the nature of a man to exercise his will in certain directions as it is in the nature of a stone for the electrons to energise in certain ways and thus give feature and distinctive characteristics to that substance.

Further, there are the limits to the Nature of the universe in which man is placed. There is an unalterable Divine pattern or order in the universe to which all life must conform. We can take some common illustrations. An experimenter is trying to find some kind of amalgam which will answer a practical purpose of hardness, toughness, lightness, or what not. He tries combining all kinds of materials in all sorts of proportions until at last he hits upon just the right thing. He has come upon a secret of Nature. Nature ordained that this one combination would have the required quality. Other combinations were failures. Nature herself has been carrying on this kind of process in her evolutionary growth. For millenniums she has, in a figure, been "making her experiments of life." Numberless forms have been produced and perished because they did not conform to a mysterious, invisible order. The ever-working loom of a Creative Force, by the holding or the failing of a thread, is showing us the Divine Pattern. So there are throughout the history of man various social experiments. Matthew Arnold suggests this in his fancy that

> Before man parted for this earthly strand,
>   While yet upon the verge of heaven he stood,
> God put a heap of letters in his hand,
>   And bade him make of them what word he could.
>
> And man has turn'd them many times: made Greece,
>   Rome, England, France—yes, nor in vain essay'd
> Way after way, changes that never cease.
>   The letters have combined; something was made.
>
> But ah! an inextinguishable sense
>   Haunts him that he has not made what he should,
> That he has still, though old, to recommence,
>   Since he has not yet found the word God would.
>
> And empire after empire, at their height
>   Of sway, have felt this boding sense come on—
> Have felt their huge frames not constructed right,
>   And droop'd and slowly died upon their throne.
>   (*Revolutions.*)

Likewise the individual tries his various experiments of living, and in the process discovers the real existence of moral law. Not every experiment succeeds. The Determinism of a Supreme and Sovereign Law asserts itself. The soul has only perfect freedom when it perfectly accommodates itself to the moral law of the universe. The figure of a balanced battle between good and evil cannot be pressed. The result of following evil rather than good is not the shaking of the Throne of the Eternal, but sure and certain moral penalty. Only harmony with the Divine Will transforms into a home what is otherwise the prison-house of the universe. By seeking only to do the will of the Eternal do we know the truth which makes us free. Man's Freedom is only to discover God's Determinism.

V

The higher doctrine of Providence rests upon this sense of the Divine Law. We must not regard Law as a soulless, mechanical thing. It has a religious significance. It is an aspect of the being of God. It represents the unalterable Divine Will. It cannot be touched by human wrong-doing and folly. We feel also that it must be purposeful and beneficent. Can there be significance in the tiny processes of life, for instance, in the growth of a plant, one stage leading on to the next, and no meaning or purpose in the whole scheme of the universe? Shall there be no sense, beneficence, or rationality in the *whole* of Law, much of which operates beyond our sight? Shall not the laws of death be as rational as the laws of life? Will not Law preserve everything really precious for the highest good throughout life, death, and the great forever? Walt Whitman was surely right in his creed:

I do not doubt that the passionately-wept deaths of young men are provided for:
And that the deaths of young women and children are provided for:
I do not doubt that whatever can possibly happen at any time is provided for.

There is nothing accidental or fortuitous in the whole length and breadth of the universe. There is Law covering great and small, near and remote.

This is the doctrine of Providence taught by Jesus: "Fear not, for your Heavenly Father cares for you. Every hair of your head is numbered." This care operates even in seeming calamity. God cares for the sparrows—not merely for those which escape the fowler's net, but the poor little things which get killed and are marketed about two a farthing, symbols, not of deliverance, but of tragedy. Jesus introduces this detail deliberately to show that the Divine Law and care will cover men persecuted and likely to be martyred. "Be not afraid of them that kill the body but are not able to kill the soul." Even if tragedy should overwhelm them, if the soul be right with the Father, they are proof against real harm. The Divine Providence covers them even in calamity, tragedy and death. Nothing can be beyond it; nothing alien can creep in by accident. The tiniest sparrow's death was provided for by the law of the universe, which is also the love of the universe. This is the higher doctrine of Providence. There may be truth in what we call "special Providence." We can well conceive that we are surrounded by unseen forces whose action can break into our human affairs. The friendship and helpfulness familiar in our common human relationships may not be limited to the action of those whom we see with our human eyes. But there are circumstances when no relief comes, and the world does its worst. Then the deeper Providence must be accepted. The Divine Law still operates, and

> Love and Law are both the same,
> Named with the Everlasting Name.

VI. The Experience of Suffering

This constitutes one of the gravest challenges to the idea of the Eternal Goodness, sensed in the cosmic consciousness. Among the suggested explanations of the facts of human sorrow and suffering one or two may be definitely rejected at the outset. We cannot accept the Gnostic doctrine of the creation of the world by evil or stupid spirits as accounting for the flaws of the world. Monism puts the question: Who in turn was responsible for the existence of these stupid or evil spirits? Who created the Demiurge who did his work of creation so badly? We cannot regard the whole universe as falling under two alien principles, the one good, the other bad, without any higher reconciling purpose or principle.

In recent times we have had another attitude towards the whole problem put forward by Christian Science—the bold denial of pain and suffering as realities. This is too violent a challenge to human experience. We know that it is possible to make men insensible to pain for the moment by the use of anaesthetics, but shall we deny the existence of pain because temporarily chloroform can deaden the senses? It seems possible to render people insensible to pain by means of Christian Science methods or by mental suggestion, but we do not solve the metaphysical problems of the world by hypnotising ourselves to blindness in regard to what we do not want to see. Knowledge must be based on normal experience and not on hypnotic or semi-hypnotic states. Mental suggestion, faith-cure, Christian Science and the like can be of limited practical value in correcting some imagined evil, morbid hypochondria, or obsession. But in the long run we are brought up against reality, and have to face a world which often enough is not the thing which we would have it. There are limitations in the use of a mental drug. Sorrow, pain and the dark things of human life are too fundamental in our experience to be laughed away airily. And if evil be non-existent, how can there be even an evil imagination?

VII

The theory that suffering is to be explained as punishment for transgression and is to be regarded as a Divine verdict upon the sufferer's personal sin, fails to cover such cases as that of Job, one who was the type of men of conspicuously pure and honourable life nevertheless suffering calamity in the highest degree. There is no question that sin has consequences of suffering. That is a different matter. All sin as an outrage upon social health brings suffering. Calamity reveals the breaking of law. Pain is a factor in the educative discovery of the laws of life. An epidemic is part of a revelation; it shows where there is something wrong in men's ways of living. We must learn the ways of living which avoid such things. A disease is a challenge to us. There is something wrong to be set right. Equally true is this of the social diseases of the body politic, slumdom, destitution, war. The world slowly finds out from its hard and painful experiences the eternal laws of divine health in all departments of life. Transgression, then, as a particular type of the breaking of law, brings its calamitous consequences. But since, apart from the special pain of remorse, innocent as well as guilty are involved in these consequences, we are compelled to believe that while the penalty of sin indicates the nature of sin, as the breaking of the law of God's order, it cannot be taken as indicating guilt, or the particular measure of it, in those who suffer such consequences—indeed, there are cases (e.g. that of Jeremiah) where suffering is involved in positive virtue and nobility of soul.

The doctrine of Reincarnation is an attempt to restore the idea that all suffering is to be regarded as a divine judgment on personal sin. If such sin has not been committed in this life, it must have been committed in a previous existence. But this hardly accounts for the suffering of the righteous. Did a noble soul like Jeremiah suffer because in a previous existence he had been a notable sinner? Did Jesus become a Man of Sorrows because in some previous existence He had been conspicuously a Man of Transgression? In these cases of the suffering of the noble in soul two principles are apparently at work: (a) the evil consequences of sin fall upon them, for were the generality of mankind upright in spirit and conduct there would be no martyrs nor the "persecuted for righteousness' sake"; but (b) the very bearing of these consequences, in as far as it proceeds from noble motive, serves to manifest a divine spirit which actually needs for its manifestation these very circumstances of need, weakness, suffering, pain. In a perfect, painless world there would be no place for courage, sacrifice, service, love. Christ and those with the Christlike spirit suffer because of the sins and follies of the world, but it is through the circumstances of this very suffering that the divine spirit in them emerges. The Cross indicates at one and the same time the world's sin and the Love of God.

VIII

We must approach the whole problem of suffering with the general principle in mind that life is a constant and many-sided education or manifestation. We have been set in the world to learn, to develop, to release a "hidden splendour." Character is the highest good, and the "struggle-conditions" of life provide a gymnasium to this end. Struggle is involved in the very idea of life. Man was not "made to feed on joy." "When the fight begins within himself, a man's worth something." Job found his soul through the very afflictions, frustrations and sorrows which at first sight seemed to have no place in the universe of a wise and loving God. The sufferings of the righteous are to be conceived in the light of a spiritual law of manifestation. "Every good has its birth of pain," for from all advance is demanded a toll which actually gives virtue its character. The self-realisation of virtue proceeds from painful struggle-conditions. The disciplines of the soul are necessary for its perfection. The "works of God" are manifest against the very tragedies of life (John ix. 3). The essence of Christianity is suggested by such words as Love, Helpfulness, Mercy, Service, Sacrifice —yet these are obviously virtues which imply and presuppose need, and the pain of need, and the sacrificial pain of relieving need.

IX

The special difficulty with this principle is presented by the fact of pain in sub-human nature. One can only say that there may be glimmerings in such sub-human nature of the faculty which in ourselves we call the rational and moral sense. One cannot help feeling that there is some continuity between higher and lower life, that "Nature makes no leaps," and that even in the lower stages of creation there is some process of moulding and developing the quality of consciousness through the experience of sub-human pain. There seems to be some ratio between the development of consciousness and personality, on the one hand, and susceptibility to pain and suffering on the other. At the lowest end of the scale, in stones, vegetables, earth-worms, there seems little or no susceptibility to pain. This susceptibility seems to increase with the ascent in the scale of values, and man, with his comparatively complete personality, has a greater susceptibility to pain because he has a moral nature to be affected. Love, ambition, idealism—the highest features of personality—expose humanity to a far greater range of suffering than that to which the lower forms of life are limited. With this ratio between consciousness and susceptibility to pain it would appear that where a creature can suffer there is, even in faint form, some glimmering of what we call personality or soul, and where there is that, there is scope for the process of discipline and education through pain; there is some nature capable of "finding itself" through the experiences of frustration and challenge. St. Paul in a moment of insight spoke of the whole creation groaning and travailing in pain together, as one great cosmic unit and for one end —namely, that the "sons of God" should be manifest. The whole process was conceived as a development in which pain had a factoral part in the working out of a nature in which ultimately divinity revealed itself. It is along these broad lines that the inquiry for the intellectual justification of the eternal cosmic soundness in the face of the phenomena of pain should apparently proceed.

X

But we return to our main thesis, and claim that Providence in the widest sense must be apprehended in some mode proper to its cosmic, eternal and infinite nature. It is true

that we can find in finite phenomena and in arguments based
thereon traces of a pattern agreeable to the intuition of our
cosmic consciousness—the sense that the universe is sound
and that all things work together for good. And if we seek to
deny this as the ultimate principle of existence we have
equal or greater problems in accounting for the good and
rational and purposeful in our experience. But if our intellectual explanations remain "broken lights," and if reason
cannot fully penetrate the mystery of suffering, the soul has
its own avenue to the consciousness that "Eternity is God;
Eternity is Love." It is a direct intuition to which millenniums of faith have borne significant witness. We believe that
Browning is right in suggesting that the ultimate conviction
of the Eternal Goodness lies beyond argument, in a sensing
of the harmonies of the universe by the musicians of Faith:

> Sorrow is hard to bear, and Doubt is slow to clear:
> Each sufferer says his say, his scheme of the weal and woe.
> But God has a few of us whom He whispers in the ear:
> The rest may reason and welcome: 'tis we musicians know.

CHAPTER VII

IMMORTALITY

I

WE have noticed that one of the marks of the Cosmic Consciousness is a sense of Eternal Life, and although this is primarily indicative of quality of life, and is to be realised here and now and not merely in the future, yet the very quality of such life involves continuance. It is too rich a life to be holden of death. It is too large in its processes and implications to be confined to the few years of terrestrial living. Further, Psychical Research may some day give us a Psychical Science which shall be able to demonstrate that there is survival of personality beyond death; but immortality in the fullest sense means more than this—it means unending existence, not merely survival *for a period* beyond death. From its very nature, lying outside "time," from its cosmic quality and implications, immortality must be a doctrine based not on finite perceptions, but on a cosmic intuition. God has "set immortality in our hearts." It is given by Faith, which we regard not as credulity nor scientific surmise of the unseen based on the things which we see, but as a definite faculty, making us aware of the Infinite and Eternal aspects of the universe. "What is man?" exclaims Carlyle. "He endures but for an hour and is crushed before the moth. Yet in the being and working of a faithful man there is already *(as all faith from the beginning gives the assurance)* a something which pertains not to this wild element of time, that triumphs over time, and shall be when time is no more!"

II

But while we believe that the broad fact of immortality comes to the soul from our mystic or cosmic consciousness, we may naturally note corresponding elements in our spheres of argumentation and finite observation, in accordance with the general principle of these studies. The pattern of the section must agree with the sensing of the whole.

The reasonableness of the universe points in the direction indicated also by the cosmic intuition of immortality. Can there be reason and purpose in a hundred of the minor operations of Nature—the preparation of one stage for another in the growth of a common flower or in the physiological development of the human body—and no meaning, purpose, or reason in the total process of living? And yet the whole idea of personality, which stands supreme in our judgment of values, appears meaningless if death be the end. "O life, as futile then as frail." The only way we can understand this puzzling life is to regard the world as a "gymnasium of the soul," to look upon its changing circumstances, its tests, battles, disappointments, losses and sorrows, temptations and trials, as forms of discipline and exercise for that which is central in human personality. Moral laws which work inwardly upon the soul of the individual as well as outwardly in the life of society, do not have that complete field of action which the moral and rational sense of man demands, unless we carry their operations into wider spheres than that of our individual span of human life.

Again, if we are to find inspiration to live out our best, we must find such rationality in life. We shall not be able to trace the whole of the rational process, but at any rate we must leave room for the working out of a process much of which may lie out of our sight. "We may well doubt," says the author of *Natural Religion,* "whether the natural and material will suffice for human life. No sooner do we try to think so, no sooner do we try to get rid of immortality, than pessimism raises its head. Human griefs do not seem worth assuaging, human happinesss too paltry at the best to be worth increasing. The whole moral world becomes reduced to a point. Good and evil, right and wrong, become infinitesimal, ephemeral matters. A moral paralysis creeps over us." With this we compare the saying of Renan: "The day in which belief in an after-life shall vanish from the earth will witness a terrific moral and spiritual decadence." Or we have the opinion of Professor Goldwin Smith, that morality is only saved in a generation sceptical of immortality by the consideration that, after all, there may be something in the belief. One could not be dogmatic and deny absolutely the possibility of an after-life, and even the bare possibility, the "may-be," saves the world from the full tragic consequences of disbelief in immortality. These consequences may also be checked as long as *some men* believe in immortality and help to set general social tradition under the influence of such personal belief. Once more, we have the opinion of Professor William McDougall (*Body and Soul*, Introduction), who says: "It seems to me highly probable that the passing away of the belief in immortality would be calamitous for civilisation. Every vigorous nation seems to have possessed this belief, and the loss of it has accompanied the decay of national vigour in most cases. Apart from any hope of rewards or fear of punishment after death, the belief must have, it seems to me, a moralising effect upon our thought and conduct which we can ill afford to dispense with. . . . A proof that our life does not end with death, even if we know nothing of the nature of the life beyond the grave, would justify the belief that we have our share in the larger scheme of things than the universe described by physical science, and this conviction must add seriousness, dignity and significance to our lives, and thus throw a great weight in the scale against the dangers that threaten advanced civilisation."

It may be that the idea of personal immortality was not pronounced in certain stages of Israel's history, in which conspicuous belief in God and stress upon His moral requirements were to be found, but the inference from this fact must be modified by the consideration that the sense of personal individuality among the Hebrews was largely undeveloped, that for a time shallow theories of the working out of God's moral processes "in the land of the living" were held—theories that came to constitute an insoluble problem to psalmists and prophets as experience opened out deeper aspects of human life. In our own day it is quite possible for a man of shallow thinking, feeling and experience to get along comfortably without belief in immortality. The sense of a need of a larger life proceeds from profounder realisations of life and personality.

The very fact that this belief seems so essential to the harmonious well-being and rationalising of the world seems itself a support of its truth. There is something to be said for a doctrine which appears to be an indispensable factor of the world's health, and is involved in the rationalising of human life and in the sense of human values.

III

It may be contended that we are not shut up to the immortality of the *individual* soul in order to justify the reasonableness of life and to have a motive for living out our best life —for is there not the immortality of human influence working out in future generations? If our bodies and even our souls should perish, is there not the possible immortality of living again "in minds made better for our presence," of "making undying music in the world"? Possibly some of the finest souls among us, with an admirable quality of self-effacement, might give up the thought of immortality for themselves without losing motive if they could feel that their labours might endure in the lives of others and in the progress of the race-life and in the achievements of future ages. But this view presupposes that the end of effort is to be found in material accomplishment rather than in spiritual discipline, education and refinement. The significance of life must sooner or later be found in terms of soul and preserved in terms of soul. Not in the thing done, but in the doing must be found the meaning of life. Pens and copybooks are needed in the human school of the ages, but the results are to be found in the mind and soul of the writer. We do not exist to create copybooks, but to discover how to write. Worn-out pens can be destroyed, the filled-up copybooks can be thrown into the flames without loss. The meaning of the process is to be found ultimately in the learner's personality and faculty. At some point in the history of the race all its efforts must be summed up in a soul, and for that soul there must be some immortality in order to conserve the meaning of the whole process. It may not be *our* soul, but it must be *some* soul. But if it be some soul in the future, which shall exist apart from the material world in order that the whole world-process shall have significance, why should we deny that possibility for our own souls?

As far as physical forms are concerned, the tide of fate will sooner or later sweep over our shore of human sand-castles. All men's labour on the physical side will ultimately be wiped out in the perishing of the physical world. "The old earth had a birth, as all men know, long ago—and the old earth must die." Unless we are to be paralysed and dismayed by that ultimate annihilation, unless we are to surrender the idea of spiritual purpose, or of any kind of purpose in life, we must postulate something beyond physical forms; we must grant an unseen life and reality; and if we do this for the whole race, why should we not grant it for the individual life, especially when the reasonable view of life as a "moral gymnasium" for the individual soul seems to require such a doctrine of *individual* persistence beyond death?

IV

At first sight, at any rate, the most formidable challenge to the doctrine of immortality seems to arise from materialism. Until recent years Science has been suggesting that Soul or Mind is but "a shadow thrown by Matter." Matter and motion, chemistry and physics, were found to explain so many things that it seemed a general principle of Nature that everything in the universe, including thought and feeling, could be explained by these forces. The theory ran that in the first place there was a great cloud of inorganic matter; presently, by physical forces, certain simple substances began to form; these exhibited chemical and other qualities, reacted upon one another, and by and by, through chance contacts and physical and chemical action, something called life appeared. Further processes led to the falling out of the less perfect forms, and highly specialised and organic types of life appeared. Nerves came into being, grew complex; brains emerged, and feeling and thought were born; but the whole process went strictly on mechanical lines, with the mere juggling of matter and motion and nothing else added. Thought was an accidental vapour from the simmering cauldron of physical matter. When the chance process came to an end, the spark of consciousness, mind, personality, soul would flicker out into everlasting night.

But there seems to be a clear setting of modern thought in the direction of a spiritual interpretation of the universe. The materialistic theory must deny even the primal mind of God. Yet how must the whole scheme be conceived without some directive intelligence at the very beginning? How did the laws of evolution come to constitute themselves? According to the materialistic theory, Mind is apparently the *last* thing which evolution has produced—its first works were poor, blind, unintelligent. Must we not place at the very commencement of the process some directive Mind—this something which materialistic evolution puts at the end of the process? If pure materialism breaks down here in the fundamental basis of the scheme, it cannot successfully carry its challenge against the existence and operation of Mind at other stages of the process. It has surrendered the principle that Matter can explain everything—even Mind.

Again, we have as perfect a right to postulate the reality of the Soul as a primary fact as we have to postulate the reality of Matter. Our knowledge of both comes from phenomena of a distinctive kind. We have no right to say that Matter has a substantiality and permanence which Mind or Soul has not. We do not know the real nature of Matter any more than we know the real nature of Soul. Matter may be a storm of electrons or resistance of other Souls, as Leibnitz suggested. It has no fixed and substantial nature which gives it the primacy of being over Soul, Spirit, or Mind. "Matter" is only a term to enable us to hold mentally certain experiences—and in the same way "Mind" is a term to cover equally certain and distinctive experiences, and the latter has as much claim to substantiality, reality and permanence as the former.

V

What may we say of the phenomenon of physical death, which is the most dramatic and elementary challenge to immortality? This involves us in some consideration of the relations of Soul and Body. Probably the Leibnitzian doctrine of Monadology provides the most helpful answer to this problem. The body, Monadology teaches, is a colony of souls, under the partial and temporary control of that hegemonic monad which is the "ego"—the something which I feel to be specifically "myself." The body represents, as it were, a mobilisation of sympathetic monads or souls, whose co-operation and mutual response so constitute a unity that other groups or colonies of souls are in comparison foreign and external. Yet the "self-contained" nature of the monads making up the body is evident from the facts, not only of the occasional insurrection of the body when it fails to be amenable to the will and develops disease and sickness, but also of dissolution and decay. The constituents of the body have previously been parts of other organic combinations. During life, in the growths and deaths of tissues there is change in relationship to the hegemonic centre or "ego," and death marks a major dissolution, which, however, may be conceived as leaving the hegemonic monad, the "ego," the "I myself," much in the position of a commander-in-chief when his army is disbanded. There is by no means extinction of the monad which we feel to be our true "ego," but the dissolution of a working partnership. This partnership, while it lasts, enables the monad to exercise its energy upon what we call "the material plane," coming into creative and disciplinary relations with the multiform material realities of human experience.

We may, with Bergson, look upon the brain, the body-seat of mental life, not as something producing Mind, but a motor-mechanism by means of which actions are carried out which the mind or monad conceives and prepares. Brain action may be largely selective, screening off the irrelevant, so that a special action in the material world may be executed. We may take the analogy of a pinhole camera, shutting out excess of light so that a definite image may be thrown and preserved upon the sensitive plate. Therefore when brain and body die, and in the process of nature decay, the perishing of Mind and Soul is not involved. Brain did not create the monad or Soul. It was its instrument for a temporary purpose. It had a transmissive not a creative function. It is a false analogy to say that the flame of the Soul flickers out when the candle of the body is burned through. It is a truer analogy to think of the Soul using the body and brain as an instrument or tool. Because man

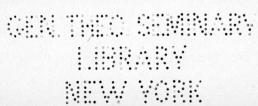

cannot dig without a spade, does man become extinct when the spade is worn out? Man cannot produce violin music without a violin, but when a particular violin becomes broken, does the man who played upon it become annihilated? It is reasonable to believe that there is an essential part of us which survives when the mechanical instrument of the body breaks down and is destroyed.

Professor McDougall in his *Body and Soul* asserts that there is not one valid argument which can really be sustained against the old-fashioned doctrine of Mind and Soul existing in their own right, apart from processes of body and matter, and goes farther to show by a wealth of detail that the universe cannot be explained unless we postulate something more than matter and motion, mechanics, physics and chemistry. There is Mind, Soul, Spirit, which can make use of mechanical law, direct and control its application, but which mechanical law cannot by itself explain.

What this "Soul" in its ultimate being is, we may not be able to say. We only know that it is of a totally different nature from matter, and that the laws of material dissolution do not necessarily touch it. Religion can tell us more of it than physics or chemistry ever can. Religion is the science of the Soul. It is spirit which knows spirit. And the deep intuitions of men's souls—the awareness that we live and move and have our being in God, the sense that He is our home and that we can share His eternity, the consciousness of the eternal worth of the Soul—these are the truest sources of our knowledge concerning the greatest part of us.

VI

For several reasons the doctrine of a merge at the moment of death into a kind of central reservoir of life, the disappearance of the Soul into the Over-Soul, does not seem a likely hypothesis. One of the reasons for belief in survival is that it

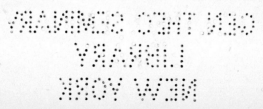

would allow a field for the working out of mental and moral processes of individual personality, broken off and left incomplete in this life. A theory which denies persistence of individuality beyond the grave gives no satisfaction for this rational anticipation of mental and moral completion. Again, although mystic experience at first sight may seem to encourage the idea of absorption, since a feature of its manifestation is an apparent merge into the Over-Soul, it is obvious that some identity must remain to receive and record the experience. Or we have the sentiment expressed—

> What an exceeding rest 'twill be
> When I can leave off being me.
> Why should I long to have John Smith
> Eternally to struggle with?

But it is doubtful whether such a sentiment will bear analysis. Complete annihilation is theoretically conceivable, but where is the subject that shall enjoy the "rest" due to the abolition of John Smith? John Smith must return to life to experience the joy of the extinction of John Smith!

Once more, we have various experiences of life when normal personality is violently disturbed—for example, the realisation of a "group-soul," a collective sentiment and emotion, or of a "falling in love"; but in these cases our personality does not disappear in order to form a new centre outside us or to constitute a new body such as might be formed by the combination of chemical substances. Contact with a new element intensifies or develops something in the individual personality. The person who falls in love does not become abolished or swallowed up in a new third person, lying midway, as it were, between lover and beloved. The individual personalities of lover and beloved become deepened and intensified. So the mystic is not lost or absorbed in God, but realises through the communion a deeper, richer personality latent from the beginning within himself.

Or, again, when philosophically we speak of the Many and the One we conceive a complementary relation—the Many in the One and the One in the Many. These must exist together. The One is what it is because the Many are what they are. If twigs, leaves, branches disappear, the tree disappears as well. There is nothing in our experience to encourage us to believe in an amorphous One in which the Many lose all form, character and identity.

Once more, the argument for survival from affection—which, after all, is one of the deep elements of personality—would fail if persistence could only be in the form of absorption in an amorphous Over-Soul. Thus Tennyson, with his dead friend in mind, was constrained to write:

> That each who seemed a separate whole
> Should move his rounds and fusing all
> The skirts of self again, should fall,
> Remerging in the general Soul
>
> Is faith as vague as all unsweet:
> Eternal form shall still divide
> The eternal Soul from all beside,
> And I shall know him when we meet.

VII

But as far as these speculations are concerned, it is wisest to take our stand upon a general principle which we feel to be profoundly true and having its base in our sense of the Eternal Goodness and of the essential soundness of the cosmos: the principle that *that which is really worth while keeping will never perish*. There must be eternal conservation of values.

> The high that proved too high; the heroic for earth too hard:
> The passion that left the ground to lose itself in the sky,
> Is music sent up to God by the lover and the bard:
> Enough that He heard it once: we shall hear it by and by.
> There shall never be one lost good . . .

Although the detailed problems of our destiny seem so immense and baffling, the religious attitude is very simple. We trust the deepest intuitions of our souls, and find the details of our future comparatively unimportant. If we knew more of the hereafter it might be far more distracting than helpful. We can be content to know that we belong to an eternal order; that to-day is not in contrast with, but is a part of, that eternal order. We can surround our daily living with that sense of eternity which is needful for the living out of our greatest life and is necessary to give reasonableness, depth and dignity to human existence. We can also feel that the chequered career, the life permanently shadowed as far as earth goes, the open grave, can have answer and reconciliation with a scheme of justice and love in the processes of a larger life. We have a few practical instincts for the day, and we find it reasonable to believe that to-day's noble living will help to fit us for the next stage. Our simple business is to do justly, love mercy and walk humbly with God. We can leave the rest to Him. Nature will do us no wrong. God knows His own scheme. Our understanding of its details will make it no wiser or better than it is. Whatever is best will be done. Whatever is worth the keeping will be kept throughout the length and the breadth of the universe. Here Epictetus may be our teacher: "Dare to look up to God and to say: Deal with me in the future as Thou wilt. I am of the same mind as Thou art. I am Thine. I refuse nothing that pleases Thee; clothe me in any dress Thou choosest."

Fear not thou the hidden purpose of that Power which alone is great:
Nor the myriad world, His shadow, nor the Silent Opener of the Gate.
(TENNYSON, *God and the Universe*.)

PART II

CHAPTER VIII

THE NEW TESTAMENT EXPRESSION OF RELIGION

I

THE story of religious faith is largely a history of this cosmic mode of consciousness, of its occurrence in men's experience, and of their attempts to express and explain it. In the following studies we are seeking to illustrate this in that vitally important period in which the Christian Church was born and its theology shaped—a period of impressive witness to these fundamental intuitions of faith and hope and love. These are not only expressed directly in Christian appeal and exhortation, but underlie the chief forms of Christian theology and practice. Much of our task will be to find this significance in primitive Christian doctrine. There will also be an attempt to make a valuation of Christian belief in the light of that "Being-Becoming" philosophy which seems involved in the phenomena of Mysticism.

II

Many of our religious difficulties in the use of the New Testament have arisen from the fact *that we have sought to find there for our religious purposes theology rather than faith.* Our study has suggested a distinction between the two. Faith is intuitional, the revelation coming from the soul's sensing of the broad cosmic facts of our existence; theology is to provide intellectual expression and satisfaction for intuitional faith, to meet the demands of the intellectual part of our nature, to justify the broad claims of intuition in the finite sphere, to fill up its details, as it were, in finite life, and to relate it to the world of finite experiences, knowledge and action. Reason may not take the place of those direct intuitions of the soul; the central elements of faith have reference to infinity and eternity, and rest upon the revelation of a Mysticism, which is a "seeing by the soul" of the Infinite and Eternal; inference by argumentation belongs to the finite world, labours under its limitations, and fails to give the last and final truths of our being, which rest in the Infinite and Eternal. What Reason may do is to show that its findings lie in the direction of cosmic intuitions, and that there is nothing in finite experience absolutely contradictory to the instincts of faith. In our studies of God, Providence and Immortality we have recognised both the intuition of cosmic consciousness and the place of reasoned argumentation as a necessary supplementing of it, a reconciliation of the "reasons of the heart" with the "reasons of the mind." Hegel was right in claiming the insufficiency for life and thought of mere intuition (see p. 43), and man will inevitably speculate, seek to express and explain his intuitions of faith, and thus theology will form with its value largely dependent on the stage of intellectual development reached by the speculator. Theology will therefore vary and change, and we need not expect its soundest, clearest, and most adequate forms in the earlier periods of human thought, even when the *intuitions* of faith may be definite and pronounced.

This distinction suggests the religious use of the New Testament. Its permanent value lies in its faith rather than in its theology. Its "faith, hope and love" abide; its "knowledge" passes away. The New Testament must be read for its witness to spiritual intuitions and not for its first-century speculations concerning them. Thus the study of the New Testament involves us in an analysis of its contents (*a*) into the witness to fundamental intuitions of faith, realised by the men who "see with their souls," and (*b*) into the theories of varying worth which have gathered round them—indeed, we must often find the significance of the latter in their testimony to the former. The explanations, however inadequate and unsatisfactory they may be in themselves, constitute a witness to the intuitions to be explained.

III

Moreover, our fidelity to the New Testament will not take the form of justifying and defending the speculations which early Christian thinkers wove concerning their spiritual experiences. Christian faith by no means commits us to a brief for first-century theologies and theosophies or for later creeds built upon them. It rather consists in the acceptance of those fundamental attitudes of faith, hope and love most simply expressed in the life and teaching of Jesus of Nazareth, and living our life and directing our desires and thought in the light of them. Primarily Christianity is a setting of soul rather than the acceptance of a philosophy of religion. But it is natural and wholesome that we should attempt what the New Testament writers attempted—to build speculative schemes upon these fundamental intuitions. Such a modern task is virtually a "translation" of the speculative faith of the New Testament theologians. We interpret their meaning, not in following the details of their first-century speculations, but in taking up and continuing their labour, and stating their truth as best we can in the light and terms of our own knowledge. The New Testament needs interpreters rather than custodians of its theological letter. We cannot do the New Testament theologians justice by a merely traditionalist attitude; we must continue their task in a creative spirit. The basic intuitions remain, and constitute the permanent element in religion, but the intellectual speculations based on them will manifest the restlessness and changes of progressive living thought. New Testament theology must therefore not be stereotyped, but translated.

IV

The first task which meets us in the study of the New Testament Expression of Religion is to set the development of New Testament thought in historical perspective; to determine, as far as we can, the nature and life and teaching of the historic Founder of Christianity, and to distinguish this from the doctrinal elaborations of the New Testament Church. Each phase of the growth has its own expression of those fundamental instincts of religion which we have already noted.

We assume with confidence that we have a genuine historical life as basis for our Gospel tradition. The contention of the "Christ-myth" writers has succeeded no farther than to show that in the natural elaboration of the accounts there are unhistorical elements, and that contemporary myth played a considerable part in the theological interpretation of early Christian thought. We do not reject the historicity of Gautama Buddha because miraculous and mythical birth stories have gathered around him. We do not regard the story of St. Francis as a myth on the ground that we find miracle of a most improbable kind in the *Lives* of the saint. And we would surely agree with Goguel (*Jesus the Nazarene*, p. 205) that although the darkness, earthquake and resurrections of the Crucifixion story are probably mythical, yet "it would be no more legitimate to conclude from this that the death of Jesus was a myth than it would be to presume that Julius Caesar never existed because numerous writers have related that his death was accompanied by signs not less extraordinary."

On the other hand, with our realisation of the way in which our Gospels were produced; of the interval between the events and the recording of them; of the fact that apparently not one of the present Gospels is the work of an eye-witness (at any rate, of the bulk of the incidents recorded); with a recognition of the discrepancies manifest even in the parallel passages of the Synoptics, and the larger differences between the first three Gospels and the Fourth Evangel, and of the theological, apocalyptic and ecclesiastical tendencies affecting the traditions in their transmission, we can no longer claim the supernatural infallibility claimed for the records by our fathers, nor even that degree of human accuracy and precision which we expect in modern biography and scientific historical account. In our quest for the historical Jesus we are confronted with the serious problem of determining, if we can, the historical facts which lie behind the records rather than on the face of them. The popular method of treating any or all of the Gospel passages as if they were unquestionable historical statements or miraculously guaranteed records is clearly unjustifiable.

V

For our quest of the historical figure behind the records it is a matter of the highest importance that the tradition of the life and words of Jesus did not come to us through a single Gospel. We have four ancient documents dealing with the same general subject-matter. We must, of course, dismiss the idea that the four Gospels represent four independent witnesses to one set of events and discourses, for it is very evident that in the parallel passages Mark's Gospel is used by the other Synoptics, and even the Fourth Evangelist seems to use Mark and Luke. But the comparison of the four records is valuable for the illumination which it casts upon the methods, interests and mentality of the several writers. We not only see the growth of sayings and narratives, but the direction of the growth and the nature of the tendencies. There are doctrinal modifications of sayings. The doctrinal colouring is heightened as we pass from Mark, where it is comparatively slight, to Matthew. The Marcan *logion*, "Why callest thou me good? There is none good but one, that is, God," becomes transformed in Matthew into: "Why askest thou me concerning that which is good?" (xix. 17). The Marcan statement that Jesus at Nazareth "could do no mighty works" is toned down into the statement that He "did no mighty works." The process finds its culmination in the Fourth and latest Gospel, which has become largely a theologian's treatise with the historical elements subordinate.

Again, in the comparison of the Gospel accounts one sees the clear tendency to magnify the marvellous. In Mark vi Jesus walks on the sea. In Matthew's version not only does Jesus do this, but Peter succeeds to a point before he begins to sink. Further, if this process of elaboration can be seen between Mark and Matthew, we may suspect it as operating even before the form of Mark is fixed. We find traces in Mark himself of what seem to be "doublets" of the same tradition, but the one more marvellous than the other. Thus we have in Mark iv a story of Jesus stilling the storm while He is in the boat with the disciples. Two chapters later He stills the storm, but He walks the sea as well. But even in the simpler chapter iv we can distinguish two elements—the self-possession, calm and trust of Jesus in the presence of danger, the faith in God for lack of which He reproved His disciples, and the miracle of commanding the winds and waves so that they obey Him. Is not the calming of the tempest in the souls of men the spiritual genesis of the whole tradition, the growth of which we can trace in three distinct further stages, each becoming more marvellous?

Once more, in Luke xiii, verses 6–9, there is recorded the parable of the fig-tree which does not bear fruit and is therefore threatened with destruction. The figure is that of the nation, Israel; she is in danger of perishing unless she brings forth fruit worthy of repentance. This parable has presumably reached Luke independently in its original form. Mark, though writing at an earlier date, has received it already transformed—it has become a miracle, and one of the most unconvincing of miracles. Jesus going from Bethany to Jerusalem seeks figs from a tree—somewhat curiously, indeed, because Mark says it was not the time for figs. Finding nothing but leaves, Jesus exclaims, "No man eat fruit from thee for ever." Next day the fig-tree is found withered away from the roots (Mark xi). In Matthew xxi the story of the cursing is repeated, but with a further element of wonder, for immediately before the eyes of the disciples the tree withers away!

VI

We must take into account these general tendencies of elaboration, not only where there are parallel passages, but where we have reason to suspect the present form of a narrative for which we have no check or comparison of parallels. Thus we are doubtful about the more astounding miracles, or the doctrinal claims made by Jesus, according to the Fourth Gospel. Certain sayings of an ecclesiastical kind may well be suspected. It is highly improbable from the nature of the case that a reference to Church discipline (e.g. Matt. xviii. 17) is an authentic saying. We doubt the present form of the *logion* promising to build the Church upon Peter (Matt. xvi. 18), or that of the Absolution passage (John xx. 23). The Eucharistic references of John vi seem to reflect the conditions of a later period of thought. Suspicions concerning some of the apocalyptic sayings in their present form are strengthened by the literary phenomena of Mark xiii. It appears fairly evident that the evangelist has incorporated some apocalyptic writing—"The Little Apocalypse"—among the words of Jesus. If certain verses (7, 8, 14–20, 24–27, 29–32) be lifted out, they constitute a continuous theme in themselves and leave behind an intelligible line of thought. But as the chapter stands, it makes on the reader an impression of confused and vacillating ideas and of definite predictions unjustified by historical consequences. The sun should be darkened, the moon fail to give her light, the stars should fall from heaven, and the Son of Man should appear with great power and glory (verse 26), and all these things should be accomplished within the lifetime of that generation (verse 30). Even the rest of the chapter, which reflects the conditions of a later period of the Church—persecutions, legal trials, false Messiahships and a world-wide missionary movement—gives one the impression of being an unhistorical section, possibly based on a few historical sentences of Jesus (verses 1, 2, 21, 28, 34 ff.). The interpretation of the "sign of Jonah" as a reference to the apocalyptic Son of Man being three days and three nights in the heart of the earth (Matt. xii. 40) is an elaboration inconsistent with the context of a refusal to give a miracle sign. The sign of Jonah is really the self-accrediting nature of the preaching (Luke xi. 29, 30).

VII

Old Testament precedent and prophecy may have played a part in the creation of tradition. A clear minor instance is found in Matthew's story of the entry into Jerusalem, in the mention of *two* animals: "They brought the ass and the colt, and put on *them* their garments" (xxi. 7). This seems to have been due to the misreading of the poetic parallelism of Zech. ix. 9. Mark xi. 7 more correctly speaks of one animal. We can just record cases where, with varying degrees of probability, the influence of Old Testament precedent and prophecy on the Gospel records has been suggested: the forty days' fast of Jesus in the wilderness, parallel to that of Moses on the Mount and of Elijah in the desert; the feeding of the multitude in the wilderness, with its Old Testament counterpart in the miraculous feedings of Israel in the wilderness; the raising of the widow's son at Nain, even as Elijah raised the widow's son at Zarephath; the supernatural Virgin Birth (cf. Isa. vii) at Bethlehem (Micah v. 1); the flight into Egypt (Hosea ii. 1), and the massacre of the Innocents (Jer. xxxi. 15). There may also have been influences from current traditions, theosophies and apocalypses affecting the story. The period during which the thought of the early Church was being born was one of strange interminglings in the lands of the Eastern Mediterranean.

Apart from all this, it is very evident that the evangelists were not too certain of their material. The variations of detail in the description of incidents show this. It is also clear that the evangelists were not sure of the incidents to be connected with certain *logia*, for they set these in quite different connections, and, indeed, interpret them in quite different ways. The "sign of Jonah" is one instance, and others are to be found in Dr. J. E. Carpenter's *First Three Gospels*.

VIII ·

In seeking the historical value of these narratives, we cannot exclude the criterion of probability as suggested by universal experience. We are warned that it is not legitimate to bring *a priori* objections to certain incidents and sayings found in the Gospels, that we ought not to come to the New Testament with presuppositions as to what could and could not happen in the case of so exceptional a personality as that of Jesus, yet if we are honestly to treat the Scriptures as we would treat any other ancient writing we must read the Scriptures in the light of universal experience. We must exhaust every possibility of explanation by normal experience before having recourse to explanations utterly foreign to normal, universal and age-long experience. We find law so constant and Nature so orderly and consistent in her operations that to shake our belief in a general normality of phenomena we need evidence much stronger than our present Gospels, as we have found them to be. They are obviously not infallible documents, but traditions gathered together by men of the second generation of Christians, and containing material of varying historical value.

We may find abnormalities in our own day. The records of psychical research are full of them, and similar abnormalities we may reasonably accept in the Gospel period. They are abnormalities, not contrary to law, but resting on less familiar law. Some of the stranger elements in the Gospel records find their most probable explanation in similar modern psychical phenomena. But concerning what goes utterly beyond such present-day experience we may not unreasonably be sceptical. This, indeed, is an essentially wholesome attitude. Moreover, such scepticism fortunately need not destroy, nor even touch, our real faith in our Lord, His message and work. We interpret these in the light of eternal moral and spiritual laws and the operations of personality in the broadest sense. This being so, we need have no theological difficulty in applying what we believe is a healthy and justifiable criterion in the reading of the Gospels —namely, that they must be studied in the light of probability and in all their detail be interpreted according to the laws of universal and eternal experience.

IX

A further observation needs to be made. The study of the biographical details of the life of our Lord leaves us with a sense of problems more or less unsolved, and some, indeed, unsolvable. Much is dubious, much uncertain. The processes of *Aberglaube* are evident. The figure of Jesus has become clouded and uncertain, except in the broadest outline. But the case seems other with the element of His practical spiritual teaching. The conclusion of Paul Wernle (*The Sources of our Knowledge of the Life of Jesus*) is that "we cannot write any biography, any so-called 'Life of Jesus.' . . . Mark is only a compiler of detached traditions, which he was the first to unite conjecturally into a whole, and he himself has no personal knowledge of the localities and no clear insight into the chronology of Jesus's life. And where Mark as a historian fails us, how should we here and to-day gain any better knowledge?" (p. 154). But Wernle proceeds to claim that we do know the spirit, mind and message of Jesus. "Out of the wealth of His parables and sayings, and out of many momentary memories of Him, Jesus speaks to us with a voice as clear and definite as if He lived among us to-day. The great discourses of the Collection of Sayings give us the same answer as the colloquies of Mark and the parables which only Matthew or Luke records. And they are always clear, definite answers, simple, unforced, springing out of the depths of feeling, not the logic of the understanding. What is crucial in the words of Jesus . . . shines forth again out of the Gospel to-day as bright and wonderful as if the sun were but newly risen to drive away with its conquering beams all ghosts and shadows of the night" (pp. 160–2).

CHAPTER IX

THE EVANGELISTS AND HISTORY

I. THE MARCAN TRADITION

OUR main source of information for the events of the life of Jesus, as distinct from His teaching, is the Gospel according to Mark. The other Synoptists rely chiefly upon him for their facts and their framework. His Gospel almost word for word reappears in Matthew and Luke. If these Marcan passages were cut out from the Synoptists' records scarcely anything in the nature of a biography would be left. "Even now," comments Burkitt ("Gospels," *Encyclopaedia of Religion and Ethics*), "many professed theologians do not seem to realise how narrow is the channel by which the Gospel history has filtered down to us."

In estimating the value of this primary record two questions must be asked: (1) Was Mark an eye-witness? and (2) What was his general mentality? Papias expressly denies that Mark was an eye-witness. "Neither did he (Mark) hear the Lord, nor did he follow Him." Unfortunately we are not quite sure of the reliability of Papias, although from internal evidence Wernle finds confirmation of his statement in his vagueness of geographical description and of the connection of events. "Even in details, the seeming lifelike picture is often dissipated into mist when we begin to examine it." This suggests that "Mark was not an eye-witness, but had only worked on the teaching— that is, on practical, not historical, discourses—of Peter" (*Sources of our Knowledge of the Life of Jesus*, Eng. trans., p. 107).

II

The argument that Mark was an eye-witness because of the vividness of some of his descriptions is not convincing. It is an argument which would prove that a capable novelist lived in many different ages and witnessed every incident which he described. Nor is the gift of vivid description peculiar to men of outstanding genius. Imaginative skill in description is often found with men of quite ordinary types of mind, incapable of any large creative intellectual construction. The cursing of the fig-tree and its consequences are vivid enough, but almost certainly unhistorical. The story of Herod and Herodias is graphic, but not only was Mark not an eye-witness, but the incident was historically ill-founded. It is precarious to build an evidence of eye-witness on the curious incident of the young man who fled away naked (Mark xiv. 51, 52). It is suggested that this young man was Mark himself, and that is why he records the incident, for it is so trivial in itself that it would hardly be mentioned by the evangelist save for a personal reason. Loisy, however, connects the story with Amos ii. 16: "He that is courageous among the mighty shall flee away naked in that day, saith the Lord." The Betrayal and Crucifixion story appears to have been largely influenced by out-of-the-way Old Testament passages (see Gougel, *Jesus the Nazarene—Myth or History?*, pp. 160 ff.), and this may be another detailed instance.

III

Further, granted that it is not impossible that Mark was actually present at some of the scenes at Jerusalem in the last days, this does not carry us very far. It does not guarantee any witness of the earlier incidents of the Gospel, the first part of which is "little more than a string of anecdotes, loosely connected together, not perhaps always in relative chronological order" (Burkitt, "Gospels," *Encyclopaedia of Religion and Ethics*). Nor does it confer absolute accuracy upon all the details even of Passion Week recorded in the Second Gospel. Hearsay and rumour would play a part in a narrative compiled even by one present at Jerusalem at the very time of these stirring events. But even this degree of contact during the last days of the evangelist with the historical Jesus is purely conjectural. In the earlier period covered by the Gospel there is not the slightest real evidence of eye-witness and much to make any eye-witness highly improbable. We may accept the tradition of his contact with Peter and of his being the apostle's interpreter on occasion without assuming that all the Marcan narrative came from Peter. Mark must have had other sources, and why should we suppose that all his information should be submitted for the confirmation of Peter? We know even from tradition next to nothing of the nature and period of Mark's relations with Peter. What we can say about Mark is that he was through association with the primitive Christian community close to the earliest tradition, and much of his Gospel appears to be based on genuine, though indirect, historical witness.

IV

But a further important question is to be considered—that of the mentality of the historian. How far was he able to appreciate the figure of his study? Is his picture a complete one, or has he missed some of the more important features because of his own limitations as a recorder? What insight have we into Mark's mind from the character of his work? There is much more in Nature than the ordinary photograph conveys; the colourings, for instance, are missed, because of the limitations of the plate. Must we think of Mark's Gospel as only catching, as it were, the black and white of the

personality of Jesus and missing His spiritual genius and
the deeper elements of His life and teaching? We believe
that there was infinitely more in Jesus than Mark is able to
suggest, and that any view of Him which is limited to Mark's
picture is sadly incomplete. Mark was simply incapable of
recognising the greatest features of Jesus, even with all the
good will possible on his part. This conclusion is not due to
mere modern idealisation; it is forced upon us by the nature
of the other parts of the New Testament. Some of the missed
spiritual colourings come back to us in the *logia*, in the
Fourth Gospel, in the Epistles. The black-and-white picture
of Mark does not give us the Figure which would account
for the spiritual wealth and the permanent qualities of the
movement which proceeded from Him. We need to bear
this in mind in view of the modern tendency to turn to
Mark's Gospel and to treat it as the reliable and authentic
presentation of Jesus; after all, it is only a very partial
picture, inadequate not merely because of its scarcity of
information, but because of its faulty emphases, its choice
of external and least significant features, the incapacity of
its author to appreciate the greatest elements in the life and
teaching of Jesus. He even left this sense upon the early
Church. The Fourth Gospel, according to Clement, was
written to remedy a lack in the Marcan tradition—to
supply "a spiritual Gospel," for the earlier Gospels had set
forth "the things obvious to the senses."

V

We may now record our impressions of the mentality of
St. Mark, based on inherent indications of his interests
shown in his record. He appears to be a simple-hearted,
simple-minded soul, perfectly honest and sincere, but without any high degree of intelligence or spiritual insight.
He has had close contact with Paul, but has caught nothing

of the latter's more subtle and spiritual conceptions of faith. He has none of the fine feeling of the Fourth Evangelist in his interpretation of the life and significance of Jesus. He remains the plain man, non-mystical, prosaic in his thinking, attracted by externals, unfitted by Nature to be a sympathetic spiritual interpreter of Jesus. He has no speculative ability; he does no theorising. This feature of his mentality has its advantage. He does not colour the narrative with his own interpretations to any serious extent. He elaborates less than the other evangelists. His "colouring" of the story is simple, obvious, and never grave. When he ventures to theorise he does it naïvely and clumsily. If people do not understand the parables of Jesus, the only explanation Mark can offer is that Jesus never meant them to understand Him! It is the explanation of a simple loyal soul; it will convince no one except those who have a similar mentality.

VI

But Mark's advantage arising from his non-interference with his sources is unhappily counterbalanced in another way. He has shown little discrimination in dealing with his sources. He does not ask whether parable has passed into miracle. He will accept a Jewish Christian apocalyptic, arising from some more imaginative mind, and incorporate it without misgiving among authentic *logia* of Jesus. Two accounts of the stilling of the tempest come to him. He sets them both down as separate events. He gives us "doublets" of the Feeding of the Multitude. From one source comes a great spiritual answer to the critics of Jesus who accused Him and His disciples of Sabbath-breaking—"The Sabbath was made for man and not man for the Sabbath"—a saying which "accredits itself" and appeals as an authentic saying of one of spiritual genius, as other bold and spiritual sayings attest Jesus to have been. From another source comes a saying with a scribal spirit and interest, with a traditionalist's

concern for a precedent from one of the worthies of Israel:
"Did ye never read what David did when he was an
hungred?" Mark appears to have no difficulty in attributing
both sayings to Jesus. He records the magnificent refusal of
Jesus to accredit His ministry by credential miracle: "No
sign shall be given to this generation" (Mark viii. 12); at
the same time he relishes every marvel tale he can find to
show that Jesus is Son of God.

As a historian he suffers not from any lack of honesty, but
from lack of discrimination. Some of his details have the
highest historical probability. The later Church would never
have invented such sayings as "Why callest thou me good?",
Jesus "could do there no mighty works," "My God, why hast
thou forsaken me?" (See also Burkitt, "Gospels," *Encyclopaedia of Religion and Ethics*.)   On the other hand, he gives a
story of the death of John the Baptist which abounds in
historical improbabilities, and side by side with a verse
which is regarded by Burkitt as one of the instances of subtle
genuine authenticity (Mark xi. 11) he gives the highly
improbable account of the cursing of the fig-tree. We do not
seem able to argue from the fact of his historical sections that
everything which he records must be taken as historical.
Apparently he deliberately colours nothing, nor tampers
with his sources for doctrinal reasons, but he innocently
accepts all that comes his way, probable or improbable, as
long as it fits into his general framework. We get convincing
historical touches; we get wild improbabilities. With his
love for the dramatic, he apparently finds it hard to resist
any tradition of action and dramatic arrest.

VII

We have here touched upon another clear and important
feature of Mark's mentality. There is a rough artistry in him.
He has a rude gift of graphic description, not uncommonly
found with men whose general thinking is prosaic and

mechanical. He has not the genius to invent interpretatively, to conceive an intellectual scheme, or to be in any sense a constructive thinker; but he has a rough artistic plan for his whole work, and he can embellish a tale with imaginative details. He is rather like a certain type of Sunday-school teacher, who would never dare to attempt any drastic reconstruction of a Bible story, but can tell the story with all kinds of inventive picturesque touches to make the account vivid and attractive. We do not conceive that Mark would have turned a single parable into a miracle story. The parable of the spiritual food has become the miracle of the Feeding of the Multitude before it reaches Mark, but Mark can give the vivid descriptions of the folk settling themselves like garden-beds at the miraculous feast, the detail of the green grass, and in other instances all those graphic touches which have been so much stressed by those seeking proof that Mark was an eye-witness. The argument is a singularly unconvincing one. The gift of dramatic narration neither implies eye-witness nor is accompanied by creative powers of a speculative or intellectual kind. There are very definite reasons for belief that Mark, despite his graphic descriptions and his chronological and geographical details, was not an eye-witness. We put down these features of the Second Gospel to Mark's dramatic gift, and to that alone.

One stresses the point that Mark was not deliberately inventive, apart from this gift of graphic and imaginative description. Given a miracle story, he would elaborate it with picturesque details, but he would never invent a miracle. Elaborations of such a kind must have taken place before Mark attempted his work. We do not know who were responsible for it. Their elaboration might be innocent enough. They did not set out to be historians. They told a story, and in human fashion the story grew. Perhaps we may put something down to the process of dramatic preaching. The conclusion that Mark himself did not invent the stories in their main outline is confirmed by the phenomenon of "doublets." The same story appears in Mark in more than one form (the feedings of the multitudes, the stilling of the tempest). Mark did not create or drastically transform his material; he accepted material already shaped, without sense of discrimination, but he allowed himself to give graphic and dramatic form to his material. There is therefore another indication here that Mark is not the direct eye-witness. A process of elaboration, which we find it hard to attribute to Mark, lies between the life of Jesus and Mark's record.

VIII

As we have already said, Mark manifests little real spiritual appreciation. He has no sense of the deeper meaning of the personality and message of Jesus. He has almost a childish love of miracle, and in tantalising fashion subordinates the spiritual teaching to the telling of miracle stories. It almost seems like an accident when we get a spiritual *logion*. To Mark, Jesus is not the giver of "the words of eternal life"; He is pre-eminently the miracle-worker, the healer, the caster out of evil spirits. In its selection of material Mark's Gospel strikes us as less proportioned than the other Synoptics. The dramatic and marvel interests are dominant. In this respect Mark represents a certain tradition of the early Church; he is representative of a primitive group of Christians who found the significance of Christ in miracle and apocalypse, but were little sensitive to His deeper spiritual values. The Infancy stories, for instance, were not Marcan, and yet they belong to his mental tradition; they were produced probably in a rather later period, or at any rate in another circle, by those who had the Marcan type of mind, the Marcan interests and principles of selection. Their absence from Mark we suppose is due, not to any historical discrimination or scepticism on Mark's part (he would have relished their insertion had he known of them); his silence is most plausibly explained by his ignorance of them.

IX

In another direction this type of mind reveals itself. We realise Mark's obvious interest in apocalypse. He thinks not in terms of religious interest, transformation of personality, spiritual and ethical law, but in a celestial drama played out on the stage of that generation. The interest which makes him choose miracle rather than discourse, parable rather then sermon, leads him to give great space in his short work to the apocalyptic aspect of the life and teaching of Christ. We are at once sensitive to the possibility of an unconscious and innocent misrepresentation of the figure and work of Jesus. Mark presents Him hardly as the preacher of a spiritual kingdom, a transformer of popular Messianic conceptions, but as an apocalyptic Messiah. We are left with Gospel hints, where we would expect Gospel emphasis upon the spiritual kingdom. Jesus in Mark's Gospel has the appearance of claimant to apocalyptic Messiahship as His chief and significant function. Although the open claim is postponed to a comparative late date in the ministry, it is nevertheless the guiding interest of the evangelist. We are made conscious of it even at the baptism. From the early days of the ministry the evil spirits are restrained from declaring the Messianic secret. This interest and emphasis of the evangelist has led scholars like Johannes Weiss and Schweitzer to conceive that this, too, was the interest and emphasis of Jesus Himself, whereas we conceive that the apocalyptic references of Jesus only indicated His use of a category for a spiritual message of a far more universal and eternal nature. Mark thinks in terms of action, movement, drama, of miracle now and of apocalyptic wonder hereafter. That is his misfortune and ours, for he created one of the great traditions of what Jesus was and did. That there was another tradition is evident from other parts of the New Testament—a spiritual and ethical teaching, wider than local forms and current expectations; a tradition which retained its worth and appeal when crude apocalyptic expectations were disappointed and fell into the background.

X

Turning to the other Gospels, there seems no question of eye-witness at all in regard to the First and Third Gospels.

1. *Matthew's Gospel.*—Irenaeus (*c.* 185) states that "Matthew published his written Gospel among the Hebrews in their own language while Peter and Paul were preaching and founding the Church in Rome." He further states that it was only after the death of Peter and Paul that Mark "also transmitted to us in writing the things which Peter preached." Papias (writing somewhere between 135 and 165) is quoted by Eusebius as saying, "So then Matthew composed the oracles (τὰ λογια) in the Hebrew language, and each one interpreted them as he could." Irenaeus is known to have read Papias, and the former's statement is probably derived from the latter. Papias derived his information from the "Elder" who, Streeter believes, was the author of the Fourth Gospel. Our present Gospel of Matthew is written in Greek, and it uses Mark's Gospel as one of its main authorities. Therefore it cannot be identified with the Hebrew or Aramaic work of Matthew mentioned by Irenaeus and Papias. Streeter (*The Four Gospels*, pp. 500 ff.) believes that our present "Matthew's" Gospel was produced in Syrian Antioch. He conjectures that the persecution of Christians in Jerusalem about A.D. 66 drove a number of refugees to this city, bringing with them the books they valued most highly. A Gospel tradition, strongly Judaistic in character, came with them, representing "not primitive Jewish Christianity, but a later Judaistic reaction against the Petro-Pauline liberalism in the matter of the Gentile mission and

I

the observance of the Law." About this time also, Mark's Gospel arrived at Antioch from Rome. There was also known at Antioch a document older than Mark—Quelle, or Q, "most probably an Antiochene translation of a document originally composed in Aramaic, perhaps by the apostle Matthew, for Galilean Christians" (Streeter).

Antioch had its stricter Jewish party and its more liberal and pro-Gentile party, but in the quarter of a century which followed the Fall of Jerusalem circumstances were unusually favourable to conciliation. Between the Judaistic party who had originated with James and the adherents of the Pauline tradition lay the moderates, who had taken their spirit from Peter. In these new circumstances the Petrine party was enabled to effect a conciliation and to produce a compromise Gospel—our present Matthew. Peter is the supreme interpreter of the new law. It is he who can "bind and loose"; it is he on whom Christ's Church shall be built. This is the interpretation put upon an earlier saying which originally must have had a quite different significance. The date of this new compromise Gospel—our present Matthew —is assigned to A.D. 85. *But this process rules out the authorship of any member of the apostolic circle for our present Matthew's Gospel. Its compilation is not the work of an eye-witness,* although much of its incorporated material may have come from some who saw and heard Jesus.

XI

2. *Luke's Gospel,* according to Streeter, was an attempt to improve upon Mark. It is to him chiefly that the reference in the introduction is made: "With the materials at his disposal, he might well consider that he could improve upon a Gospel which had no account of the Infancy and the Resurrection appearances and very little discourse; but to say this bluntly would have been tactless, for Mark's was the Gospel on

which many of his readers had been 'brought up.' By the
vague and general 'Forasmuch as many have taken in
hand' . . . nobody's feelings could be hurt" (p. 599). In
Luke's introduction he acknowledges that he himself belongs
to the second generation—παρέδοσαν ἡμῖν. The sense of the
passage makes οἱ ἀπ᾽ ἀρχῆς αὐτόπται refer to the subject of
παρέδοσαν. *Luke was evidently not an eye-witness. There are no "we"
sections in the Third Gospel.* Mark, apparently much in its
present form (for the Ur-Marcus theory is now vigorously
denied by Streeter, Burkitt and others) formed a source used
by Matthew and Luke. The former used Mark's framework,
introducing into it non-Marcan material in alternate blocks.
Thus, as Streeter says: "Matthew may be regarded as an
enlarged edition of Mark; Luke an independent work
incorporating considerable portions of Mark." Matthew and
Luke have a considerable amount of material in common
not found in Mark (the Quelle sections). Streeter conjectures that Luke prepared a work earlier than our present
third Gospel—a proto-Luke, independently of Mark and
approximately of the same date, making considerable use of
Q. We may thus have here an historical witness apart from
that of Mark's tradition. Later, Luke produced an enlarged
edition of his earlier work, making use of Mark and pre-
fixing an account of the Infancy.

XII

3. *The Fourth Gospel.*—It would not be easy for an actual
Apostle, as John, the son of Zebedee, was, to allegorise the
story as this evangelist does. It would conflict too severely
with the actual human history of Jesus. Such a treatment
requires a stage of remoteness from the actual facts. It is an
achievement only possible in the second generation. At the
same time, the work must be done by one who is sufficiently
in a well-recognised line of continuity to be able to speak with

some authority on what the mind of the historical Jesus was. These conditions seem satisfied by attributing the work, as Streeter does, to John the Elder, disciple of the Apostle John, writing about A.D. 95, when he was nearing the age of eighty. Streeter thinks that John the Elder may have come into personal contact with the Apostle John without perhaps having seen a great deal of him, for most of the incidents recorded in the Fourth Gospel seem to have been derived from Mark and Luke. He conjectures that he may as a young lad in Jerusalem have even witnessed some closing scenes in the life of Jesus (*The Four Gospels*, p. 431). But of one fact we may be reasonably certain: the author is no eye-witness, at any rate of the great majority of the events which he describes—probably not of any. "Many of the apparently life-like details . . . are in reality but veiled allegorical allusions. Their picturesqueness may be set down, not to the absolute memory of the eye-witness, but to the fine instinct of the literary artist" (E. F. Scott, *The Fourth Gospel*, p. 19).

XIII

In the Fourth Gospel, whoever the author may be, there seems to be no attempt to confine the narrative to historical sayings and happenings. The historical elements are subordinate to spiritualisation. The "truth" of the Fourth Gospel is the allegorised truth of spiritual facts rather than the historian's precision and accuracy in the description of events. The author appears to have made use of Marcan and Lucan materials, very freely treated, and he has perhaps other sources of incident, but he has obviously used all these as parabolic and allegoric vehicles for the conveying of ideas arising from quite independent sources and circumstances. It is clear that the Fourth Evangelist is continually alluding to situations and tendencies of thought found in the Christian Churches of Asia Minor nearly a century after the death of the historical Jesus. We are aware of the existence of Gnosticism, of a partial sympathy with it, and also a sensitiveness to its dangers. We are conscious of theological and ecclesiastical controversies which had arisen with Jews and with the disciples of John the Baptist, with Scriptural literalists, and with sacramentalists. The work has polemical and ecclesiastical aims arising out of conditions which do not belong to Christ's own generation and to the theatre of His historic ministry (E. F. Scott's *Fourth Gospel*, chaps. iii and iv). It is quite clear that the theological and ecclesiastical ideas put into the mouth of Jesus are, at any rate in large part, the ideas of the author, and possibly of a school gathered round him, rather than the ideas of Jesus Himself. The Gospel has as its background the Logos conception of the Prologue and the Christological speculations of Paulinism, which we conceive to be foreign to Christ's own original teaching. In large part the Fourth Gospel is not the story of the historical Jesus and His teaching, but the allegorically presented history of the first century of Christian speculation as experienced in the Ephesian centre.

XIV

The question thus arises as to what historical value in regard to the actual life and teaching of Jesus the Fourth Gospel possesses. Are we dealing with purely "imaginary conversations" grafted on to the Synoptic sayings and incidents, or have we also genuine, and in some measure independent, reminiscences of the historical life and teaching of our Lord?

(1) On the one hand, the author is not an eye-witness, at any rate for the main part of his story. The most we can grant is Streeter's conjecture that the author as a young lad may have actually caught a glimpse of Jesus. It is very difficult to conceive an intimate associate of Jesus speaking of Him in the highly artificial fashion of the Fourth Gospel. Nor is

it likely that an eye-witness would fall back upon the Synoptics like Mark and Luke, who were not themselves eye-witnesses. (2) The Fourth Evangelist bases a good deal of his incident upon the Synoptics, but in many places where he departs from them, his narrative suggests fanciful elaboration and historical improbabilities. In dealing with the early phases of Christ's ministry, John's presentation of events and sayings, where they differ from the Synoptic record (e.g. in regard to the Messianic claims of Jesus or to His relations with John the Baptist), is much less historically convincing than that of the earlier Gospels. Or, again, such an independent narrative as that of the raising of Lazarus is full of historical improbability. (3) Much of the Fourth Gospel, as we have seen, reflects later conditions and ideas inappropriate to the historical situation of Jesus. The author's motive in writing is therefore in large measure doctrinaire rather than purely historical.

XV

On the other hand, have we echoes of the actual historical teaching of Jesus, derived from sources quite independent of the Synoptics, elements of our Lord's message unappreciated by Mark and the men of Marcan mentality, but noted and preserved by some more spiritual listener with whom the Fourth Evangelist was in direct and fairly intimate contact? Have we an independent and authentic tradition of Jesus as a Mystic, whose mystic teaching (in the sense of Mysticism in which we have used the term) has been preserved in many of the phrases of the Fourth Gospel and has guided the evangelist's attitude in regard to problems of a later date? In support of this point of view are the following considerations:

(1) There are hints of an independent and superior historical tradition underlying the Fourth Evangelist's account of the Last Days. This suggests that the author

knew someone who had fairly full and, at any rate, independent information of Jesus in the last phase of His ministry.
(2) It is quite possible that the Fourth Evangelist had access
to *logia* uttered throughout the ministry of Jesus, even
though he had only very imperfect knowledge of events.
This phenomenon is found in the First Gospel. For events
the author of our present "Matthew" goes to the Marcan
tradition, but for sayings he relies on another source, Q,
which had apparently little or nothing to say about events.
So the Fourth Evangelist may have had, for the earlier part
of Christ's ministry at any rate, no independent knowledge
of events and yet have possessed a reliable and authentic
set of *logia*, from some source independent of the Synoptics,
and more definitely mystic in nature than the sayings
preserved in the First Three Gospels. (3) One of the tendencies seen in the Fourth Gospel is a claim for the real historicity
of Jesus against the Docetist teaching that He was but a
phantom form. The author can allow himself to elaborate
the picture of Jesus found in the Synoptics to the point of
unreality, and yet he remains emphatic that an historical
figure lies at the foundation of his Gospel. From this characteristic it seems reasonable to suppose that in dealing with
the teaching of Jesus he can allow himself to elaborate with
the utmost freedom and yet work round a kernel of actual
historical *teaching*. Somewhere he must touch an historical
speaker. (4) We may understand the writer's freedom in
dealing with what we suppose are authentic *logia* of Jesus,
together with this respect for history, by calling to mind the
Greek way of writing history. "Plato, who felt that he owed
everything to the teaching of Socrates, never, as far as we are
aware, made any attempt to hand down to posterity the
ipsissima verba of his master. . . . It is probable that in the
earlier dialogues the speeches of Socrates, though written in
the style and language of Plato, do not inadequately represent opinions entertained by Socrates. But in the later
dialogues Plato had developed his system far beyond any-

thing which is at all likely to have been in the mind of the historic Socrates" (Streeter, *The Four Gospels*, p. 370). Streeter believes (p. 372) that the author of the Fourth Gospel "must have meditated year after year, not only on the Epistles of Paul, but on certain *logia* of Jesus which had come to him as being of special and profound significance. He appears to have had a tradition of events independent of the Synoptics; it would be strange if this did not include some sayings as well." (5) That the Fourth Evangelist was working on some older sayings is further suggested by a line of internal evidence. Sayings are found which suggest to us greater spiritual genius in their original form than in the evangelist's use and interpretation of them. We may suggest as instances (*a*) the answer by Jesus to the Jews who asked Him for a "sign" to authorise His cleansing of the Temple: "Destroy this temple and in three days I will raise it up." We conceive that this was the fine answer of a reformer who rightly claimed the authority for His action, in its spiritual nature. It was part of a self-accrediting religious zeal, constructive as well as destructive. It had power to build up as well as cast down. But the evangelist's interpretation compared with this was weak and improbable: "But He spake of the temple of His body. When, therefore, He was raised from the dead, His disciples remembered that He spoke this" (ii. 21, 22).

(*b*) "And I, if I be lifted up from the earth, will draw all men unto Myself" (xii. 33) suggests an exaltation similar to that of the Sermon on the Mount—the servants of God must bear their witness, and be seen as cities set on hills and lamps placed on the stand. But the evangelist finds this a reference to being lifted up upon a cross: "This He said, signifying by what manner of death He should die."

(*c*) Or we have recorded a conversation with Nicodemus, the point of which seems to be a challenge to the idea that one sent from God must be accredited by signs and wonders.

The real credential is by the spiritual appreciation of man's highest nature. But the evangelist finds the saying serving the Platonic doctrine of Two Worlds and a sacramental gaining of the Spirit, and so far forgets what seems to be the original idea of Christ's answer that he fills his evangel with miraculous signs to accredit Jesus as the teacher sent from God.

(d) After His resurrection Jesus breathes on the disciples, saying unto them: "Receive ye the Holy Ghost; whose soever sins ye forgive, they are forgiven unto them, and whose soever sins ye retain, they are retained" (xx. 23). This appears to be an ecclesiastical turn given to a simpler teaching of Jesus, of which Synoptic expressions are to be found in His teaching that a spiritually minded man, in virtue of his harmony with the mind of God, may pronounce sins forgiven (Mark ii. 1–12), or that he has the power of "binding and loosing"—that is, of making sound moral judgments (Matt. xviii. 18).

XVI

One gets the impression from the whole work of uneven spiritual genius, as if two minds were being expressed—one that of a spiritual mystic, the other that of a sacramentalist and theologian, with interest in miracle, and holding a Platonic scheme of two worlds, with Christ as a mediating Logos (see p. 251). The explanation of the phenomenon may be that the writer is combining authentic *logia* of Jesus, derived from John the Apostle, with elaborations proceeding from a different and on the whole a less spiritually acute mentality. In general we are dealing with a work of unreconciled positions. "Ideas flow in upon the writer from various sources—from primitive Christian tradition, Paulinism, Alexandrian speculation—and he does not attempt to reason them out or to co-ordinate them into a system" (E. F. Scott, *The Fourth Gospel*, p. 14).

XVII

We believe, then, that a tradition from the Carpenter of Nazareth—simple, spiritual, mystic, but untheological and unecclesiastical—has been preserved by a writer who has other interests and attitudes, some of which have almost passed into contradictions of the original tradition. We conceive that the more mystical and spiritual elements of this original tradition were unappreciated and missed by Mark or by his informers; they were, however, received and preserved by a disciple who was able to understand Jesus—the Apostle John, the "disciple whom Jesus loved." With him the spiritual message was primary; events fell into the background. A second generation, inheriting this mystic and spiritual Johannine teaching, had the teaching without much of the history, and had to fall back upon the Synoptic narratives for details. In a way, in the Fourth Gospel the two traditions, the Marcan and the Johannine, had come together again—the Johannine teaching gathered within the Marcan framework, but not in such a way as to restore the original figure underlying both traditions. For, on the one hand, the Marcan tradition had incorporated unhistorical elements; on the other, the Pauline development, the contact of Christianity and the Hellenic world, the speculations of the Ephesian school and the problems of the Christian Church during the first century—all these had affected the simple, original teaching of Jesus as handed down by the earlier John, and have made the Fourth Gospel allegorical rather than historical.

XVIII

But the value of the Fourth Gospel for our study is that we seem to have preserved in it the authentic tradition of Jesus as a prophet of definite religious mysticism, and founding a school of men taking the mystical attitude towards life, conscious of mystical intuitions in their own souls, and meeting the later problems of the Christian Church with the solutions of the mystical tradition. We may nowhere be sure of the actual mystic utterances of Jesus, but we conceive that they underlie large sections of the spiritual teaching of the Fourth Gospel and are embedded in passages which are elaborated by a later hand and mind. We can eliminate the known Pauline and Alexandrian features, the ecclesiastical and doctrinal elements; the rest we may take as representing substantially the spiritual and mystic message of One who stressed the Fatherhood of God and the Brotherhood of man; love for God and communion with Him, and the realisation of strength, joy and peace following therefrom; the mystic's union with the Father and the realisation of the greatest realities of life through fellowship, love and service. This teaching appears without the characteristic mystical features in the Synoptics, but we believe that its more distinctive mystic statement, as suggested in the Fourth Gospel, is an authentic element in the ministry of the historical Jesus, strengthening His appeal to the hearts of kindred spiritual souls throughout the ages, and deepening the meaning in experience of His evangel of love to God and love to man.

CHAPTER X

THE HISTORICAL FOUNDER

I

It is obviously beyond the scope of our study to attempt a full historical biography of Jesus in the light of the foregoing consideration of the Gospels, their nature and origin. We intend to confine ourselves to those aspects which bear upon the question of New Testament perspective and theological development. We want to see, if possible, the nature of the religious teaching given by Jesus up to the time of His death, and to distinguish this from the additions of the evangelists, reflecting the theological elaborations of the early Church. We want to see the nature and the limits of the claims made by Him. We also need to note the elements of the evangelical tradition having historical credibility, which might set at work processes of theological development, and to trace the origins of those conceptions upon which the attention of the early Christian speculators seized.

THE INFANCY STORIES

It is natural that the historical tradition becomes most questionable when it attempts to deal with the earliest years —indeed, here reliable tradition fails us almost completely. The process of pious invention which showed such wild play in the apocryphal Gospels of the infancy and boyhood of Jesus has begun even in our canonical records of Matthew and Luke. In filling up the blank of the early days and years possibly both Old Testament prophecy and contemporary myth played a creative part. The expectation that the Messiah must be David's son provided a genealogy. Prophecies connecting the Messiah with Bethlehem, David's city, were to be satisfied with a Bethlehem birth story. "Out of Egypt did I call My son" may have started the tradition of an Egyptian sojourn. The prophecy of Rachel weeping for her children possibly created the detail of the massacre of the innocents. The influence of Old Testament prophecy did not stand alone; there was also the suggestiveness of contemporary ideas. The Mithraic tradition told of a Deliverer born in a cave and adored by shepherds; miraculous birth stories were familiar in the pagan world; and there were Old Testament passages which would help a Hebrew mind to accept the idea—abnormal births of some of the Old Testament worthies and the Isaiah prophecy of a virgin who should conceive and bear a son whose name should be called Immanuel, although the context showed that in the writer's mind the situation anticipated was utterly different from that of the Gospel story, and it is improbable that the Gospel story had its actual origin in the prophecy. It is not necessary to trace exact parallels; the stories themselves bear on their very face the marks of their nature. The traditions as we have them in Matthew and Luke are drawn from different sources, it is true, and there can be a divergence of traditions which may indicate independence of testimony, and consequently the multiplication and strengthening of witness—the argument made familiar to us in Paley's *Horae Paulinae*. But the divergencies of Matthew and Luke are too many and too extreme to serve this argument. In nothing do they agree except that the birth was a miracle and that it took place at Bethlehem—statements that have an intelligible doctrinal origin. They bear independent testimony to an early tradition, but this is very different from bearing independent witness to an historical fact or set of facts. The tradition itself may be quite unhistorical. Moreover, the differences are of such a nature as to make it quite clear that the Church had no firmness of historical knowledge for this period of our Lord's life. Its beginnings lie in myth and uncertain legend, and it is precarious in the extreme to attempt to build history, and still more, vital and essential faith, on these early incidents of the records of Matthew and Luke. We must treat the stories as we do the similar tales of the birth and infancy of Buddha—namely, as tributes to an outstanding personality and religious genius. The Infancy stories *reflect* historical truth, even if we cannot say that they directly *state* truth. The "light of sacred story" gathers around the cradle as well as around the cross, and the virgin birth and the other marvel stories are testimonies to the impression of the God-nature in Jesus manifest in later years.

II. THE BAPTISM AND TEMPTATION

Definite historical tradition seems to begin with the mention of John the Baptist—"that good man, who commanded the Jews to exercise virtue, both as to justice towards one another and piety towards God, and so to come to baptism" (Josephus, *Antiquities*, xviii. 5. 2). The baptism of Jesus by John is historically credible. Such an incident would not have been invented later. The idea of the "submission" of Jesus to a "baptism of repentance" was obviously felt to be a difficulty by the early Christian community, and the First Evangelist tries to explain away the stumbling-block (iii. 14). The prediction by John of the coming mightier one may have been simply a disclaimer that he himself was the Messiah (cf. Luke iii. 15), or it may have signified nothing more than the spiritual instinct of a prophetic soul that God would complete through other workers the task of reformation started by himself but not finished (cf. Savonarola's saying, "The truth shall triumph but not by me," or Whittier's

> Others shall sing the song: others shall right the wrong:
> Finish what I begin, and all I fail of, win).

The description of the Coming One's work as baptizing with the Holy Spirit rather than with water may be a reflection of such later incidents as that recorded in Acts xix. So also the vision and the voice may be later elaborations introduced into a fitting situation of intense religious experience. Mark gives the vision as subjective. The only one who could say, then, what happened was Jesus Himself, and the description hardly seems like His. At any rate, we can build little upon the saying, either on theological lines or even to indicate the date of the dawning of Christ's Messianic consciousness.

A season of temptation following an intense religious experience of crisis and call is psychologically natural, but the ministry of angels and the elaborate details of the three temptations in Matthew and Luke are obviously allegorical in nature. They are not in the style of Jesus, yet, if the events happened, the descriptions could only have come from Him.

III. Miracles of Healing

Mark soon leads us up to the problem of the credibility of the works of healing in the Gospels. In this connection we need to notice the following points: (1) The testimony of the Gospels to miracles of healing is so abundant that we are bound to respect the witness or throw over practically all historical reliability for the Synoptics. At the same time we cannot rely on all the details of the narratives. We are dealing with second-hand traditions. In some cases there are, of course, considerable discrepancies in the different Gospel accounts of the same incident. Other miracle stories are quite beyond reasonable credibility. (2) Granted the possibility of "mind-cures" by suggestion and telepathy, for which there is now so much modern evidence, we have little difficulty in accepting some historical basis for most of the narratives. In view of the fact that we are dealing with accounts which we cannot regard as precisely accurate in every detail, we are unconvinced that the facts "go beyond any parallels from the records of modern spiritual healings." (3) There are two evangelistic traditions concerning the significance of such healings. The one which is the more historically probable does not present Jesus Himself claiming these acts as credential signs to His teaching and person. When the Pharisees ask for a "sign" Jesus declares that no "sign" shall be given—that is, a "sign" of the physical miracle type. Either (a) no miracles of healing were performed at all (which, in view of the records, it is not easy to believe), or (b) the kind of faith-healing wrought was not regarded either by Jesus or by His critics as having evidential value. Even "the sons of the Pharisees" could "cast out devils."

But a second and inconsistent miracle tradition, which gives the miracles as "signs," appears. They are mentioned expressly as "signs" by Jesus Himself to convince John the Baptist (Matt. xi. 2 ff.), although the culmination of the series of marvels—"the poor have the Gospel preached to them"—is curious, and may indicate that the original saying referred to spiritual transformations rather than physical healings. The evangelists clearly attach evidential value to the miracle stories, which they find it important to record. Why should they crowd their pages with miracle tales if they found no doctrinal significance in them? In the Fourth Gospel the tendency to find the miracles as "signs" apparently reaches its culmination, although even here we are not sure how far the writer intends us to make a spiritual interpretation of the miracles. An authentic tradition appears in the story of Nicodemus. The credential of Jesus as a teacher sent from God must be found, not in physical wonders, but in His response to an awakened faculty of spiritual appreciation. A man must be born "from above" in order to realise the spiritual evidence lying in the words and deeds of Jesus. The physical wonder cannot prove the spiritual truth. "That which is born of the flesh is flesh; that which is born of the spirit is spirit." (4) The question may suggest itself: Granted that Jesus had abnormal powers of faith-healing, did this give rise to the impression of that supremacy which we would fain confine to the moral and spiritual sphere? These facts may be taken into account: (*a*) The "sons of the Pharisees" also worked miracles, but did not win such tribute; (*b*) Jesus Himself, according to the more probable tradition, stressed the moral and spiritual elements of His teaching rather than the thaumaturgist features of His ministry; and (*c*) the tradition which the influence of Jesus left upon the early Church was pre-eminently a moral tradition. The emphasis of the Epistles is not upon the thaumaturgic, but upon spiritual and ethical elements. The former is severely subordinated to the latter. Jesus made life morally and spiritually new to men, and it is this fact which compels the varied tributes of all the New Testament writers.

IV. The Ban of Silence

A curious feature appears in connection with some of the accounts of healing in Mark's narrative. Jesus is said to have forbidden the evil spirits to reveal their knowledge of His identity. "I know Thee who Thou art—the Holy One of God!" Perhaps we have here a reading back into the pages of Christ's biography of the practices of the later Church when spiritualism and theology entered into a curious association (1 John iv. 1 ff.; Acts xvi. 17, xix. 15). But however the tradition came into Mark's hands, why does the evangelist make Jesus so anxious to suppress this witness to His exalted identity?

If we may regard the case by itself, we may conjecture that Mark is impressed by this witness from the supernatural; at the same time he is sensitive to the incongruity of basing the claims for the Holy One of God upon demoniac witness. He records and obviously appreciates the witness; in almost the same breath he displays the abhorrence of the source: "The devils bear their testimony, yet—silence, ye evil spirits!" But there are other cases in which Jesus imposes silence:

in the case of certain healings—that of the leper (i. 44), the daughter of Jairus (v. 43), the deaf man (vii. 36), the experience of the Transfiguration (ix. 9) ; and Wrede believes that we have in all these cases a subtle indication that Jesus was not recognised as the Messiah during His lifetime, and that Mark accounts for this by supposing that Jesus did not wish to be so recognised. Wrede's argument loses strength when the instances are examined individually. It may be contended that the common feature is not to be accounted for in every case by a common explanation. In the case of the healing of the leper the suggestion of Mark is that Jesus was in danger of being overwhelmed by the demands for His healing help, for the injunction was disregarded, and Jesus was compelled to seek refuge in desert places. It is natural to suppose that Jesus was physically exhausted and that He enjoined silence lest a fresh batch of cases should follow this striking healing. The healing of the deaf mute (vii. 36) took place at a time when Jesus was seeking privacy (v. 24). A case of healing at Tyre had made this city impossible, and Jesus went on to Decapolis. Publicity of the healing of the deaf mute here would only lead to the repetition of the experience of Tyre; hence the natural desire for secrecy. In the case of Jairus's daughter—a raising from the dead—Mark's note may have an altogether different significance. One suspects evangelistic exaggeration for the whole incident; if such an astounding event occurred exactly as narrated, it must have made an impression throughout the community far more profound than the ordinary cases of healing. That such a story was not more widely spread required some explanation on the part of the evangelist, and one conjectures that Mark, in order to explain the general ignorance of the community concerning this amazing case, says that Jesus forbade mention of the matter outside the family.

Possibly Wrede's argument may be allowed in reference to the Transfiguration, which in Mark's account seems to be an elaboration of some simpler experience. The detail of the imposing of silence upon the disciples until after the Resurrection may really point to a post-Resurrection date for the story as we have it. The entry into the story of Moses and Elijah may be considered in connection with the tradition, dealt with later, of the suffering Son of Man. But even in the cases where we may feel doubtful about historic reliability the evangelist's readiness to use the explanation of the injunction of silence may bear witness to a genuine tradition that there was a period during which Jesus was unwilling to make a Messianic claim.

V. The Spiritual Significance of the Miraculous

In regard to the question of the Gospel miracles in general, our modern apologetic will be less concerned in proving or denying the fact of miracle than in asking whether these marvels, if historical, have any religious significance. What have they to do with faith? What credential do they give to Jesus? His real credential lies in the moral contents of what He said and did and in the moral and spiritual power which His message still has for men. His "sign" is the "sign of Jonah." His credential for cleansing the Temple is the spirit of the act. His credential as a teacher lies in the teaching itself. One Rabbi Eliezer, says a Jewish story, being unable to convince his brethren in argument, worked several miracles. He moved a tree by his word; he caused a stream to run backward, and performed similar miracles to accredit his teaching. But at the end the other rabbis said: "What has miracle to do with the truth of doctrine? What Rabbi Eliezer has wrought only shows that we do not quite understand the natural laws underlying these apparent marvels, but the true credential to doctrine lies in its appeal to our mind and reason, which God has implanted within us for this special purpose." The attitude of Jesus in refusing to give a "sign" to accredit His message on certain occasions, though perhaps not inconsistent with the working of miracles, does seem most definitely inconsistent with the tremendous apologetic value attached to miracle by the Church in later time. Surely Jesus taught most emphatically, like the other great religious founders, that essential faith does not rest on physical miracle.

But if there should be no significance in miracles themselves, there is significance in the fact that these stories were either invented, enlarged or found credible and appropriate by people who were accustomed to associate miracle with the greatest souls, the messengers and ambassadors of God. We can adopt a general principle of interpretation which minimises the importance of the often difficult question of the literality of the abnormal in the Gospels. The traditional tendency of Scripture reading is to find the miraculous as proofs of doctrine; there is more probability in an inversion of the argument—namely, that doctrines are the real source of miraculous tradition or interpretation. We may perhaps judge the situation best in the mirror of another religion. In the Buddhist Scriptures there are tales of Buddha's miraculous birth, of how he fed five hundred disciples at once out of a small basket of cakes prepared by an old woman for herself and her husband, of how he healed the blind and the like. Yet other traditions tell how Buddha disliked miracles, protested against them, and forbade his disciples to work them. This second tradition seems the more historically probable, yet the former tradition, stating and exalting miracle, is not without significance. It testifies to the impression of the greatness of Buddha which was made upon his disciples on counts other than those of miracle.

Similarly the significance of the miracle stories of the Gospels is not to be sought in their historical literality, but in the spirit which so exalted Jesus in virtue of His moral and spiritual supremacy that such stories were felt to be fitting with such greatness. The miracles, whether historical, or non-historical, or semi-historical, were not the source of the doctrine; their invention or interpretation can be regarded as significant expressions of a doctrine which had its real source in other facts of a more spiritual nature.

VI. THE MESSIANIC CLAIM

We may now consider more fully the problem raised in regard to the Messianic claim by the conversation at Caesarea Philippi. When Peter confesses "Thou art the Christ," Jesus, while apparently accepting the title, "charged them that they should tell no man of Him" (Mark viii. 29, 30). Various explanations of this imposition of silence have been offered.

(1) Wrede finds in the detail an indication that the title of Messiah was never claimed by Jesus, and that Mark tried to account for men's ignorance of this Messiahship during His lifetime by saying unhistorically that Jesus kept His Messiahship a close secret except to a chosen few. On the other hand, it is hard to believe that no Messianic claim of any kind was made for or by Jesus during His life. This would involve the jettisoning of a number of incidents in Mark which have intrinsic probability to commend them.

The blind man at Jericho hails Jesus as Son of David (x. 47), a title which apparently had a Messianic significance (xii. 35). The Marcan tradition describes Jesus as deliberately arranging a Messianic entry into Jerusalem. The significance of the entry upon an ass is rightly connected by Matthew with the Old Testament prophecy: "Behold, thy King cometh unto thee, meek and riding upon an ass and upon a colt, the foal of an ass." This was probably the passage in the mind of Jesus when He arranged this detail of His approach to Jerusalem. The action is apparently taken as having Messianic significance by the Passover crowd (though this has been challenged); its Galilean members may have been prepared for this by previous teaching in Galilee.

Mark includes in the acclamation the words: "Blessed is the Kingdom that cometh, the Kingdom of our father David. Hosannah in the highest." At the trial before the High Priest Jesus is deliberately asked, "Art Thou the Christ, the Son of the Blessed?" and Jesus answers, "I am." The trial before Pilate seems mainly concerned with the question whether Jesus had made some claim to kingship. "Art Thou the King of the Jews?" Pilate asks the crowd: "Will ye that I release unto you the King of the Jews?"; or again, "What shall I do unto Him who is called King of the Jews?"

The condemnation of Jesus by the Roman authorities is made intelligible by supposing that He was charged, not with a purely religious offence (what had Rome to do with Jewish orthodoxy or heresy?), but with an offence which might be regarded as political. The treatment of Jesus as pseudo-king by the soldiery, "Hail, King of the Jews!"; the superscription over the Cross, "The King of the Jews"; and the mocking cry, "Let the Christ, the King of Israel, now come down from the Cross!"—all these constitute a cumulative, impressive witness to the tradition of an open Messianic claim—at any rate in the last period of the ministry.

VII

(2) A second explanation of the imposition of silence as to Christ's Messiahship is offered by Burkitt, who argues that "the office of Messiahship is essentially different from that of prophet or seer. Properly speaking, it cannot be claimed. The Messiah, if He be Messiah, will be in some way evident King of Israel and Judge of the Nations. . . . When the crowds found out that Jesus, the prophet of Galilee, had thought of Himself as Messiah, they lost interest and called for Barabbas" ("Gospels," *Encyclopaedia of Religion and Ethics*). Thus at this period Jesus was unwilling to make a Messianic claim. Men must guess the secret even as Peter had done. But it is not

easy to see the rational justification of such a belief. Why should not the Messiah make a proclamation and claim, if He were to accomplish the restoring again of the kingdom to Israel in the way popularly expected? Or, if the belief was so deep set, how was Jesus induced at a later date to make some kind of Messianic proclamation? Would He not know that it would be fatal to His success and influence, and defeat its own ends at the very moment of proclamation?

VIII

(3) Two alternatives still remain. If Jesus deliberately intended to transform the current expectations of Messiahship, and to choose the way of conquest through purely moral influence and humiliation, He might well suppress a claim likely to be misunderstood until He had further educated His disciples in a new ideal of Messiahship. The hour was not yet come for proclamation.

There is a second and, on the whole, more likely explanation. It is possible to suppose that at the time of the Caesarea Philippi incident, the Messianic consciousness had dimly dawned in the mind of Jesus without its having fully developed. It was a period, we may conjecture, in which Jesus was still struggling with conflicting ideas and ideals. Jesus felt that He must wait for a clearer consciousness. For the moment His own mind was not sufficiently made up to take the bold course of proclamation which apparently He favoured later. The authentic Marcan tradition of retreats and avoidance of collision with the civil and religious authorities until the last days gives countenance to this interpretation. We have no reason to believe that the Messianic consciousness of Jesus was clear and full from the very beginning of His ministry. There were stages in its development for Jesus Himself, and the diverse and conflicting current conceptions of Messiahship provided cause for much

mental struggle and uncertainty. Even at Caesarea Philippi
we may suppose that the last stage of Messianic consciousness had not been fully reached. Into the complex conception the idea of the triumph of the Messianic Kingdom
through sacrificial suffering was forcing itself to a place of
prominence; there must be time allowed for a complete
determination of conception and policy. Hence the temporary
injunction for silence.

IX

Schmiedel (*Jesus in Modern Criticism*, p. 41) believes that
the Messianic consciousness of Jesus only ripened slowly. At
first He only conceived Himself to be a reformer, engaged in
a struggle with the Pharisees. It was a great advance from
the thought of being a reformer to that of being Messiah.
Schmiedel thinks that this step was forced upon Jesus by the
need of combating the law of Moses. He had to set His
authority as high as that of the Mosaic law, and this drove
Him to the assertion of Messiahship. This view is not too
convincing. His challenge to Mosaic tradition arose from
the sense of the inwardness of religion and revelation. It
hardly needed the claim that He was Messiah, nor does one
like the idea that the claim was born from the desire to
authenticate a teaching which would not have been spiritually convincing in its own right. This is hardly consistent
with Christ's own teaching concerning His "sign."

X

It seems more reasonable that the Messianic claim arose
gradually out of the transformation of the current ideas of
the Messianic Kingdom. "Jesus came into Galilee, preaching
the Gospel of God, and saying, The time is fulfilled and the
Kingdom of God is at hand. Repent ye and believe the

gospel." The teaching of the Kingdom preceded any Messianic claim. But the conception of the Messianic Kingdom was fundamentally transformed in the hands of Jesus. It was not the political Kingdom of men's hopes. It was to come gradually and without observation, as a spiritual movement. It was to be established not by force of sword, but by force of character. Its strength was in love, and in overcoming evil with good. One may cite as instances of this transformation of the expectation of the Messianic Kingdom the following: (*a*) Luke xvii. 20: "The Kingdom of God cometh not with observation: neither shall they say, Lo here! or, lo there! for the Kingdom of God is within you (or, in the midst of you)." (*b*) John xviii. 36 may represent an authentic saying of Jesus: "My Kingdom is not of this world: if My Kingdom were of this world, then would My servants fight" (cf. Matt. xxvi. 52). (*c*) The reply to the sons of Zebedee (Mark x. 35 ff.). This indicates that Jesus had used the figure of a Messianic Kingdom in which He would be King, but the Kingdom and the Kingship were utterly unlike those of the world. "They which are accounted to rule over the Gentiles lord it over them, and their great ones exercise authority over them. But it is not so among you, but whosoever would become great among you shall be your minister, and whosoever would be first among you shall be servant of all." (*d*) The answer to the scribes: "Render unto Caesar the things which are Caesar's, and unto God the things which are God's" (Mark xii. 7)—a repudiation of the Messianic idealism which found salvation in the throwing off of the yoke of Rome. (*e*) The entry of Jesus into Jerusalem as King of Zion, yet "meek and riding upon an ass." One may compare Matt. xii. 19, where the methods of Jesus are contrasted with those of a Messianic military conqueror: "He shall not strive, nor cry aloud: neither shall anyone hear his voice in the streets!", etc. (*f*) It is the little flock of humble followers to whom it is the Father's good pleasure to give the Kingdom (Luke xii. 32), and the seeking of the Kingdom is obedience to the laws of righteousness, "Seek ye first the Kingdom of God and His righteousness." The scribe accepting the moral supremacy of the commandment of love is "not far from the Kingdom" (Mark xii. 34). These and kindred passages show the preaching of the Kingdom of God by Jesus as in part inspired by Messianic expectation, but given a spiritual interpretation, which set His view of the Kingdom in contrast, in almost every detail, with the current political expectations of the Messianic glory.

This transformation affected the idea of Messiahship. The place in the current political conception given to the political and military Messiah, throwing off the yoke of Rome, must be taken, in a scheme of spiritual counterparts, by the prophet and reformer, calling the nation to repentance and to this new idealism of a spiritual kingdom. The Messiah was not the anointed monarch of the political and military type, but the one "anointed to preach good tidings to the poor, to proclaim release to the captives and recovering of sight to the blind, to set at liberty them that are bruised, to proclaim the acceptable year of the Lord" (Luke iv. 18; cf. Matt. xi. 2 ff.)—a passage which may have played a considerable part in the transforming of the Messianic conception of the Gospel and the identification of Jesus with the Messiah. The military and political Messiah was not the only idea of the "anointed" one.

XI

The identification of Jesus as Messiah followed, then, from the process of giving spiritual counterparts to the elements of the popular and false Messianic expectation. Jesus naturally fell into the place of spiritual Messiah in virtue of His relations to the new movement. His acceptance of the title became, indeed, part of the preaching of the new Gospel of the Kingdom. It was one way of making men realise the spiritual nature of that Kingdom. At the same time we must not allow ourselves to think that the identification was lightly regarded and accepted as merely involved in a kind of literary parallelism. We may conceive that this was the way in which Jesus came to the consciousness of His Messiahship, but, once reached, that consciousness was of revolutionary import to the mind and personality of Jesus. It was a profound, sobering, and even terrifying thought, for Jesus shared His countrymen's reverence for the fact of Messiahship. He felt Himself now to be not merely a prophet of God for His generation. His was a deeper and larger commission. He was chosen by God to be the special figure of the ages.

The incident at Caesarea Philippi is generally regarded as a revelation merely to the Apostles. It would seem that it was equally a new self-realisation on the part of Jesus. It is true that He is said to have spoken of the "Son of Man" before, but it is doubtful that this had any Messianic significance, at any rate, in Christ's former use of it (see section on "Son of Man," p. 187). There was a divine Messianic commission given at the baptism, according to Mark, but this seems an unhistorical supposition on the evangelist's part. As Schmiedel pertinently says: "Had Jesus at the moment of the baptism felt conscious that He was the Messiah, He must afterwards, if we are to credit most of the records about Him contained in the Gospels, have almost entirely forgotten the matter." We must rather conceive the Messianic consciousness of Jesus dawning later—probably only just before Peter's confession. His question suggested that the thought was breaking in His mind. His imposition of silence upon the disciples finds its most likely explanation in the fact that it was for a period not sufficiently formed, set and confirmed to be published to the world. The soul of Jesus was troubled; the discovery was too new, too sobering, too amazing even for Jesus. If we try to explain the imposition of silence as due to the fear of consequences or to the doctrine that the Messiahship must not be claimed but only discovered by others, it is difficult to understand why Jesus made the public claim at a later date. But make the discovery as new to Jesus Himself, and it throws light upon the sudden seeking of privacy, the silence imposed, and then, when time was given for the thought to deepen into fixed conviction, upon the new policy and approach to Jerusalem.

XII. The Causes of Christ's Death

In view of the doctrinal importance attached to the death of Jesus in the New Testament Church, an important question arises in reference to the historical reasons of Christ's death. There were quite intelligible historical causes, operating from the early days of His ministry. (1) There was the challenge to Mosaic Law, which brought Jesus into collision with the orthodox Jewish religionists. Particularly "sabbath-breaking," of which Mark gives us several instances, seems to have irritated the Pharisees. The fraternising of a prophet with publicans and sinners would be a further cause for scandal. This difference of attitude would lead not only to a hostility of Pharisees to Jesus, but to a deepening hostility of Jesus to the Pharisees and their traditions, moral evasions, formalism and hypocrisies, culminating in the chapter of woes. (2) A more formidable enemy had been raised in the shape of Herod Antipas. The antagonism of Herod was partly on moral grounds. He had imprisoned the Baptist and consented, though apparently with reluctance, to his death. "He feared John, knowing that he was a just man" (Mark vi. 20). An uneasy conscience drove him to an abandoned attitude of hate and murderous passion against all who showed affinity of character and aim with John the Baptist. But deeper lay a political enmity and fear. The Baptist and Jesus were one in preaching a Messianic Kingdom, and the Herodians felt that the establishment of the Herodian Kingdom under Rome was jeopardised by popular Messianic talk. This political reason was probably fundamental in Herod's treatment of John the Baptist, although other causes (rebuke of Herod's matrimonial relations) may have contributed. To Herod, Jesus was perpetuating John's work and witness and agitation for a Messianic Kingdom. This hostility of Herod finds many expressions in the Gospel tradition: (a) Luke xiii. 31, "Depart hence, for Herod will seek to kill Thee," followed by the reply of Jesus, contemptuously likening Herod to a fox. (b) Mark viii. 15. Jesus warns His disciples against the leaven of Herod. (c) Mark iii. 6. Early in the ministry the Herodians are said to have joined with the Pharisees in plotting against Jesus, and even though Cheyne may be right in suspecting such action at this period, we have doubtless preserved here a more general historical tradition. (d) A note in which Herod is said to have recognised, in Jesus, John the Baptist risen from the dead is followed by certain wanderings of Christ, suggesting an avoidance of Galilee. Thus Jesus passes through Tyre and Sidon (vii. 24), Decapolis (vii. 31), Bethsaida (viii. 22), Caesarea Philippi (viii. 27). (e) The account of the trial of Jesus before Herod, which, though not without its historical difficulties, bears witness to the tradition in the early Church that Herod Antipas was regarded as the enemy having a hand in the causes which led to Christ's death. (f) Acts iv. 27 specifically couples Herod with Pilate as the opponents of the "Holy Servant Jesus." (3) The charges brought up against Jesus at His trial were apparently two: (a) His claim to destroy the Temple. This was presumably understood quite rightly as a challenge to the religious order which had come to centre around the Temple. The teaching of Jesus was felt to be a threat against Mosaism, as interpreted by its contemporary exponents. Jesus would destroy the standing faith and create a new one. So we must interpret the famous saying, "Destroy this Temple made with hands, and in three days I will build another without hands." In the case of the populace, this was probably understood as the blasphemous challenge to ancient and established religion, although the Christians at a later date found in the saying a subtle reference to the Resurrection—a clearly erroneous interpretation. But the saying indicates the real cause of the murderous opposition of the scribes and Pharisees—Jesus was apparently intending to destroy the Law and the Prophets! Matt. v. 17 witnesses to such a popular impression.

(b) But in the eyes of the Herodians and Pilate the offence of Jesus was His Messianic claim. There had been a deliberate assertion of such a claim in Christ's final coming up to Jerusalem. The definite conviction had at last formed in the consciousness of Jesus that He was Messiah, and that there was need of a bold and new proclamation of the Kingdom at Jerusalem. The saints must claim their Kingdom. The hour was come for the "Son of Man" (the "elect" of Daniel vii) to be glorified. Jesus would raise His standard for the spiritual Messianic Kingdom. He would be lifted up in publicity to draw all men to Himself. We may dismiss the idea that Jesus made the journey to Jerusalem to die there as a sacrifice and propitiation. As Goguel (*Jesus the Nazarene*, p. 203) says: "So far was Jesus from coming to die at Jerusalem that He carefully organised His entry into the Holy City to impress the spectators, and by His action and public teaching did His best to rally the crowd to His cause. Doubtless He must have perceived how dangerous was the part He played. If He failed, His death was certain, for His enemies would not disarm. He did not retreat while there was time, but accepted in advance the sacrifice which might have been demanded of Him. Nevertheless, so little was His death a dogmatic necessity for Jesus that in the precaution of quitting Jerusalem every evening He attempted to escape from His enemies, and perhaps had it not been for the treachery of Judas He would have succeeded. The Gethsemane episode (Mark xiv. 32–42) is in this respect very characteristic. At the last moment, when Jesus sees the circle of His enemies closing around Him, He is appalled. The scene in its essential details is certainly historic; it is too much in contradiction with the idea of Christ accepting with serenity, almost with impassivity, the necessity of His sufferings, to warrant the belief that it was created by tradition."

XIII. The Resurrection

For the Resurrection of Jesus the evidence, though conflicting in some details, is much stronger than for the Infancy marvels. Unlike the Virgin Birth tradition, it enters deeply and widely into New Testament thought. Its records are found, not only in every Gospel, but in Paul. At a later stage the parallel ideas of the resurrection of the vegetation gods of the Mysteries may have played a part in the *interpretation* of the Resurrection, but we cannot think that they played any part in *creating* the Christian tradition. The story has a clear Jewish setting. The first use of it was to make it serve as a miracle-credential for Jewish Messiahship. There is some evidence noticed elsewhere (p. 197) for an older Jewish tradition for the Resurrection of the "Son of Man" "after three days," arising from the imagery of Daniel, and finding expression in the Book of Revelation (chap. xi). But there are differences between this tradition, as far as we can trace it, and the stories of the Resurrection of Jesus so striking that we cannot think that it gave rise to the latter, although the two naturally became related in the Gospel narrative. But we believe that the Resurrection stories of the Gospel point to some abnormal, if possibly not quite unique, psychical event occurring shortly after the death of Jesus. What we have already come to know of psychical phenomena makes the main outline of the Resurrection narratives quite credible. There are abundant records of the appearance of the so-called dead to the living in our own day, and the situation, as far as we can realise it in the New Testament documents, on principles of literary and historical criticism, seems to demand such a happening as a definite historical event. This does not mean that our present Gospel narratives can be accepted as historically accurate in every detail. There are well-known discrepancies in the stories. The actual process of elaboration is to be detected by comparing the account of Matthew (with its story of the military watch, etc.) and the other narratives. The tradition of the empty tomb may well be suspected. There are hints that the risen body was hardly the actual flesh and blood, in spite of the tradition of Thomas Didymus. According to the Fourth Gospel the risen Christ passes through closed doors, and Paul puts the Resurrection appearances on a level with his own vision of Jesus at Damascus.

But the whole subject needs to be approached from a pragmatic standpoint. What relation has the Resurrection of Jesus as a miracle to our vital faith? Apart from it, have not His words abiding power? Do we not still believe in the continued life of Jesus beyond death on other grounds? Because of our conviction as to the eternity of personality, we believe that He still lives and loves and acts. We cannot conceive that the power of death should hold such a life. Paul, of course, finds in the Resurrection of Jesus a guarantee of our own. If we regard the Resurrection as of the character of the appearances recorded by psychical research we may find some such support for our belief in our own survival of personality, unless we insisted on too great a difference between our nature and that of Jesus. Yet even for such a guarantee we should prefer some modern and well-investigated instance of the resurrection of someone whose nature was unquestionably like our own. But Paul has hardly this modern idea in mind. He is thinking and speaking in the terms of his cosmic scheme of salvation. Since Adam the world had been in bondage to elemental "world-rulers of darkness," Death being one of these and representative of the rest. Jesus by His dying and Resurrection had broken the power of Death and of the associated "world-rulers of

darkness," and had made it possible for those with whom
He—the risen Christ—was mystically united to share His
victory over the world-principalities of darkness and death.
The resurrection cults of paganism may have had no small
influence in shaping this theory in the mind of Paul; but
the Rabbinical, semi-Gnostic doctrine of the Apostle hardly
belongs to the permanent elements of Paulinism.

It would seem, then, that though many profound truths
have gathered around the Resurrection stories—Easter
thoughts of the undying life of Jesus and ourselves, and of
the victory of light after darkness, the spring-time of all
spiritual and moral values after the temporary winter of
separation, loss and disappointment—these thoughts find
their symbol rather than their origin and guarantee in this
story of the Resurrection of Jesus—a story which we accept
substantially, as literal and authentic, but which, if denied,
would by no means involve the collapse of vital faith. Jesus
holds us on other grounds. We see in Him the grace and
truth of God, apart from any marvel, even the most stupen-
dous. If we do not see the essential values of Jesus in the
beauty and appeal of His life and message, no physical
marvel of rising from the dead would melt our stony hearts!

L

CHAPTER XI

MYSTICISM AND THE TEACHING OF JESUS

I

ONE of the most illuminating sayings in regard to the interpretation of Jesus and His teaching is that of Matthew Arnold. Jesus, he claims, came "to open out the choked-up wells of human intuition." He must be regarded not as a bearer of unique theosophic revelation coming from beyond the range of human discovery, but as a prophet of universal faith, based on what is deepest in the human soul. Thus He appealed, for the confirmation of His teaching and the validity of His message, to the instincts of man's deepest nature. He refused to give physical "signs from heaven" to accredit His claims. His "sign" was the "sign of the prophet Jonah"—the approval of conscience and reason, the confirmation of man's faculty of spiritual appreciation. Deep must answer to deep. Essential Christianity must be a matter of experience. The "authority" of Jesus is derived simply from the correspondence of His teaching with this universal experience. Jesus is the interpreter of man's spiritual nature, helping men to recognise for themselves the spiritual elements of human consciousness and experience. His teaching was not to impart a theosophy from without, but to awaken a faculty within. He came not merely to give the Water of Life to men, but to help them to find within themselves "the wells of Living Water, springing up unto Eternal Life."

Christianity is no power or revelation alien to human personality; it is rather to be regarded as the culmination of the development of human personality. In its essential character Christianity is universal religion, having its

sources, its tests and confirmations within the spiritual nature
of mankind. Our Lord's teaching, despite all the local
Jewish circumstances and thought-forms of the period of its
origin and the metaphysical and ecclesiastical elaborations
which gathered round it in its passage through Hellenistic
and other civilisations, retains so much of that universal
character that it makes its appeal to the souls and minds of
men of all races, and even creeds, and in our own civilisation to men outside as well as inside the Churches. Jesus is
essentially a citizen of the whole religious world. It is not
certain how far He Himself was conscious of a programme
of spiritual world-conquest. His appeal to the world proceeded not from deliberate intention of a missionary cam-
paign in our modern sense, but from His simple fidelity to
the universal and eternal elements in religion. The expansion
of Christianity as a world-religion proceeded from that
fidelity to the natural instincts and intuitions of a world-
faith. The Judaistic features fell off from it, and yet its
vitality and appeal persisted. New features of the Hellenistic
world came to be associated with it, and some of these in
ages of free inquiry and criticism have been challenged and
largely discarded, and yet the religion of Jesus has maintained its value and appeal. He is still revered by our most
iconoclastic writers and by the critics of Churches and
creeds. Even more striking is His influence upon non-
Christian communities and upon those whose thought is
deeply embedded in other systems. It is said that India is
not being proselytised by Christian missionaries, but that it
is being Christianised. Western ecclesiastical interpretations
of Christ are not being accepted, but the spirit of Jesus
is stimulating a purification and re-centring of Hindu
religious thought, and together with the rejection of Christianity as a system, an admiration and love for the personality
of Jesus Himself has been repeatedly manifest. The Mohammedan Imam of Woking Mosque has recently claimed for
his fellow-Muslims that "our love for Jesus is in no case less

than that cherished for him by those who pass under his name," but "we Muslims assert that all that was believed and taught about various deities in the pagan world thousands of years before Christ—in India, Egypt, Greece, Persia and Rome—has become incorporated in the pure and simple faith of Jesus, and his blessed name soiled with things he never knew or taught" (*The Sources of Christianity*, Kamal-ud-Din, p. 20). This attitude, whether historically well based or not (and this it is partly our task to consider) testifies at any rate to the presence in the Gospels of a large element of "universal religion," existing apart from ecclesiastical, apocalyptic and sacramental features which have been associated with it from earliest times and found even in its New Testament literature.

II

We may now recall what has been said previously concerning the nature of universal religion, arising from that world-wide phenomenon of Mysticism, in the definite and specific sense of Cosmic Consciousness. We have seen that Mysticism is an experience found in all ages and races, with features of spontaneity and naturalness, and fundamentally independent of traditions and current philosophies, although tending to create a philosophy of its own. Its quality involves belief in the universe as an organism, each part related to the whole, and each part ultimately capable of feeling itself within the whole. We "live and move and have our being in God." From the finite parts a way can be found to the heart of the Infinite, and one of the most characteristic features is the sense of communion with God, with the consciousness of peace and power realised therefrom.

There is an ultimate soundness and health in the unified scheme of things, although in the section and process there will emerge elements at first sight inconsistent with the perfection and health of the whole. This phenomenon is involved in the very nature of progressive development— that progressive development which is life itself, for there must be a movement from the less developed to the more developed; but all things, if not "good," "work together for good," and the mystic consciousness issues in a profound optimism and sense of the "love of God" operative in the scheme taken as a totality.

There are in the truest forms of Mysticism two characteristic avenues to the central reality of God: there is an inward way, finding illumination, reality, sacredness, power, in that which is deepest in the soul—an exact opposite to religious externalism and outward revelation and authority; there is also the way of broad sacramentalism—a discovery of the Infinite through the forms of the Finite. It is a false Mysticism which strips off all human elements by asceticism of thought, feeling and practice in order to reach the Infinite. True Mysticism will find the material world of time and sense an approach to that which transcends time and sense. It will find God in Nature and in human life. It will not despise and abhor the graces and affections of the world, but rather find in all these a way to the discovery of God. The joy of life will not be mortified, but sanctified. The way to God will not be repression, but love.

III

These features of Religious Mysticism, it would appear, provide the key to the interpretation of the teaching of Jesus, and explain His appeal and authority. He was an original and freshly thinking soul, who made a "Return to Nature" in the spiritual realm, and brought back a world, thinking in traditional and artificial ways, to the fundamental faith which lies deep in human personality. The faith of Judaism was growing to be a faith of external authorities;

the work of Jesus was to restore a faith of the Spirit—not a faith of psychic emotion, too often confused with the faith of the Spirit in religious circles—a faith which demands suppression of personality, so that some mysterious inward "Spirit" may enter and take possession of the individual soul. This idea lends itself to an unwholesome "mediumistic" Christianity and to a paralysis or mutilation of personality. The faith of Jesus meant the development of personality until it yielded its revelation, stimulus and spiritual power.

(1) We may state as the first feature of the characteristic "Mystical" attitude of our Lord this clear emphasis upon the *inwardness* of morality and faith. The sources of spiritual life, illumination and power were to be found within. Tradition was subordinated to the authority of the wholesome soul. The healthy-minded man is "lord also of the Sabbath." Man must turn from the traditions of the scribes to the native goodness which stressed truth and sincerity and comradeship (Matt. xv. 3–6; xxiii). It was even the privilege of the healthy minded to declare the forgiveness of sins (Mark ii. 9–10). The argument of the incident is to claim such "authority" not only for Jesus, but for every commoner in the Kingdom of God. Man must look within his own soul for confirmation of the truth of the message of Jesus. His credential was the "sign of Jonah," the appeal to the deepest spiritual elements in men's hearts (Luke xi. 29). "The unpardonable sin is to deny the word of God within" (Mark iii. 29). In the Fourth Gospel this tradition of our Lord's teaching has abundant expression. A man must be born from above to realise that Jesus is a teacher sent from God. The power of spiritual appreciation must accredit Him—no mere physical signs and wonders (John iii. 1 ff.). The water that Christ gives shall become in the hearer a well of water, springing up unto eternal life (iv. 14). There can be a vain searching of the Scriptures—the native spiritual instincts of the heart must lead men to Jesus (v. 39). In the discourses of the fourteenth and following chapters the

doctrine of the Inward Light, and Strength, and Peace, and Joy is stated in familiar detail. The Holy Spirit should teach the disciples all things, convict the world in respect of sin, of righteousness and judgment, and guide men into all the truth. This is the genuine mystic tradition—the stress upon the inward light and authority, and reliance upon the guidance of that likest God within the soul. Externalism and traditionalism are foreign to the genius of the Gospel. Man must be true to his deepest self, and find the Holy of Holies in his own soul.

Only with such a "Return to Spiritual Nature" was Christianity able to release the new movement from the bondage of scribal disapproval, the letter of legalism, the hampering jots and tittles of Jewish traditionalism. Sane Mysticism tends to liberty of mind and soul, wholesome self-reliance and spiritual independence.

(2) The feature of *Natural Sacramentalism* in the attitude of Jesus should also be noted. He found beauty in life. The world was God's world. The common sights of Nature conveyed the sense of the Presence and Providence of God. There was something of the Greek joy in life and grace in the spirit of Jesus. Most striking was the contrast between the austere Baptist and the Prophet of Nazareth "at home in the universe."

(3) Mysticism lays stress on the idea of *Communion*. The whole stress of the Gospels upon prayer and the spiritual and psychical consequences resulting therefrom is an expression of this spiritual intuition. We must regard the central element in such prayer to be communion. This kind of exaltation may put the soul *en rapport* with forces and energies of a larger world, to which Jesus attributed almost limitless powers, but the central idea of Christian prayer is not in mere petition, nor in the gaining of seemingly miraculous powers, but in communion with God. It is striking that in the ideal prayer taught by our Lord the clauses are more or less appeals to our own thought and will and idealism,

to prepare the soul for that silent communion with God which is the essence of prayer. Surely we have not to persuade God to hallow His name, favour His own will, and cherish His own Kingdom. It is we who must hallow His name, desire earnestly the establishment of His Kingdom, forgive them that trespass against us. When we have thus put our hearts in the right condition and mood, then the soul is "in tune with the Infinite" and in harmony with God: the soul possesses God in its communion, and with God has everything. In such experiences we know that we are in the Father and the Father in us. The peace of soul, newness of existence, "eternal life" resulting from such communion, finds abundant statement in both Synoptics and the Fourth Gospel, although with characteristic differences of expression.

(4) The *Optimism* associated with the mystic outlook upon life is prominent in the Gospel traditions of Jesus. The earth is the Lord's and the fullness thereof. Providence rules all the details of existence. Not even a sparrow falls without the Father's knowledge. The very hairs of our heads are numbered. All worry is forbidden (Matt. vii. 24), because the Father knows all our needs. The ultimate triumph of righteousness is never in doubt. It is the Father's good pleasure to give the saints the Kingdom. The current apocalyptic figures, spiritualised, we conceive, above their crude literality, are employed to suggest the ultimate Sovereignty of God. The Kingdom will be established. The Lord shall judge the earth. Jesus can speak of His joy and peace amid the most distressing of human circumstances. His stilling of the storms of the human heart gives rise to a story of miracle. The saint can experience an "ataraxia"—"Let not your heart be troubled."

(5) The mystic sense of *Eternal Life* is one of the favourite themes of the Fourth Gospel. It underlies the Synoptic teaching equally clearly—a newness of life here and an existence which is not closed by bodily death. Jesus has no

sympathy with the Sadducean doctrine. God is not the God of the dead, but of the living, for all live unto Him (Luke xx. 27 ff.). Men may kill the body, but the soul is beyond their power (Luke xii. 4).

(6) The mystic feature of the *Solidarity of the Race* as the basic root of Christ's ethical teaching will be dealt with in the following special study.

CHAPTER XII

MYSTICISM AND CHRISTIAN ETHICS

I

Underneath Christ the Divine I see
The dear love of man for his comrade, the attraction of friend
    to friend,
Of the well-married husband and wife, of children and parents,
Of city for city, and land for land.

In these words the mystic Walt Whitman interprets the
message to the world of Another who was essentially a
mystic in His attitude to God and man. We have here the
master-principle of Christian ethics.

Mysticism implies the consciousness of the organic unity
of the universe. "Perpetually telling of the unity of man and
God, the speech of the mystic classics antedates language,
nor do they grow old" (W. James). But there is also a corresponding sense of organic unity between the individual and
the human race which has vital practical consequences.
The association of mystic religion and morality in the most
developed faiths suggests some inherent relation between
the two.

If, on the one hand, mysticism means enlargement of the
soul, on the other hand the master-principle of morality is
the recognition of the larger units of life, and the effect this
has on interests, motives, affections and will. A man is
immoral when he thinks, feels, acts merely sectionally. He
may even divide out his own life into temporary phases, and
act for the moment instead of from the whole span of human
life. He may become, as it were, "his own enemy." His acts
become more moral when he takes in another life with his
own, and thereby finds a truer, larger "self." A higher

morality arises from devotion to a great cause, a race-"self," a race-interest. The growth of moral conception is associated with the expansion of the unit from which we derive our interests and motives.

II

This master-principle of both mystic faith and morality —resting upon the sense of the organic unity of all life, human and divine—finds no clearer or more striking expression than in the message of Jesus of Nazareth. Man's relation with God, according to Him, could be suggested by the pregnant phrase, "Our Father." If we may take the Fourth Gospel as preserving a tradition, if not the actual words of our Lord, its abundant mystical expressions lead us to give a mystic interpretation to the term "Father" in the Synoptics. God is not merely like a father in tenderness and care, but there is one nature holding us kin; we "live and move and have our being in Him; . . . we are also His offspring." He can come and make His abode with us, and reveal Himself "closer than breathing and nearer than hands and feet." Jesus gives us the arresting conception that whoso deals compassionately with the least and humblest of men is doing his deed of mercy to the Lord Himself. Or, again, man must realise that his largest, truest "self," the larger life which he must gain at the sacrifice of his smaller life, is to be found in that organic whole in which lies his own life, the God he worships and the neighbour whom he can serve. That seems to be the significance of the two supreme and kindred commandments: "Thou shalt love the Lord thy God with all thy heart and with all thy soul, and with all thy mind, and thy neighbour as thyself." Man must love God and his neighbour as part of his own true life. The practical inference is the "royal law": "All things whatsoever ye would that men should do to you, do ye also unto them." This was the summing up of that spiritual body of teaching—the "Law and the Prophets," which Jesus conceived that it was His own task to "fulfil." The new element in Christian ethics was not a new law, but the consistent application of an older one, bringing up the imperfect details of the Old Testament to the standard of its own highest spirit. The working out of the root-ideas found beneath the best Old Testament morality went farther than the Old Testament moralists had conceived. The idea of organic unity, human and divine, struggling into expression on the heights of the "Law and the Prophets," grew into a revolutionary evangel of the Fatherhood of God and the Brotherhood of man in the teaching of Jesus.

III

These master-principles, laid down on two recorded occasions (Matt. xxii. 38–40, vii. 12) found illustration in wealth of detail. Jesus proclaims Himself Herald of a Kingdom of God the laws of which show its nature as a Commonwealth of Love. We must will for others the good we will for ourselves. The individual is not set against the rest of the universe, but must act as a corporate part of it. Would we receive mercy in circumstances of misfortune and human weakness—then we must show it. Would we be leniently judged—then we must be lenient in our judgment of others. We rejoice in our own well-being—therefore we must enter into the joy of the angels over one sinner that repenteth. The prayer thanking God that we are not as others strikes a false note in the Commonwealth of Love. The conception of pre-eminence and greatness must be formed in the light of the thought that we are members one of another, that humanity is one, with a co-operative aim as its ideal. He is greatest who serves the most. The Son of Man came not to be ministered unto, but to minister.

The Hindu mystic, it is said, trains himself to contemplate ever-increasing circles of interest and affection, beginning with that of family and friends, and reaching out through city, nation, race and world to the all-embracing God Himself. The same principle is seen in the teaching of Jesus. We must not be satisfied with confining our interest and affection to the circles naturally nearest to us. Mere family ties must be transcended. Those who do the will of His Father are the mother, the sisters, the brethren of Christ. Even more, our brotherly concern must go beyond our circle of friends. In a spirit of striking comprehensiveness Jesus bids us "Love your enemies"; the just and the unjust belong to the family of God. So also the sinners and the prodigals are not unclassed for him who has the mind of Christ. They are "lost sheep," but still belonging to the house of Israel; they are the "sons of Abraham." The prodigals are still children of the Father and members of the family. The exemplary son and the wastrel are still related—"This —thy brother." The Master's interest was not confined to the groups of respectable and sympathetic folk. He conceived that His work lay with a wider circle. He came to seek and to save that which was lost. Nor must the truth of His message be confined to the chosen nation. In contrast to the Jewish spirit of exclusiveness the genius of Christianity lay in its universality. Men should come from the east and the west and the north and the south, and sit down in the Kingdom.

IV

This master-principle created a radically new attitude towards religion. The faith of the Jewish Church had become a selfish competitive striving for heaven, a striving *against* others rather than a striving together *with* others and *for* others in a Commonwealth of God. Judaism found the principle of religion that of the market. Pray, fast, give alms, and you shall have the glories of heaven in strict proportion to the price which you pay. "Works" will be the purchase price of Paradise. Jesus, on the other hand, found the figure of religion in the family circle, where the children are with the father and all that he has is theirs, in virtue of their oneness with him and with one another. The good life of a disciple is not to gain discipleship's reward, but to express the fact of discipleship. The commercialism of the Jewish faith had its challenge in the parables of the Labourers and the Prodigal Son. In spiritual relations legal equity may find itself entirely out of place. In these parables Jesus challenged the venerable Covenant relationship between God and man because it was not the highest. Jewish ethics were based on the principle, God has a bargain with us; if we do certain things God will do others in return. The ethics of Jesus rested on the principle, Become one with God, and you will do the Father's will.

V

Another aspect of the same master-principle of the ethics of Jesus is seen in the fact that His was a ministry of reconciliation. His work was to restore the broken family of God and man. The peacemakers are the children of God. If a man has a quarrel, he is in no fit mood to worship. "Let him first be reconciled with his brother, and then let him come and offer his gift." Forgiveness of injuries, the forgetting of wrongs, the putting aside of feelings of revenge, the "gaining" of another by understanding and love—these were the burden of saying after saying and parable after parable.

There is, of course, a sterner side to this ministry of reconciliation. One would betray a very superficial view to make it merely a matter of toleration. The question must sooner or later present itself to earnest reconcilers: How far can reconciliations go? At a certain point are we not in danger of unwholesome compromise, of the attitude: "Let us kiss and be friends, for nothing matters very much. Let us have peace and harmony at any price. We will tolerate anything or anybody as long as the world is not disturbed." This is an attitude which Christian men will not and dare not take up. To ignore real and grave differences, to call black white for the sake of reconciliation, may betray culpable moral blindness or cowardice, slothfulness and weakness. Sometimes the true way of reconciliation may take the paradoxical form of further division as a stage towards a new synthesis. The way to peace may be through strife. The angel who heals may be the angel who troubles the waters. And thus one aspect of the work of Jesus was the bringing not of peace, but of a sword—the symbol of mental conflict and division. The temporary Separatists have some-times been the ultimate Unifiers. Jesus could roundly de-nounce the scribes and Pharisees with startling intensity of language. Yet even such stormy philippic ended on a note of yearning : "Jerusalem, Jerusalem, thou that killest the pro-phets and stonest them that are sent to thee, how often would I have gathered thy children even as a hen gathered her chickens under her wing !" Our Lord claimed that He came not to condemn the world, but that the world through Him should be saved. He came not to denounce, but to reconcile. Even the strife-spirit of Jesus was involved in His ideal of the creation of a Kingdom of Love. No separation is a justifiable one which does not thereby aim at harmony on a higher plane. No schism is worthy if not controlled by the object of an ultimate union.

The more characteristic methods of reconciliation used by Jesus are seen in His confidence in the power of love and forgiveness to cast out evil; His refraining from public denunciation ("Neither do I condemn thee—go and sin no more") when He saw the chance of silence helping the process of healing ; His trust that His own suffering and death, and not the destruction of those opposed to Him, would establish the Kingdom of God; or in the difference between

Christ's idea of Messiahship, with its moral forces, and the ideas of military Messiahship common in His age.

VI

Some of the most striking *logia* of the Sermon on the Mount are to be interpreted in the light of this master-principle. It is quite true that we cannot take the Sermon on the Mount literally, but it is a strange inference from this that we need take no notice of it at all. It is a strange argument to say that Jesus put His meaning into such strong hyperbolic terms that He really could not have meant anything at all! We have a good illustration of the hyperbolic style in the *logion*: "I say unto you, whosoever is angry with his brother" (the original *logion* seems to have been without the modifying clause "without cause") "shall be in danger of the judgment; whosoever shall say to his brother Raca shall be in danger of the Council, and whosoever shall say Thou fool shall be in danger of the Gehenna of fire." "Raca" was hardly a word at all; it was more or less the suggestion of a sneer in the inflection of the voice. The underlying meaning is obviously—beware that ye despise not human personality; beware of contemptuous, unbrotherly attitudes of mind. Even the sneer is heresy against the law of love and co-operation. Prejudices, rivalries, misunderstandings, misrepresentations, deceit, trust in brute force, follow.

VII

The same idea of respect for personality provides the key for what is perhaps the most puzzling section of the Sermon on the Mount—the *logion* on non-resistance. "Ye have heard that it was said, An eye for an eye and a tooth for a tooth: but I say unto you, Resist not him that is evil: but

whoso smiteth thee on thy right cheek, turn to him the
other also" (Matt. v. 38). Jesus knew the law that like tends
to beget like—that if you present the harsh, exacting side of
your nature to another he tends to show you the same kind
of nature in return. Hit a man and he tends to hit back.
The method suggested by Jesus is to attempt to break the
vicious circle of harshness answering harshness, by a higher
application of the law of "like begetting like." Overcome evil
with good; answer wrong with kindness; show a positive
new attitude to beget a new attitude. There is no virtue in
a passive non-resistance considered by itself, apart from the
positive principle of love, and apart from a deliberate
intention to overcome evil with good. There may be cases
where non-resistance may be immoral. We can make a
mechanical fetish of non-resistance. It may come to be merely
weakness. As a universal law of conduct it might be, at this
stage of evolution, actually mischievous. Non-resistance may
only be useful as a striking method of making love articulate.
The story of the saintly bishop in Hugo's *Les Misérables* is
not to encourage the leaving open of silver chests and the
giving away of silver candlesticks to thieves as a general rule of
conduct—indeed, if that had been common conduct, these
particular acts would have failed as expressions for the good
bishop's attitude of positive love. The unusualness of the
deed provided language for a spirit of positive love-energy
potent to evoke a response of repentance and reformation.
The innermost meaning of non-resistance was a positive
law which on occasion may take the very form of resistance.
Love may sometimes find it needful to resist as well as non-
resist; but love will never allow itself to hate, to perpetuate
hatred, to become revengeful and vindictive, to be blind to
the possibilities of good, or to lose faith in itself as the
strongest redemptive power in the world.

Our Lord desired to show something more. He had to
answer the immoral moralists and meet the objections of
justice as commonly understood. The highest morality con-

M

ceived by them of old time was "an eye for an eye and a tooth for a tooth"—a morality based on the idea of possession and blind to considerations of the redemption of personality. Normally, respect for property is a wholesome rule of conduct, but there might be cases when the lower morality of justice and the higher morality of redeeming grace might conflict. Christ's law was that in such cases the morality of grace must prevail. If the prodigal had been treated with justice, his father would promptly have sent him back into the far country, but the love of the father made him turn the other cheek—"Bring forth quickly the best robe and put it on him." The elder son complained naturally that this was not justice. He was right, but it was something greater. If Valjean had had justice meted out to him in respect to the bishop's silver, back he would have gone to the galleys. In the spirit of Christ the bishop showed him, not justice, but the higher morality of grace, which has as its object the winning and redeeming of personality and the unifying of the race-family.

VIII

The emphasis laid by Jesus upon absolute sincerity and truth ("Let your Yea be Yea and your Nay, Nay") may also be regarded in the light of this principle which we are seeking to trace under the whole ethical teaching of Jesus. Falsehood not merely has awkward utilitarian consequences, and works badly in social life; it is also an offence against the idea of the common family; it is an attempt to think and speak sectionally, to overreach and gain unfair advantages, to serve the sin of covetousness. Falsehood is unbrotherly and schismatic, and that fact condemns it. Truth is a quality characteristic of real fellowship, the essential for wholesome cooperation and a healer of divisions and misunderstandings. Love and untruth are inconsistent. Untruth is a strife-maker. Sincerity is a peace-maker and peace-preserver.

IX

The *logion* "Seek ye first the Kingdom of God and His righteousness" may be considered in the light of this general principle which we find underlying the ethics of Jesus. We have recognised two ways in which men may seek to express the mystic impulse to seek the Absolute. The one is to cast off the limitations of the finite, strip oneself of its affections and interests, and seek the supreme experience of communion with God by an isolation from the world. This has been the way of religious asceticism. The other way is that of developing the soul by contacts with life, relations with other men, by social usefulness, character and service. God is to be found through social integrity and fellowship. To the first type, morality as we know it becomes a superfluity; the only virtue is to disentangle oneself from the whole field of social relations. The mystic quest of Jesus did not lead Him in this direction. He sought the alternations to work and service—namely, meditation and a quietist's communion with God, but refused to build tabernacles on Mountains of Transfiguration. His Gospel implied social contacts; it was a message of social character, fellowship and service. The way to God was the path of duty among men. He was ever preaching single-hearted devotion to the highest and unlimited sacrifice for its sake, but this is very different from an ascetic withdrawal from life and an indifference to social duties and virtues.

It is true that our Lord bids His disciples not to be anxious concerning their material conditions. Our materialistic state in its large aspects is in the hands of Nature, and we must trust that Nature in her broad operations will do us no wrong. Our business is to seek first the Kingdom of God and His righteousness. But this does not mean that we are to be indifferent to the material sides of life, where human will and energy can affect life and welfare. The chief end of man is to glorify God and to discover his own soul, but God must be glorified in the right use of the body and of the material field in which it can work, and the soul must "find itself" in a certain useful attitude towards the mundane, material things of life. The aspirations and idealisms of men must be touched and stimulated by the facts that there are wrong things to be righted, bad material conditions altered, heavy and patient work to be done to make the world a better place to live in. It is in a world of material things that character must be developed, the Kingdom of God served, and practical righteousness be called for and expressed. We may interpret the promise, "All these things shall be added," in the light of the truth that Christianity shall stimulate material progress, check idleness and waste, challenge world-suicidal ambition and anti-social greed, and make for sobriety, steadiness, mutual consideration and social health in material matters. Among the consequences of seeking the Kingdom of God and His righteousness for its own sake shall be a wholesome and happy society. And in such a sanctified quest of the Kingdom, in the process of sympathy, courage, fellowship and service, the soul shall discover itself and God. Love and Service are the ways to the truest and healthiest mystic experience.

X

In the Johannine interpretation of the teaching of Christ we have further emphasis upon the relations of mysticism and morality. In the Fourth Gospel the way to the mystic experience of the Father is through ethical discipleship: "If a man love Me, he will keep My word, and My Father will love him, and We will come to him and make Our abode with him." There is an appeal to the "works of the Father" done by Christ "that ye may know and understand that the Father is in Me and I in the Father." Those who have seen Christ full of grace and truth have seen the Father. Thus the ethics of Christ lead to the mystic experience of God. The mystic experience reveals itself in the ethics of Christ.

This Gospel teaching was preserved and stressed in St. Paul. Fellowship with Christ produces the works of the Spirit. Thus the doctrine of Salvation by "Faith-Communion" also adequately covers Morality. The special argument of the First Johannine Epistle also brings into prominence the relations of Christian Communion and Morality. The Epistle is aimed against a Docetic Gnosticism which not only challenged the reality of the Incarnation but divorced Morality from Faith. The Spirit could be indifferent to the works of the alien Flesh. This challenge leads to a wholesome emphasis upon the doctrine that Communion with God is no mere corporeal or semi-corporeal or psychical union, but harmony of spirit, affection and purpose. The conditions and fruits of mystic fellowship must be purity of life and love of the brethren. "Whosoever doeth not righteousness is not of God, neither he that loveth not his brother" (iii. 10). Love is the test of sonship, salvation, fellowship with God and Christ. "He who loves God will love his brother also. He who loves not his brother whom he has seen, how can he love God whom he has not seen?"

XI

All this corresponds with a well-defined mystic tradition that "there is a discovery of God in His creatures," and that "where Love is, there God is." The Eternal Oneness is most truly discovered through the forms of earth, through service, through sympathies with a creation which is "crammed with God." "All creatures are a theophany of God," says Erigena. The mystic will see God in the "flower of the crannied wall" or in the hazel-nut, where Juliana of Norwich saw Him. "He prayeth best" (and prayer is most truly conceived as mystic union with God) "who loveth best all things both great and small." He specially has learnt high wisdom who can say with Whitman, "In the faces of men and women I see God," and acts in the light of that vision. We must love God and our neighbour, and we must love God *in* our neighbour.

The mystic tradition melts and forms in the alternations of the love of God and of the love of man. Like sets of black and white squares in a check pattern, sometimes one aspect, sometimes the other starts up, but the effect is due to their close interrelation. The mystic and the man of faith knows a Jacob's ladder, with angels of God ascending and descending upon it—angels ascending from the love of man to the love of God; angels descending from the love of God to the love of man.

> No one could tell me what my soul could be;
> I searched for God and God eluded me;
> I sought my brother out, and found all three.

CHAPTER XIII

THE PROBLEM OF CHRIST'S APOCALYPTIC TEACHING

I

WE have left over for fuller consideration the question of the highest importance: Did Jesus Himself preach a "Second Coming" in apocalyptic glory and with apocalyptic accompaniments, within the generation of His hearers, as the evangelists and the New Testament writers generally suggest? We have seen reasons for attributing to Jesus in the late period of His ministry a Messianic claim, but must we also attribute to Him a claim to literal Enochian Messiahship, the manifestation of Messiah as given in the Similitudes of Enoch, the coming of a supernatural Son of Man on the clouds, Judge of all mankind, the Opener of the graves, the Establisher of the Millennium? Was the expectation which was so deeply rooted in New Testament conceptions literally shared and preached by Jesus Himself?

Some will claim that the matter is of less importance than appears at first sight. They may acknowledge that the belief in its literal form was a mistaken one, but will assert that we must accept it as part of that general mental background of the day which Jesus shared, in a way, quite naturally; and that we must interpret it as Christ's expression, even if in crude terms, of the instincts of faith in God and the Divine working. It was a belief born of the intuition that God was in His heaven and that He would not leave the world in its misery and impotence. His own arm would get Him a victory—dramatic, sudden, imminent, complete, in a situation in which human resources were exhausted. Thus the "mistake" of Jesus was not altogether a mistake, for it expressed faith and hope in the power and love of God.

Or, pressed by the fundamental inconsistency between this apocalyptic element and the finer and more spiritual elements of our Lord's teaching, these apologists may attribute the teaching to different periods of our Lord's development, or they may point to the common phenomenon of religious genius, which, as seen, for instance, in the case of Paul, does not work at a uniform level or consistently with the expressions of less exalted moments. They will claim that our Lord may very well at certain times have thought with the mind of a Jew, and with the limitations of that mind, and yet have arisen on great occasions to those fundamental and universal spiritual truths which we now particularly associate with Him. They will claim that we must judge the values of a general teaching from the highest elements in it, and that inferior elements, even though they came from the lips of Jesus, do not represent the genius of Christ; in the working out of Christian thought they fell away as less significant, unimportant, and belonging to the mere race tradition of His time. They represent a half-developed stage, later outgrown. In seeking the message of Paul, we are not unduly worried by his Rabbinical exegesis or his views on women's hair. His genius and message can be detached from such mental dross. Similarly, the significance of Christ's teaching must be judged from its highest levels. The admixture of inferior elements does not in reality detract from the value of His greatest words, which stand, as it were, in their own right. If we were compelled to receive the inferior teaching attributed to Jesus by the evangelists as His *verba ipsissima*, we should be forced, with reluctance, to accept this point of view. But the knowledge of how the Gospels came to us relieves us from any such necessity. We have evidence of mechanically minded and unspiritual reporters and interpreters shaping the original tradition to express their own conceptions. Whether is it more

natural to attribute the inferior elements of the Gospel
tradition as we have it to them, or to the Founder, whose
mind and spiritual genius are seen so conspicuously in the
Sermon on the Mount and in a multitude of parables and
logia? We may grant that Jesus said *something* to start trains
of apocalyptic expectation. It is conceivable and probable
that He clothed some of His prophetic teaching in apocalyptic
forms, and used current terms of this kind to express spiritual
ideas. But we cannot conceive that the connotation He
intended by His use of these terms ever drew Him beyond
the consistency of His spiritual teaching or into any real
challenge to His prophetic message. Those further steps were
taken by interpreters of the Marcan mentality.

II

We have another school—that of Johannes Weiss and
Albert Schweitzer, who would go farther in apocalyptic
emphasis in their reading of the Gospels. They would not
regard apocalyptic as a "secondary" element creeping by
accident into the teaching of Jesus side by side with a higher
message. They would find it not only authentic, but central.
According to them, the "prophetic" reading of the teaching
of Jesus is the erroneous and indefensible method of liberal
theologians. If Weiss and Schweitzer are right, Jesus is no
spokesman of eternal religion. He commits Himself to crude
Jewish apocalyptic hopes. He shares an apocalyptic indifference to the present order. He only bids men look forward to
the imminent coming of the apocalyptic order and to
the workings of a God who is virtually divorced from all
human life, endeavour and action. Jesus, instead of being
the prophet of universal faith, is to be ranked with the
mechanical religionists, the men of artificial religious thought,
the enthusiasts of apocalypse whose hopes have been
repeatedly disappointed by the issue of events; the men who

find no real place in their system for the presence and
working of God in the order that now is. Human life is a
strange existence alien to God; there is no divine significance
in its operations, beauty and wonder. There is nothing to be
consecrated, not even human will. The one virtue is to expect
divine action from without, and wait passively for that. All
this stands in such contrast to all the other elements of the
Gospel, which lay stress on human action, brotherhood, sacramentalism of life, injunctions for a wholesome social order
based on spiritual principles, that, if we make the apocalyptic elements central, no place can be found for the prophetic spiritual elements. The former exclude the latter. At
every point they are in contrast and opposition. The coming
of the Kingdom is mechanical, not spiritual. The universe
is no united organism of God. It is cut into hopelessly unrelated "ages." God is not immanent in the present order.
The mystic principles of Divine Fatherhood and Human
Brotherhood lose that basis which lies in an organically
unified cosmos. The Divine does not permeate the world,
expressing itself in human grace and functioning in consecrated human effort. Christianity becomes the preaching
of a crude drama of the skies, paralysing all healthy human
endeavour, contradicting wholesome human instincts, and
presently discredited by the issue of events. The "Gospel"
is the acceptance of an apocalyptic theosophy, not the
"Way" of Love and Service indicated in the Sermon on
the Mount and similar teaching. The problem with those
who would interpret the message of Jesus on purely apocalyptic lines is that they are confronted with a great mass
of spiritual and ethical teaching in the Gospels which is
fundamentally inconsistent with the spirit and philosophy
of apocalypse. It has no place in their scheme—and yet it
is a clear and convincing element in the Gospel tradition.
The spiritual and the apocalyptic really belong to different
worlds. The spiritual involves an inward transformation of
personality in order to establish the Kingdom; the apoca-

lyptic involves external operations, celestial action from without; the stress is removed from human will, self-consecration and effort. The Kingdom is not to be established by the steady, patient exercise of the law of Love, the cultivation of social virtues with a spiritual basis. The apocalyptic Kingdom is to be established from without; the only virtue required is passive pious expectation. There is too much of the former element in the teaching of Jesus, too much stress on personality and on the inwardness of essential religion to allow us to accept an apocalyptic teaching, fundamentally inconsistent and incongruous with this, at any rate in the form we find it, as a genuine and authentic element in His message. We believe the process can be traced step by step, and that the first of the stages was created by certain ambiguities connected with the use of the New Testament term "Son of Man."

III

It is perhaps too readily assumed that the term "Son of Man" in the Gospels is a title definitely claimed by Jesus for Himself individually and with a specific Messianic import. Our study, however, is to suggest that *Jesus consistently used the term in a collective sense, and that He did not apply it to Himself as an individual in a specific and exclusive way; that it was not for Him a Messianic title, although even in the Gospel period His interpreters, anxious for the identification of Jesus with the Messiah and familiar with such an identification in the Similitudes of Enoch, came to think of it as a personal title for Jesus, with certain very misleading results.*

It is natural to connect the New Testament use of the phrase with Daniel vii, where in the dramatic imagery of world events there appears, following the mention of various world powers symbolised by beasts, "one like unto a son of man" to whom is given an everlasting kingdom. In verse 18 this "one like unto a son of man" is obviously identified with the saints of the Most High, who, though worn out by their oppressors (verse 25), for a period designated as "a time and times and half a time," finally receive the kingdom and dominion for ever. But the whole imagery may have been inspired by current apocalyptic ideas, and the figure of the "one like unto a son of man" may have been originally an angelic power, possibly Michael (Dan. xii. 1), warring against the chaos monsters. (So N. Schmidt, *Encyclopaedia Biblica*, art. "Son of Man.") In a later period, in the Similitudes of Enoch (generally attributed to the first century B.C.), the "Son of Man" becomes specifically a supernatural power, sitting on the throne of His glory and executing judgment on men and angels, and establishing a kingdom of blessedness for the saints. There is a similar Parousia and Judgment in Mithraism, where Mithra takes the part of Deliverer, Judge and Founder of the kingdom of the elect. We have thus in pre-Christian times a double conception of the "Son of Man," (*a*) a personification and symbol, a collective name for the "saints of the Most High," and (*b*) a supernatural person, an angelic individual with an apocalyptic function, one of the heavenly powers who in some Jewish circles became apparently identified with the Messiah, although such identification was far from being general. To an intelligent and spiritual reader of Jewish Scripture the language of Daniel would clearly indicate a personification of righteous men rather than a specific individual person, as the meaning of "the Son of Man."

IV

It is most natural to believe that this was the sense in which our Lord originally used the term. Jesus could appropriately apply it to the "little flock to whom it was the Father's good pleasure to give the Kingdom," and, indeed, to the righteous men and women of all time. The "Son of Man," one suggests, was not in the mind of Jesus a special person, but a group of persons, parallel to the "saints of the Most High." In the earlier period of His ministry, at any rate, our Lord did not apparently lay stress on personal claims. These were only made as the preaching of the Kingdom and the transformation of current ideas compelled them. The thought of the Kingdom seems to have been His first interest and theme. The term "Son of Man" appears to have been used before the declaration at Caesarea Philippi, but evidently did not convey to the minds of the disciples or of others the implications of Enochian Parousial Messiahship. It was a term presumably used openly at a time before Jesus made any public Messianic identification with Himself. As Westcott remarks: "It is inconceivable that the Lord should have adopted a title which was popularly held to be synonymous with that of Messiah, while He carefully avoided the title of Messiah itself." But is it certain that He used the term in any exclusive personal sense at all? A collective meaning suits the sense of many of the "Son of Man" passages as well as, and in some cases better than, the strictly personal and individual meaning. It has been pointed out that in Aramaic the common prose title for man was *Bar nasha*, "son of man," and it has been claimed that Jesus, speaking Aramaic, could not have made a distinctive title of it; but the substitution of "man" for the "son of man" destroys the intelligibility of the passages where the phrase is used, except possibly in the cases of Mark ii verses 10 and 28. But this objection does not apply if we understand by "son of man" not man in general, but the class of righteous men, saints, reformers, souls filled with the spirit of God. In nearly every case (the few exceptions will be noted later) such an interpretation suits the context. (*a*) The argument of the conversation leading up to the statement "The Son of Man hath power on earth to forgive sins" (Mark ii. 10) is that the privilege is not exclusive to Jesus alone. It is easier to say "Thy sins are forgiven thee" than to say "Rise up and walk," for it is the common authority of a saintly soul to declare to a penitent sinner the forgiving love of God. It is the privilege of the "saints of the Most High"—the "Son of Man." (*b*) The claim, "The Son of Man is lord also of the Sabbath," is a defence of the *disciples* of Jesus plucking corn on the Sabbath-day. (*c*) To a would-be follower, presumably not prepared for the sacrifices and hardships of discipleship, the warning is given that the "Son of Man hath not where to lay his head." The "Son of Man" is not merely Jesus, but the community which the would-be followers desired to enter, the company of reformers, idealists, pioneers, who have known scorn, privation, discomforts from the foundation of the world. (*d*) The rule of greatness among the disciples is that of service and sacrifice, "for verily the Son of Man came not to be ministered unto, but to minister and give his life a ransom for many"—not exclusively Jesus, but the men of the Kingdom personified as "the Son of Man." The sufferings of the righteous should atone for and save the community (Isa. liii and several passages in Maccabees). (*e*) "When men shall hate you for the Son of Man's sake" (Luke vi. 22) may reasonably be taken as referring to persecution through fidelity to the cause of the Kingdom of the "saints of the Most High." In all these cases the possible interpretation is to be gained by regarding Jesus as identifying His disciples, together with Himself, under the collective personification, "the Son of Man."

V

Again, the Son of Man seems to have been identified in the popular mind with certain outstanding prophets in the history of Israel—Elijah, Jeremiah, John the Baptist, some ancient, some practically contemporary. Such identification may point back to the conception of the Son of Man as a collective idea, "the saints of the Most High," finding expression in one and another typical and representative figure. When Jesus hears the disciples saying, "The scribes say that Elijah must first come," He answers: "Elijah indeed cometh first and restoreth all things: *and how is it written of the Son of Man that He should suffer many things and be set at nought?* But I say unto you that Elijah is come, and they have also done unto him whatsoever they listed, even as it is written of him" (Mark ix. 9–12). The reference to the Son of Man comes in strangely here, if it is meant to apply to Jesus Himself. Elijah is mentioned immediately before and immediately after, and the second reference is obviously to the suffering and rejection of Elijah (here meant to signify John the Baptist), and the passage manifests continuity of meaning if the "Son of Man" is taken to signify, not Jesus, but the righteous who suffer and are rejected, specifically in this case John the Baptist. He is identified with Elijah because both are identified with the "Son of Man," the suffering and rejected "saints of the Most High."

VI

The theory that the Son of Man is meant to be a collective term rather than an exclusive title of Christ's is further supported by the phenomenon of the distinctions drawn apparently between Jesus as a historical individual and the "Son of Man." One is struck by the passage from the first to the third person, e.g., (a) "Ye which have followed *Me*, in the regeneration when the *Son of Man* shall sit upon the throne of His glory," etc. (Matt. xix. 28). (b) "Whosoever shall be ashamed of Me and of My words, of him shall the Son of Man be ashamed, when He cometh," etc. (Mark viii. 38). (c) Even the reply before the high priest (Mark xiv. 62 and parallels) preserves a distinction between the historical Jesus as Messiah and the Son of Man: "And Jesus said, I am (the Christ) and ye shall see the Son of Man sitting at the right hand of power and coming with the clouds of heaven."

J. E. Carpenter (*The First Three Gospels*, p. 369) comments:
"It is remarkable that Jesus, whether in encouragement or
threat, should never say 'Ye shall see Me coming.' Why
should He name an apocalyptic symbol, not Himself?" If,
however, the coming of the Son of Man signifies the coming
of the "saints of the Most High" to their Kingdom, and the
triumph of righteousness over the forces of evil oppression,
the passages may bear an intelligible sense. "Undaunted,
Jesus confronts the anger of the Council, the wrath of the
high priest, as though He said: 'You may kill Me, but you
cannot baffle God! The Messiah may perish, but the Son
of Man will come.' "

With this interpretation of the "Son of Man" as a collective
term for the "saints of the Most High," and of "the coming
of the Son of Man" as the open triumph of righteousness,
we avoid the strangeness of those passages where Jesus (who
had already come) speaks of the Son of Man *as yet to come*:
"Ye shall not have gone through the cities of Israel till the
Son of Man be come" (Matt. x. 23; cf. xvi. 28); "In an
hour ye think not the Son of Man cometh" (Matt. xxiv. 44;
cf. xxiv. 27, xxv. 31, Luke xvii. 30).

VII

We believe that these sayings, with this peculiar and
striking feature suggesting distinction between Jesus as an
individual and the Son of Man, have preserved an original
tradition going behind the thoughts and interpretations of
the evangelists themselves. For one concedes that it is almost
certain that the Gospel writers took the term "Son of Man"
as a specific title claimed by Jesus, and identified Christ with
the coming Parousial Son of Man. In one instance of the
later Gospels of Matthew and Luke the term Son of Man
seems applied specifically and unambiguously to the historical Jesus: "The Son of Man (as contrasted with John

the Baptist) came eating and drinking, and they say, Behold a gluttonous man and a winebibber, a friend of publicans and sinners" (Matt. xi. 19; Luke vii. 34). Mark viii. 38 speaks even of the Parousial Son of Man as "coming in the glory of His Father," thus suggesting identification with Christ, although the use of the third person reveals an older tradition and significance. Matt. vii. 32 also seems to identify Jesus with the Judge of the Parousia: "Many will say unto Me in that day, Lord, did we not prophesy in Thy name?" etc. Jesus seems also identical with the King who declares at the Judgment, "when the Son of Man shall come in His glory," "Come, ye blessed of My Father, inherit the Kingdom prepared for you from the foundation of the world," etc. (Matt. xxv). In Matthew's parable of the tares the Son of Man is mentioned as sowing the seed, and it is also the Son of Man who directs the Parousial Judgment at the harvest (Matt. xiii. 37, 40), yet the first Son of Man seems a reference to the historical Jesus.

But one best explains the use of the third person in general and the many suggestions of distinction between Jesus and the Son of Man as due to the older and original tradition of the Son of Man as a collective term for the "saints of the Most High," not, of course, excluding Jesus, but including others as well. At a later stage, not altogether unnaturally (for Jesus was an outstanding representative of the righteous sufferers, redeemers and conquerors indicated by the term), the evangelists identified Jesus as *the* Son of Man, but did not succeed in altogether obliterating the traces of the original use. *But when the exclusive identification was made, the Son of Man tradition of the Similitudes of Enoch would begin to play its part.* Jesus became the supernatural, apocalyptic Messiah, the Christian counterpart of the Persian Mithra or of the Jewish archangel Michael. The foundations of the unfortunate and unspiritual Second Adventism of the New Testament were laid. The figure of Jesus was given over to wild apocalyptic, and attracted even into Mark's Gospel such extraneous matter as the "Little Apocalypse" of the evangelist's thirteenth chapter (see p. 115). The birth of Christological apocalyptic becomes intelligible, but we believe that all this was a quite unhistorical elaboration of misunderstood sayings of Jesus. The simple, spiritual, prophetic teaching of our Lord was perverted, and a conception was introduced into Christianity which, when taken into Hellenistic circles, reduced Jesus to the level of a Greek deity.

CHAPTER XIV

THE SUFFERING SON OF MAN

I

ONE line of development of the idea of the Son of Man leads, as we have seen, to a Parousial figure, coming in glory, treading down the powers of evil, judging the quick and the dead, and establishing an everlasting Kingdom of blessedness for the saints. But another line of development brings us to the conception of a very different figure—that of a suffering Son of Man, who comes to His triumph only through persecution, death and resurrection. Following the confession at Caesarea Philippi, Jesus "began to teach that the Son of Man must suffer many things and be rejected by the elders and chief priests and scribes, and after three days rise again" (Mark viii. 31). The statement is repeated after the Transfiguration (Mark ix. 9 f.). The prediction of suffering, death and resurrection after three days recurs in the secret passage through Galilee (ix. 31) and on the journey to Jerusalem (x. 32, 34). Prediction passes to fulfilment. The Passover arrives, when "the Son of Man is delivered up to be crucified" (Matt. xxvi. 2). The stages of the betrayal are linked with the mention of the Son of Man: "The Son of Man goeth even as it is mentioned of Him, but woe unto that man through whom the Son of Man is betrayed" (Mark xiv. 21). "Sleep on now; the hour is come. Behold, the Son of Man is betrayed into the hands of sinners" (xiv. 41). Judas is met with the words, "Betrayest thou the Son of Man with a kiss?" (Luke xxii. 48). The women at the sepulchre are reminded by the angel of how Jesus spoke to them in Galilee, saying that the Son of Man must be delivered up into the

hands of sinful men and be crucified, and on the third day
rise again (Luke xxiv. 7).

II

These sayings are apparently referred back to a previous
writing: "The Son of Man goeth *as it is written of him*"; "*It
is written* that the Son of Man must suffer many things and
be set at nought" (Mark ix. 12)—a passage which we have
suggested refers to Elijah or John the Baptist as the Son of
Man. The passage proceeds: "But I say unto you that Elijah
is come, and they have done unto him whatsoever they have
listed, *even as it is written of him*." The reference here does not
seem to be Malachi's prophecy, which did not predict any
special sufferings of the forerunner, but presumably to some
lost apocalypse which told of a suffering Son of Man,
identifiable with "Elijah, Jeremiah, or one of the prophets."
There is, of course, the striking Old Testament passage of the
Suffering Servant (Isa. liii), who is a man of sorrows and
acquainted with grief, whose sufferings and death may be in
some way regarded as an offering for sin (cf. the atoning
value of the sufferings of the righteous in Maccabees, or
"The Son of Man gives his life a ransom for many"), and
whose days after his travail are to be prolonged. The fifty-
third of Isaiah may well have played an important part in
the development of the Son of Man conception, but one seeks
other indications of literature of an apocalyptic kind suggesting more clearly the sufferings, death and resurrection of
the Son of Man.

Behind the general apocalyptic thought of the period
stands the legend of anti-Christ, resisted by some power
of righteousness who suffers through such witness. In
Daniel vii "the saints of the Most High," symbolised, as we
have seen, by "the one like unto a son of man" (cf. verses
13, 18), are "worn out" by some adverse tyranny (anti-
Christ?) (verse 25). The tradition of the "birth pangs of the

Messiah" applies, it is true, to the woes preceding His
coming rather than to His personal sufferings, but this
tradition may be regarded as a special form of a larger idea
of the sufferings of the righteous at the hands of anti-Christ
in a period before the triumph of the everlasting Kingdom.
But of special interest for our purpose is the eleventh chapter
of the Revelation, where we seem to find traces of an apocalypse of suffering, death and resurrection after three days
apparently quite dissociated from the events of the Gospel
narrative. The "Son of Man" is not mentioned, but Moses
and Elijah, or figures like them, undergo the process
"written" concerning the "Son of Man" in the Gospels.
In a period of exceeding distress two mysterious witnesses
prophesy. These have the power to shut the heavens that it
rain not during the years of their prophecy (Elijah ?),
and they have powers over the waters to turn them into
blood and to smite the earth with every plague as often as
they shall desire (verse 6), an obvious reference to Moses.
The "two witnesses," then, appear to be Moses and Elijah.
The beast, however, comes out of the abyss, wars against
them, overcomes them and kills them. Their dead bodies lie
unburied "in the street of the great city which spiritually is
called Sodom and Egypt, where also their Lord was crucified." Men look upon their dead bodies three days and a
half, and suffer not their dead bodies to be laid in the tomb.
And after the three days and a half the breath of life from
God enters into them; they stand on their feet and go up
into heaven in a cloud, their enemies beholding them
(Rev. xi. 7–11). These details are clearly not borrowed from
the death and resurrection precedents of the Gospel. There
are two witnesses. The bodies are unburied; they rise up
after three and a half days. These particulars testify to some
quite independent apocalyptic tradition, in which Moses
and Elijah play the chief part, a drama of suffering, death
and resurrection "after three days" (cf. Daniel xii. 7, the
period of power for the adversaries of the holy people shall

be for a time, times and a half). One connects this account
with the Son of Man passage (Mark ix. 9–13), in which
Jesus speaks of Elijah (John the Baptist) as having come, "and
they have done unto him whatsoever they have listed, even
as it is written of him."

One is inclined to find the same tradition in the Transfiguration story. Elijah and Moses—the "two witnesses" of
Rev. xi—talk with Jesus; Luke adds that the topic of their
conversation was "His decease, which He should accomplish at Jerusalem"; the first thing of which Jesus speaks
after this experience is "the rising again of the Son of Man
from the dead" (Mark ix. 9). In the Transfiguration story we
appear to have a reminiscence of a "Son of Man" apocalyptic
tradition of suffering, death and resurrection in some way
associated with Moses and Elijah.

III

We believe that this tradition of the suffering Son of Man
was much in the mind of our Lord as hostility gathered
and persecution began to press upon Him and He became
conscious of rejection and the possibility of danger and death.
He saw His own betrayal, sufferings, sacrifices, triumphs
through pain and sorrow *as representative experiences of the
Son of Man*. It was not merely He, an individual, who was
betrayed and suffered as it was written of Him. The Son of
Man was a cosmic element wider than any individual life,
but finding expressions in individual lives and in particularly
significant acts in them.

Foretold by prophets and poets in their most rapt prophecies and
    poems . . .
Many times have I been rejected, taunted, put in prison and crucified,
    and many times shall be again,
All the world have I given up for my dear brothers' and sisters' sake,
    for the soul's sake. . . .
                    W. WHITMAN, *Chanting the Square Deific.*

Our Lord used the familiar imagery of the drama of the apocalypse to express His conviction that righteousness triumphs through suffering and sacrifice, that truth apparently fallen in the streets shall rise again, that death cannot hold that which is greatest in life. *He was making no prediction as to what would happen to Him physically as an individual.* But when the disciples and evangelists identified Jesus more closely and exclusively with the figure of the Son of Man, this teaching received a new interpretation. It is not the cause of righteousness, but Jesus Himself who must suffer, be slain, and after three days rise again.

IV

We conceive that one school may seize upon this as the genesis of the whole Resurrection account. Later Gospel events must be made to correspond with a misinterpreted teaching of the Son of Man suffering and rising again after three days. We are not inclined to take this view. We believe something abnormal happened after the death of Jesus, some psychical appearance which gave rise to the deeply embedded New Testament tradition of an historical resurrection. The "Son of Man" Resurrection tradition and the Resurrection stories of Jesus, despite a surface similarity, differ in an important particular. Jesus is said to have risen *on* the third day, but the whole period of death was only one day, two nights and portions of two days. The Son of Man tradition gives a Resurrection "*after* three days" (compare particularly the "sign of Jonah" saying, "The Son of Man shall be three days and three nights in the heart of the earth"), probably derived from the Daniel tradition of time and times and half a time, or the three and a half days of Rev. xi. If the Son of Man resurrection-apocalypse led to the invention of a resurrection-"myth," we should not have expected such a discrepancy. We conceive that it was only after some abnormal psychical happening following the death of Jesus that the "Son of Man" teaching of Jesus, conveying the spiritual principle that righteousness can never be destroyed, that it proceeds through suffering, persecution, seeming defeat to triumph, came to be taken in a literalist sense as applying to the physical resurrection of Jesus, and constituting His own prediction of that event.

V

With the view we have taken, we have an explanation of a feature of the Gospels which is puzzling, with the usually accepted interpretation of the Son of Man passages. In the attitude and behaviour of the disciples and followers immediately after the death of Jesus—a situation of dismay and despair—there is little support for the evangelist's presentation that Jesus had definitely been predicting on occasion after occasion His own martyrdom and resurrection immediately following. After the crucifixion, despair seemed complete, and the resurrection appearance of Jesus utterly unexpected. Nothing seemed to have prepared them for such an experience. This is quite consistent with the idea that Jesus, though He had spoken of the Son of Man suffering, dying, rising again, had never given the impression that He was making predictions concerning His own physical individuality—indeed, it is even doubtful if He contemplated an actual martyrdom at Jerusalem until almost the hour of the tragedy itself. If the predictions made by Jesus had been so definite and detailed that He knew He was going up to Jerusalem to die, we must consider the point made by Pfleiderer and others: that the conduct of Jesus at Jerusalem "makes the impression that He journeyed thither, not in order to die, but to fight and conquer, and that in looking forward to the conflict His own death presented itself not as a certainty, but at the most as a possibility" (*Primitive*

Christianity, vol. ii, p. 34 f.; cf. Goguel, *Jesus the Nazarene*, p. 203).

VI

We may now summarise our conclusions. (1) Jesus was faithful to the collective idea of "the Son of Man" found in Daniel vii, obviously a personification of the righteous people to whom should be given the everlasting Kingdom. It was used on the lips of Jesus to include His disciples with Himself. It could also be applied to the men of righteous heroism in the past—Elijah, Jeremiah and the Prophets—and to John the Baptist. (2) Jesus prophesied the ultimate glory and triumph of the people of God as the "coming of the Son of Man." (3) The disciples at a later date came to regard Jesus as the "Son of Man" in a specific personal sense, and to identify Him with the Messianic Son of Man of the Similitudes of Enoch, who, as a supernatural being, should manifest Himself at a literal Parousia. (4) By this error Christian Second Adventism was born and the way prepared for a further Hellenistic development. (5) Hellenistic deification was due to the translation of the apocalyptic Son of Man into Hellenistic thought forms. (6) There was a tradition (probably in a written form now lost) that the Son of Man—the righteous people—should suffer persecution and death, but rise again "after three days." This expressed the spiritual principle of the triumph of the righteous after seeming defeat and disaster. (7) His own experience led Jesus to stress this tradition in the later stages of His ministry. He never intended, however, to predict His own physical resurrection, which apparently came to the disciples as an altogether unexpected experience. (8) In the light of that experience, the early Church took the statement of the tradition as a definite prediction by Jesus of His own death and rising again. These conclusions give a more spiritual character to the teaching of Jesus on "apocalyptic" themes; they save

us from regarding Him as the source of the strange and
unspiritual Second Advent teaching which played so unfortunate a part in the mental life of the Church; they present
Jesus as a sane, intelligible and inspiring prophet of spiritual
and eternal religion, finding echoes in abiding and universal
experience, and keeping His value and appeal in the passing
away of all that was local and temporary in the forms of
Christianity.

CHAPTER XV

THE FIRST STAGE OF NEW TESTAMENT SPECULATION

I

HOWEVER the identification of Jesus with the Enochian Messiah came about, it had, we believe, most momentous consequences for the thought of the Christian Church. The more obvious of these was the creation of the tradition of the Parousia or Second Coming in the early Church, to which every New Testament writer bears his witness. The picture of the Thessalonian Church shown in St. Paul's Epistles gives us some idea of the tremendous hold which these apocalyptic expectations came to have upon the mind of the primitive Christian community. But a less apparent though an even more momentous consequence was manifested when the doctrine of Enochian Messiahship passed out into a Gentile world familiar with *Kyrioi*, who in many ways were not dissimilar from the supernatural Enochian Messiah of Jewish apocalyptic expectation. The Hellenistic *Kyrios*, generally regarded as a secondary and mediating deity in hierarchical polytheistic systems, was a kind of natural translation of the Enochian "Son of Man" in Jewish literature. Both conceptions, in fact, went back more or less to common sources. The roots of the supernatural "Son of Man" presented in the Similitudes of Enoch apparently lie in Persian schemes of polytheistic mediation. The Enochian "Son of Man" may be regarded as "first cousin" to Mithra, whose cult, proceeding from Persia, reached Anatolia probably well before the Christian period, where it made amalgams with Anatolian and Hellenistic cults, and thereby gained new mediational, sacramental and communion features.

Such a process as here suggested may throw light on the surprising phenomenon that in a Christianity arising from so strict a monotheistic faith as Judaism, the idea of Jesus, as virtually a "second God"—a *deuteros theos*—arose. The first stage was the identification of Jesus with the supernatural "Son of Man," the semi-Persian Messiah of the apocalyptic Similitudes of Enoch. It is very improbable that the Jewish Christians of the first generation passed beyond this stage. The deeply rooted monotheistic tradition would prevent it. As Schweitzer remarks: "Jesus, it cannot be sufficiently emphasised, is not thought of as a God, but only as a heavenly being who is entrusted with the mission of bringing in a new world. It was only later in the Greek and Gnostic theology that He was deified. For Paul He is the Son of God in the simple Old Testament and apocalyptic sense" (*Paul and His Interpreters*, p. 194). The apocalyptic "Son of Man" was a super-angel, and not a God. There could be no God but one. But as the conception passed into Hellenistic circles, familiar with polytheistic figures and ways of thinking, the mental restrictions in Judaism were naturally thrown off. Some commentators believe that this stage was reached even before Paul's conversion, and that it was to this type of Christianity that Paul himself was converted; that the Church even at this early date had been so influenced by Hellenistic mysteries that it had come to worship Christ as the Hellenistic cults worshipped Attis or Serapis, giving Him the definite technical divine name *Kyrios*, or Lord, and already attaching to the Church Meal the values of the communion and assimilative rites of the Gentile *thiasi*. (*a*) Dr. Morgan (*The Religion and Theology of Paul*, p. 50) claims that from the beginning Paul stood on the ground of Hellenistic and Gentile Christianity, and that Christ worship and the *Kyrios* title was generally accepted by the primitive Church before he became converted to Christianity. James, Peter, Barnabas—all accepted this set of doctrines. "While we read of a conflict of opinions regarding the law, we read

of none regarding the person of Christ and the homage to
be rendered to Him." (*b*) Other scholars find the *Kyrios* cult
established within Christianity before Paul's conversion, but
claim that it was only to be found within the Hellenistic
branch of the Church. There was in these circles a Hellenistic type of Christianity which stood in some contrast to the
Judaistic type of the Jerusalem disciples. Bousset says that
it is not sufficiently realised that between Paul and the
Palestinian Christian Church stands the Hellenistic community in Antioch, Damascus and Tarsus. With the former
Paul's relations were of the slenderest nature. The autobiography of Galatians seems witness to this. The Apostle
is independent of flesh and blood at Jerusalem, but the case
is different with the Hellenistic community. The Christian
"tradition" of 1 Cor. xv has been derived by Paul, not
directly from Jerusalem, but from Antioch. And it is from
this Hellenistic community, which has already introduced
the *Kyrios* title and worship for Christ, that Paul has received
his Christian faith and practice (*Kyrios Christos*, pp. 92 ff.).
(*c*) Loisy (*Les Mystères Païens*, pp. 303 ff.), following the
Galatian autobiography, finds Paul three years after his
conversion going up to Jerusalem to make the acquaintance
of Peter in order to reconcile his own type of faith, which
was Hellenistic, with that of the Jerusalem community. His
motive was a certain concern for what might be called
Christian unity. So diverse were the types that the mission
was only partially successful. Paul was not asked to preach
publicly at Jerusalem, for his semi-foreign Christianity would
not have been acceptable. Thus he only saw Peter and
James; to the rest he remained unknown by face. When Peter
came to Antioch, Paul resisted him publicly (Gal. ii. 11).
"Before certain from James had come, he had eaten with
the Gentiles," not, so Loisy thinks, in a mere social way,
but at the Lord's Supper. He had recognised the spiritual
fellowship with the Hellenists. Now, however, Peter had
withdrawn from this attitude. Again, the existence of a

"Peter-party" at Corinth leads one to suppose that the Apostle of the circumcision never completely shared Paul's views. Loisy further finds the explanation of Paul's persecution of the early Church (that is, rejecting the historicity of the Jerusalem persecution) in his hatred of the Hellenistic features which had appeared in it. It was a Hellenistic type of Christianity which he persecuted and to which he later became converted. "In one sense he was nearer to the Jewish party before his conversion to Christianity than when he himself made a Christian profession."

II

We believe, however, that in the earlier period of New Testament thought, up to the writing of the second group of Pauline Epistles at any rate, the use of the term *Kyrios* had no Hellenistic cult significance, nor had any worship or deification similar to that of the "Mystery gods" become attached to Jesus. Paul became converted to the common Christianity of the early Jewish Christians, but not to Hellenistic Christianity, with its *Kyrios* and communion features, which probably was not yet born. His preconversion zeal against Christianity was against such liberalism and stress upon a spiritual interpretation of religion as was found in the speech of Stephen (*Passing and Permanent in St. Paul*, pp. 72, 73 ff.). His "conversion" was from traditional Jewish orthodoxy to Christianity as a "religion of the spirit," not from monotheistic Judaism to a new Hellenistic Mystery cult with Jesus as the *Kyrios*. The Jerusalem visit (Gal. i), the relations with Peter, the nature of the Jerusalem Council, are all sufficiently intelligible with this simpler explanation. There was no *Kyrios* issue between Paul and the other Jewish leaders at the Jerusalem Council, not because the latter had come to accept *Kyrios* doctrines, even before Paul's conversion, as Dr. Morgan suggests, but because, as yet, neither Paul nor anyone else apparently had conceived such doctrines. The trouble seems to have been over circumcision and Jewish externalism alone. We cannot stress the early use of the term *Kyrios* to prove that at this period Christianity had been transformed into anything like a Hellenistic Mystery cult. The term is common enough in the Gospels to signify *dominus* (master, sir), and it would be natural to apply such a term to Jesus as the head of the company of the disciples. Even a larger connotation is possible, without resort to the Mystery cult hypothesis. The psalm from which the quotation "The Lord said unto my lord" came was evidently taken as having Messianic reference, as is shown by Christ's use of it (Mark xii. 36), and in Peter's speech in Acts ii "Lord" and "Christ" seem synonymous terms. Here *Kyrios* is *the* Lord, the Messiah, the Enochian Son of Man.

III

In favour of assigning a distinct Hellenistic origin to the early Christian practices of the adoration of Christ and the invoking of Him in prayer, Dr. Morgan (*Religion and Theology of Paul*, p. 46 f.) claims that "of a worship of a Messiah, Jewish apocalyptic knows nothing," and that "to Judaism even angel-worship is foreign." But in the angelology of the pre-Christian period can be seen, as Fairweather points out, "the germ from which has sprung the widespread invocation of angels and spirits in the worship of the Christian Church." In Rev. xxii. 8 John is rebuked for falling down to worship an angel, but the very rebuke bears witness to a current tendency. Angel-worship is specifically condemned in Col. ii. 18, but the passage need not be taken as an indication that none but the Supreme must be invoked, but that the angels must not usurp the mediating function of Christ. These instances (cf. also Dives' appeal to Father Abraham, Luke xvi) show how readily the human mind may come to adore and invoke not merely the Supreme but supernatural beings conceived as possessing special functions affecting human destiny. It may be thus realised how readily, even along purely Jewish lines, invocation to Christ as apocalyptic Son of Man, exalted in the heavens, might naturally creep in. We need not postulate influences from Hellenistic Mystery cults for explaining this phenomenon. It may even be questioned whether in New Testament times the practice was at all widely established. Believers are described as those who call upon the name of the Lord Jesus (1 Cor. ii. 2), but this may be read to signify prayers to God in the name of Christ, for, as Dr. Morgan concedes (p. 45), in general, "Christ is introduced only as presenting the prayer to God. . . . In the New Testament the standing practice is not prayer to Christ, but prayer to God in Christ's name. . . . Not until a comparatively late period did the practice of prayer to Christ receive the sanction of the Church. Origen assumes that this is common, but opposes it, insisting on prayer in the name." It is not *to* Jesus, but in the name of Jesus, every knee should bow (Phil. ii. 10), and there was, further, the idea that special potency was to be found in the use of the name of Christ (Heitmüller).

IV

But *grant the idea of Christ as supernatural apocalyptic Son of Man, and the passage to deification in Hellenistic circles, and more or less in the Hellenistic sense, becomes intelligible.* In Gentile circles the name *Kyrios* would be a suitable equivalent for such a Jewish technical term as "Son of Man" (that is, the Enochian apocalyptic Messiah), and it is significant that in St. Paul's writings the title "Son of Man" has completely disappeared. But the term *Kyrios* comes into prominence, e.g. "If thou shalt confess with thy mouth Jesus as *Kyrios* and shalt believe in thy heart that God raised Him from

the dead, thou shalt be saved" (Rom. x. 9). Every Epistle,
even the earliest, the Thessalonian letter, opens and closes
with the name "Lord Jesus Christ" in the salutation and
benediction: "Every tongue shall confess that Jesus Christ is
Kyrios, to the glory of the Father" (Phil. ii. 11). It is true that
Kyrios is also the Septuagint equivalent of the Old Testa
ment Jahveh, but the term as applied to Christ in the early
speeches of Acts or in Thessalonians, and possibly throughout the Pauline writings, is most naturally taken as signifying
the functions of Jesus, more or less as Enochian Son of Man.
Later it probably came to imply deity in the Hellenistic sense
and to carry the connotation of the *Kyrios* of Hellenistic
Mystery cults, but such a *startling transition must be explained
by the part played in the process by the conception of the Enochian
Son of Man*. In Judaism itself it was a disguised polytheistic
figure issuing from Israel's Persian contact; later, in new
polytheistic circles, it naturally reverted to its original
significance.

V

The tracing of this development is necessary for the adequate conception of the two stages of New Testament
speculative thought. Each has its own value; in each the
universal intuitions of religion find a separate and characteristic expression. The expression in both is distinct from that
we have sought to show in the teachings of the historical
Jesus. Even with the earlier of these two stages speculation
has begun, removing the thought of the young Church beyond
the simple teaching of our Lord, though naturally incorporating much of its essential values. The great speculative
development of Christian thought in the hands of Paul
started out from an earlier speculative stage. Some development had already taken place. Speculation began early,
and had already reached a definite point in the primitive
Christian community before Paul embraced Christianity.

Schweitzer is right in pointing out that in some respects the religion of the primitive community had become a new thing—a faith with the emphasis on the death and resurrection, and that this new element was not brought into Christianity by Paul. He found it there before him, and what he did was to think out its logical implications.

VI

We may now summarise the teaching of the primitive community in this earlier speculative stage, as a preliminary to tracing in it its distinctive expression of the elements of universal religion. We find this earlier stage represented by Acts, the Synoptics and the Thessalonian Epistles. Jesus is Jewish Messiah, a prophet of the seed of David (Acts xiii. 23) announced by the Old Testament prophets (xiii. 27), the Son of God whom He raised from the dead (1 Thess. i. 10). He is "Jesus of Nazareth, a man approved of God by mighty works, wonders and signs, whom lawless men did crucify and slay, whom God raised up. God hath made Him both Lord and Christ, this Jesus whom ye crucified" (Acts ii). After His death He assumes other features. He becomes a heavenly being, sitting at the right hand of God, witnessing His servants and protecting them. Finally He will return in glory to the earth, bring to life the dead, overthrow anti-Christ, judge the world, destroy the wicked, and reward the faithful with everlasting life. This apocalyptic event, though not immediate, is near at hand, and is expected within the lifetime of the first generation. This Second Adventism of the early Church seems involved in the two different forms of Messianic expectation. In the earliest thought the Messiah was to be a human Deliverer of Israel, a second David, a warrior or prophet, or both. After the contact with Persia, the conception of the Messiah became rather that of a supernatural deliverer, coming on the clouds, raising the dead, and establishing a millennium. The latter idea was hardly consistent with the former, but could not the double expectation be realised at different times, in two phases of being and operation? Jewish Christians, familiar with the double tradition, naturally urged that since Jesus had come only as the Jewish Messiah, He must come again in glory to fulfil the apocalyptic expectation. The first coming was in humble human form, with none of the dramatic consequences expected. Faith in the open Messianic deliverance and apocalyptic appearance could only be restored and maintained by the hope of a Second Coming.

VII

In this earlier stage of New Testament speculation two distinct ideas of Salvation may be recognised. The one is that of deliverance from sin, associated with the function of Jesus as prophet; the other is that of the apocalyptic transformation of the world by the Parousial coming of Christ. The former is a spiritual and ethical process. Jesus has been "exalted to be a Prince and Saviour for to give repentance and remission of sins"—that is, as a prophet, leading the people to repent, and thus, according to certain Old Testament conceptions (e.g. those of the eighth century B.C. prophets), to bring about the forgiveness of their transgressions. Even the message preached by John the Baptist was one of repentance "unto the remission of sins." A further theory, however, must have begun to form at an early date —the idea that there was some propitiatory value in the death of Jesus. The ignominious death of Christ, as if He were under a curse, the influence of the Servant passage (Isa. liii)—at first probably used as a prophetic identification-mark of the Messiah by the early Church—and the theory which had prevailed from the time of the Exile that there was a propitiatory value in the sufferings of the righteous, would probably lead to some early doctrine of a general undefined kind that the death of Jesus had a propitiatory value (1 Thess. v. 10). But the doctrine of Salvation, through a mystic death and resurrection, such as we find later in Paulinism, is as yet unstated, probably because unconceived. We can see, however, how naturally such a theory would grow from the theological material lying in this first version of speculative thought, and would seem to throw light on vague and isolated elements found in the thought of the earlier period. As yet the resurrection of Christ, though emphasised, had no mystic soteriological significance. It was merely taken as a credential sign of the Messiahship, the fulfilment of prophecy (Acts ii. 21), and a sign of God's approval and adoption.

VIII

Religious thought in this period seems to have mainly gathered around a Parousial Salvation. Salvation was not so much a process of transformed personality working by moral laws, as a cosmic revolution effected by dramatic, external, divine action. It has its affinities with the politico-religious tradition of the Old Testament, and proceeds step by step from that. It may be contended that even repentance is not the sign of salvation proceeding on spiritual and ethical lines, but that it is the moral preliminary to allow God to come back and act apocalyptically through Christ, His appointed "Servant." There may be an undercurrent of moral influence and transformation proceeding from the personality and spiritual and ethical teaching of our Lord— this was an element never lost in the most speculative stages of New Testament thought—but this flows, as it were, apart from the main current of religious interest. It is the more important element from the standpoint of eternal religious values, but not the element recognised and stressed by this school of religious thought as was that of apocalyptic salvation. Its operation was more or less unconscious, unadvertised and indirect. The disciples would seek to live in the spirit of Christ, because He was felt to be a Divine Benefactor *in other directions*—not because they recognised that this way of life was central in His Gospel and independent of all apocalyptic theories and hopes. The phenomenon of Churches stressing elements of secondary importance, while unconscious of their real strength, on the practice of the spirit of Jesus, is not unusual. So while the real power of this early Church lay in the spiritual and ethical influence of its Master's life of love and sacrifice, its *interest* was centred upon a Parousial Salvation.

IX

Its doctrines were controlled by that supreme guiding interest. The emphasis upon Christ's Messiahship had behind it the thought of the Salvation to be effected by the Messiah. Prophecy and miracles were to accredit Jesus as the instrument of the Messianic Soteriology. The Resurrection itself had this value. Paul's mystic interpretation of it was as yet unknown. Only later did the terms and conceptions brought into Christianity by this special interest of Messiahship with the Messianic Parousial Salvation involved begin to invite further explanation and interpretation in their own rights, and demand their place within a more or less consistent system of Christian doctrine.

The Incarnation interest, such as we find it in the Fourth Gospel, had not arisen. A simple Adoptionist view was taken of the person of Jesus. He gained His significance as an agent of the apocalyptic deliverance. He was an "approved" Messiah, a man chosen to do a supernatural work. The ultimate interest was in the deliverance to be effected rather than in the person effecting the deliverance, in His own right. The Logos speculations in relation to Christ were as yet unconceived. All mystic and metaphysical theories concerning the relations of Christ, God and mankind were remote from the interests of the Church at this stage. Jesus found His significance simply in His relations to the apocalyptic acts, the Parousial manifestation, the ending of the "age," the introduction of the new cosmic order, the judging of the quick and the dead, the creation of the new heavens and the new earth.

In this earlier stage there seem to be no signs of those mystic and sacramental ideas which are found in the Roman and Corinthian letters and in the later history of the Church. Baptism and the Church Meal were features of the life of the Churches from the beginning, but as yet no mystic and sacramentarian significance had become attached to them. Faith was belief in the Messiahship, not a "gnosis" or a mystic communion "*into* Christ." Christ's death and resurrection were not yet worked into a scheme of mystic salvation parallel to that of the Mystery cults.

X

In many ways this central Parousial hope was not only illusive (for it turned out that this confident expectation was unfulfilled by events), but it was also spiritually misleading and mischievous. Some of its consequences were seen in the demoralisation of the Church at Thessalonica. It disturbed sober thought; it interfered with steady labour. Behind it lay the false philosophy that the action of God was to be expected in human affairs, apart from the moral laws, the consecrations and efforts of human life. His working was not through personality, will, ideal, vision, but through external breaking of skies and marching forth of heavenly armies. The apocalyptic view obscures the truth of the sacredness of life, of God operating in unadvertised ways in a seemingly commonplace world. His works are conceived as sudden, arresting, dramatic, cataclysmic. The attitude of faith is presented, not as consecrating will and labour to serve the Kingdom of God, but as pious passivity—waiting for God to act, and not presuming to take the work out of His hands. It makes for impatience and dissatisfaction with steady toil, robs common life of its profounder meanings, and hides from us the profound truths of the evolutionary immanental workings of God. Parousial expectation is virtually a denial of God's indwelling within us to will and to work His good pleasure.

Nevertheless there is religious significance in this apocalyptic Parousial expectation when we recognise that it is the expression of one of those fundamental intuitions of faith— that of cosmic optimism; a projecting of the sense that the universe is essentially sound, and that "a sun will break the thickest cloud earth ever stretched." Thus "Mark Rutherford" speaks of this New Testament "dream—an absurd dream let us call it—of an immediate millennium and of the return of the Master surrounded with divine splendour, judging mankind and adjusting the balance between good and evil. It was a baseless dream, and the enlightened may call it ridiculous. It is anything but that—it is the opposite of that. Putting aside its temporary mode of expression, it is the hope and prophecy of all noble hearts, a sign of their inability to concur in the present condition of things." We have here expression of that eternal and universal intuition of the Eternal Goodness. Things must get better, for God is God; Love is "creation's final law." Now abideth not only Faith and Love—but *Hope*.

CHAPTER XVI

THE SECOND STAGE OF NEW TESTAMENT SPECULATION

I

AT some point before the writing of the later groups of the Pauline Epistles and of the Fourth Gospel a further speculative development took place. Christianity had definitely assumed in some of its centres certain theological forms which suggest Hellenistic influence. It had discovered new categories of expression and incorporated new ideas; it had found a Gentile interpretation which henceforth makes what amalgam it can with the older Jewish presentation. The Logos doctrine emerges in Christian literature, new doctrines concerning Baptism and the Church Meal similar to those of the Mystery cults appear, ideas of communion and assimilation with the Divine are manifest, and the conception of a Christian "gnosis" comes to the fore—a set of doctrines of a theosophic rather than a theological nature, described as a "mystery" and tending to induce a mystic "union." Theosophic knowledge begets mystic experience, as "gnosis" was conceived to do. Sacramentalism apparently assumes a new importance. The Platonic and Philonic idea of the "Two Worlds," with the necessity of a mediating Logos, Wisdom or World-Soul, lies behind the new Christian literature produced from this time onward. The earlier phase of speculative thought, with its Adoptionist theology, its Messianic stress, its Apocalyptic expectation, partly sinks into the background before these new interests, and partly disappears. Christ as apocalyptic Enochian Son of Man finds a Hellenistic interpretation and becomes a mediating Logos or functions as a *Kyrios*, in the Mystery cult sense. This development was gradual, and its steps are intelligible. The first stage was that of liberalising primitive Christianity to allow its expansion into the Gentile world; the freeing of Christianity from its Jewish limitations and handicaps, especially the challenge to circumcision as essential to real faith. One sees this process at work in the early chapters of Acts. Peter has to learn the lesson of a universal faith, for which circumcision is not essential. Stephen is a significant figure; apparently it was his liberalism which at first irritated Saul of Tarsus, and later transformed his whole religious standpoint. The adoption of Stephen's spiritual liberalism by Paul sufficiently explains the historical situation given in the early chapters of the Book of Acts without supposing that at this date any deeper Hellenistic development had taken place either in some sections of the Church or in the mind of Paul himself. The Jerusalem Council was concerned only with this problem of the relaxation, for Gentile converts, of circumcision and other Jewish ordinances. From this fact Schweitzer concludes that Paul had no Hellenistic elements in his teaching. "The primitive Christian community at Jerusalem did not discover anything new or essentially foreign in his thought; it was never made a charge against him that he had 'heathenised' the Gospel." We believe that this contention may be held, against Morgan and Loisy, up to the period, at any rate, of the writing of the second group of Pauline Epistles. For many years Paul's views on the person of Christ, Baptism and the Church Meal lay within the doctrinal circle of the primitive Jewish-Christian Church. Peter, James, Barnabas, Paul, all shared the common faith of the first stage of speculative thought described in the last chapter. Hellenism had up to this point little or no influence on Christian speculation.

II

In another study—*The Passing and the Permanent in St. Paul*—we have argued that the development of Christian thought from this set of beliefs held by the primitive community to a further stage, definitely influenced by Hellenistic ideas, took place between the writing of Paul's first and second groups of Epistles. One dates this development more exactly during Paul's stay at Ephesus on his third missionary journey. We suggest that Paulinism as a distinctive system was born there and then. There were many preparations for it; on the one hand, a number of ideas brought together by Messianic apologetic invited elucidation; they needed to be worked up into some kind of system, notably the doctrine of Salvation, the significance of the Death of Christ, the Resurrection. Again, there were "germs" of Hellenic thought deposited in Paul's mind from boyhood and college days. He may have been acquainted in Tarsus not only with Stoic speculation, but with the local Mystery cult. At Jerusalem he probably became familiar in Gamaliel's school with some of the Jewish Alexandrian books, with their Wisdom-Logos doctrine (e.g. "The Wisdom of Solomon"). But as yet these were merely germ-thoughts, needing the stimulus of new conditions to develop them. In the "Wisdom of Solomon," the "Wisdom" doctrine was hardly sufficiently pronounced to shape Paul's thought, but its presence in a Jewish religious writing which had won respect and a measure of religious authority in Jewish circles was valuable as a "sanction" when other influences brought a developed Logos doctrine from the Alexandrianism of Philo's time to Paul's attention. The Apostle might entertain a Logos conception without feeling it absolutely foreign and without any sense of disloyalty to his father's faith and traditions.

III

Special personal conditions at this time were favourable to such a development. The situation in the Churches of Galatia led the Apostle to a passionate claim for independence from tradition and the right to think afresh and freely. He challenged the bondage of Judaism, and even of more recent Christian traditions. Moreover, new influences were at work upon him. For two years at Ephesus he was in daily touch with Gentiles, "reasoning" with them in the school of Tyrannus (Acts xix. 9), and it is significant that at the end of his long stay at Ephesus he had gained friends among the Asiarchs, the high priests of Asia (v. 31). So sympathetic were the relations between Jews and Phrygians that the worship of the Phrygian Sabazius had actually been blended with that of the Old Testament Jahweh in a cult possessing Mysteries like those of Attis (Ramsay, *Historical Commentary on Galatians*, pp. 193–6). It is tempting to suppose that Paul had gained through his friendship with these Anatolian priests a deeper appreciation of the spiritual significance and values of their Mystery ritual.

Here also at Ephesus Paul met Apollos, the Christian Jew of Alexandria—Philo's city and the home of the Logos speculations. At Corinth Apollos had actually drawn about him a following, sufficiently numerous and influential to be compared with the Paul party and the Petrine party in that city. There are indications that there were considerable theological differences to account for this partisanship. Paul finds it necessary to defend himself against the charge that "wisdom" is absent from his teaching (1 Cor. i; ii. 1). This suggests that "wisdom" was characteristic of the teaching of one of the other parties in the Corinthian Church. Moreover, in attempting to demonstrate in his own teaching a parallel "wisdom," he significantly couches his language in gnostic terms (ii. 6 ff.). Does not this suggest that the rival teaching was gnostic in character?—the Corinthian teachers declaring this could hardly have belonged to the Peter or the Christ party (if this name indicated a fourth group among the Corinthian sects), but it is teaching which we might have expected from the Alexandrian Apollos. The differences between the teaching of Paul and Apollos *at Corinth* had been sufficient to create rival schools; but later, at Ephesus, when Paul writes his letter to the Corinthians *after contact with Apollos* (1 Cor. xvi. 2), there appears to be no serious doctrinal difference between the two men. Paul speaks of Apollos as his fellow-workman (1 Cor. iii. 9), watering where he has planted (v. 5), and one to be regarded as part of the valuable possessions of the believer (v. 22). Why, then, had those acrimonious "divisions of Christ" arisen between the followers of Paul and the followers of Apollos at Corinth? The situation becomes more intelligible if we may think of the Corinthian Church comparing the *earlier* teaching of Paul, the preaching which they had heard at the founding of their Church, with that of an Alexandrian teacher presenting a new Alexandrian version of Christianity. But now, at the time of writing the Corinthian letter, after his personal contact with Apollos, Paul himself, we may suppose, has felt the appeal of the Alexandrian thought, and can speak of it as supplementing his own. In the Corinthian letter itself and in the later Epistles his own teaching has marked Alexandrian features, of which there are no indications in the Thessalonian Epistles or in Acts (which we believe represents Luke's theological views received from Paul in the *earlier* period of the latter's ministry; see *The Passing and the Permanent in St. Paul*, pp. 84–9).

In short, there is much to suggest that Paul's own thought was influenced by Apollos at Ephesus in an Alexandrian direction, and that this marks the beginning of a definite period of more or less Hellenistic development, though the Judaistic roots remained, and for men like Paul, at any rate,

the development was conceived to be with Jewish "sanction"
and to lie within legitimate Jewish limits.

IV. ALEXANDRIANISM

Long before the birth of Christ there was in Alexandria
a large colony of Jews who, while remaining enthusiastic
for the faith of their fathers, were nevertheless inclined to
incorporate into their religious thought intellectual elements
from the Gentile world around them. These Jews of the
Dispersion so completely made Greek their language
that it was necessary to translate the Old Testament Scriptures into that tongue. When religious and theological
works came to be written, Greek ideas became grafted in
upon the old Hebrew faith. These books in Paul's day were
studied even at Jerusalem, and his acquaintance with the
"Wisdom of Solomon" and his use of it, even if not con-
clusively established, is highly probable. The tendency of
combination reached its culmination in Philo, born twenty
years before Christ, and therefore more or less a contemporary of Jesus and Paul. The main body of his literary
work was in existence about A.D. 38. His position has been
described as that "of the Egypto-Greek theo-cosmosophy
as far as was practicable, compatibly with the Jewish
Scriptures" (Flinders Petrie). He was ready to borrow from
any system which attracted him, and allegorical interpretation helped where logical consistency failed. Differences
between allegory and fact, person and personification, were
frequently ignored. "The Logoi—parts of the Reason
which operates in the world—became identified with the
Jewish angels and the Greek daimons," the slight point of
contact being that all these were regarded, although in quite
different senses, as intermediaries between God and the
human race.

V

For five hundred years before Christ the early Greek speculators, from Thales onward, had been seeking the fundamental Reality (*phusis*). It became felt that there must be something other than matter, water, mist or fire; there must be that which would mould the fundamental substance into its many forms and constitute and maintain them. Until Aristotle's time the thought did not seem to come into prominence that movement and constitution must arise from the inherent nature of the units making up the universe. It was natural that the aspects of constitution and motion should be regarded as further entities, although in some way they must still be composed of the basic "Phusis." The name "Word" or "Logos" was given to this creative and controlling Force and Law—some Reality, in a way distinct from that which it created and controlled, and yet itself composed of the one universal substance. All things were created by the Logos; in it all things were held together. It was with the whole; it was part of the whole. The Logos became a mediator between the two worlds of matter and spirit, and was experienced in man's higher mental and spiritual life. These early thinkers were struggling with the age-long problems of the One and the Many; Matter and Law and Motion; the Body of the Universe and its Soul. As the idea passed into less philosophic circles, the Logos became personalised and identified with all kinds of secondary and mediating gods.

The Logos appeared in the late pre-Christian Jewish literature under the name "Wisdom." In Prov. viii "Wisdom" is made to cry: "The Lord possessed me in the beginning of His way, before His works of old. I was set up from everlasting, or ever the world was. Then I was with God, as a master-workman" (300–250 B.C.). The idea reappears in Ecclesiasticus, written in Hebrew but under Greek influence in the second century B.C. "Wisdom" is represented "as an emanation from God, and standing alongside of God" (Fairweather). In the Alexandrian "Wisdom of Solomon" (first century B.C.), with which it is possible that Paul was familiar, a supreme God is conceived, "Sovereign Lord of all," yet "Wisdom" sits by Him on His throne, is the artificer of all things, and is identical with the Spirit of the Lord, who binds all things together. "Wisdom" can be inwardly experienced: "From generation to generation, passing into holy souls, she maketh men prophets and friends of God."

There was thus preparation for the idea of a Logos Christ even in Jewish Scriptures, although it seems unlikely that Paul would have created his doctrine from such scanty references had not his thought been stimulated from some other source. But these Jewish references would be a factor in the acceptance of new ideas. They provided "sanction," among the writings of a nation that possessed the "oracles of God," for ideas which Paul might otherwise have hesitated to build into his system.

The particular exponent of the Logos doctrine was Philo. Sometimes he treated it in a philosophic way, finding the Logos an inward mediating manifestation of God, realised by the pure in heart. But other conceptions of mediatorship had arisen: in Persia, Mithra was mediator between mankind and the Supreme Ahura Mazda, and Mithra had his Jewish counterparts in the apocalyptic Son of Man, or Michael, or Metatron, "the angel of God's face." The two conceptions of mediatorship are combined in Philo. The common feature led to a loose identification of the hypostatic and the personal conceptions. The Philonic Logos is not only experienced in a man's higher nature, his holiest emotions, his mystic exaltations: the Logos is also personal, an angelic mediator, even a *deuteros theos*, a second god, the creator of the world. "God, as Shepherd and King, deputes His own Logos, his first-born Son, to take charge of the sacred flock. He, contemplating the archetypal patterns, fashions the species."

VI

The way was thus prepared by Alexandrian thought, whether Philo's own or not, for Paul, the Fourth Evangelist and other Christian writers to make a similar identification. In Paul's second and third group of Epistles a conception of Christ distinct from the human and even from the apocalyptic Messiah is introduced. He has been creator of the world. "In Him were all things created: He was before all things, and in Him all things hold together." He serves as mediator between God and man: God sends His Son into the world (Romans viii. 22), and yet the latter functions as the Supreme, besides whom for the strict monotheistic Jew there could be no other (1 Cor. vii. 4). Christ's original status was equality with God (Phil. ii. 6), and yet a certain subordination of the Son is implied, not merely during an earth phase, but at the end of the age, for the Son is subjected to the Father, that God may be all in all (1 Cor. vii. 4). Paul's Christ, in the "second version" of New Testament thought, has thus a peculiar relation to God. In some sense He is distinct from Him; in another sense He is an aspect of Him. It is the characteristic "Wisdom" or Logos relationship. "The Word was with God: the Word was God." Again Christ, like the Philonic Logos, is a presence and power within human souls. Christ in man is the hope of glory (Col. i. 26). "It is no longer I that live: it is Christ that liveth in me" (Gal. ii. 20). In many ways His functions are identical with those of the Holy Spirit. He has entered into historical relations with Israel in the past. In an allegorising fashion which reminds us of Philo, Paul states that the spiritual rock which followed the host in the wilderness was none other than Christ (1 Cor. x. 14). These are features of Paul's Christology which appear after his contact with the Alexandrian Apollos, but not, so far as we can trace, before that event, and they are features so similar to those of the Alexandrian Logos that we can hardly avoid the conclusion that this Alexandrian contact had much to do with stimulating this particular development of Paul's thought.

VII. The Mysteries

But there was an influence other than that of the "Wisdom" or Logos conception, which seems to have entered into Paul's thought—the influence of the Mysteries. At the beginning of the Christian era there existed a number of cults which bore a sufficient degree of resemblance in doctrine and practice to the early Christian Church to raise the question of possible relationship with the latter. Early Christians, noting the doctrines and rites of these pagan cults, the teaching of a salvation effected through mystic communion with a deity dying and rising again, commented that "the devil also has his Christs." Loisy speaks of Jesus Christ as "a saviour god after the manner of an Osiris, an Attis, a Mithra. Like them, he belonged by his origin to the celestial world: like them, he had made his appearance upon the earth: like them, he had accomplished a work of universal redemption, efficacious and typical: like Adonis, Osiris and Attis, he had died a violent death, and like them he had been restored to life: like them he had prefigured in his lot that of human beings who should take part in his worship and commemorate his mystic enterprise; like them he had predestined, prepared and assured the salvation of those who had become partners in his passion" (*Hibbert Journal,* October, 1911).

Our knowledge of these cults is limited by the fact that the essence of their more inward rites was secrecy. Inscrip-

P

tions only bear witness to the outer and more formal public proceedings. The references to them by the Christian fathers belong to a post-apostolic period and are coloured by prejudice and polemical bias. The literary remains are few, and it is not easy to determine dates. Schweitzer claims that Paul cannot have known the Mystery religions as we know them because in his time they did not exist in their elaborated form. But Kennedy sanely remarks (*Paul and the Mystery Religions*, p. 70): "The elaborated form which we can trace in the second or third centuries A.D. postulates a lengthy development, and it is hazardous to dogmatise what was and what was not possible, say from the period of A.D. 30 to A.D. 100, or even earlier."

The origin of these cults lies far back in the region of Nature myths and "sympathetic" magic. The changes of the seasons were explained by early speculators in terms of the life and death of the gods. This theory involved certain practices of "sympathetic magic." There were ceremonies to revive and ensure the divine energies. The life and action of man had effects upon the life and action of the gods. Human acts of fertilisation were deemed to produce the general fertilisation of Nature (Frazer, *Adonis, Attis, Osiris*, pp. 4 ff.). The notion of "sympathy" between the life of the gods and of human beings came later to have an obverse significance. The phenomena of autumn and spring gave rise to the conception of vegetation gods who died and rose again, suggesting some kind of triumph over darkness and death. This victory and salvation of the gods could be shared by their mystic worshippers, united to them by means of certain assimilative or communion rites. The Mysteries thus had their Blood Baths (Taurobolia) and Communion Meals, *the object of which was to establish a union between the worshipper and the god he worshipped*, so that the former might share the latter's life, conquests and immortality.

VIII

This feature of assimilation or union, the most characteristic feature of the Mystery doctrine, came also to characterise Paul's developed thought. Apparently it led him to new interpretations of older Christian conceptions and practices. The rite of Baptism, which seems originally to have been a "sympathetic" act of cleansing, then a sign of moral reformation and entry into a new order, gained a specific significance of assimilation with a buried and risen Christ. In the Mystery of Attis the image of the buried god was restored on the evening of the third day, and the worshippers were bidden to rejoice because the resurrection of their god implied their own salvation. So Paul comes to regard Baptism as a re-enactment of the death and resurrection of Jesus, accompanied by an appropriation of His life and triumph, through communion with Him. "We who were baptized into Jesus Christ were baptized into His death: we were buried with Him through baptism into His death: that like as Christ was raised from the dead through the glory of the Father, so we also might walk in newness of life. For if we have become united with Him in the likeness of His death, we shall also by the likeness of His resurrection," etc. (Rom. vi. 3 ff.).

The Church Meal of the early Christian community was apparently of the nature of a church social gathering. We may suppose that Paul felt that it ought to have another kind of significance—and it is a significance similar to that of the communion meals of the Mysteries. With his doctrine of the revelation of the inward Christ, Paul states in 1 Cor. xi. what he believes Christ intended the meal to be. It must be an occasion of solemn religious communion. A *logion* from the Gospel tradition, probably originally illustrating the "dying-to-live" teaching of Jesus, and signifying "My life is like a loaf which must be broken before it can nourish" (cf. "Except a grain of wheat fall into the ground and die, it abideth by itself alone, but if it die, it beareth much fruit"), came to have the Communion significance : through the eating of the bread, Christ's worshippers were in some way united to Him and to one another. In the old covenant the shedding of sacrificial blood effected a nation's salvation. We conceive that Christ at the Last Supper used this figure, familiar to every Jew, to suggest that His own blood-shedding might, beyond the tragedy of sacrifice, effect the salvation of men and the bringing of them together in a new fellowship. But what was with Jesus a parable seems to have taken on deeper meanings in Paul's mind, in the light of Mystery customs and doctrines. "The cup which we bless, is it not a participation in the blood of Christ? The bread which we break, is it not a participation of the body of Christ, seeing that we who are many are one bread, one body, for we all partake of the one bread?" (1 Cor. x. 16 ff.). The Apostle knows the doctrine that eating of the pagan religious food unites one with the idol (verses 20, 21).

IX

It is not easy to determine how far these striking parallels should take us. Paul was clearly conscious of the Mysteries and their doctrine of the union of worshipper and deity by means of assimilative rites. He seems familiar with the vocabulary of the Mysteries. But he may only be using their figures in a literary way to illustrate spiritual truths gained and held quite independently of them. On the other hand, he may have found in these doctrines certain sugges-tions, stimulating his mind to think along these lines of assimilative salvation in the creation of new theological forms. He may have "baptized" the ideas into Christianity. There were experiences of mystic communion with the Divine which were immediate and first hand. Did not these give a justification to Paul's interpretation of Baptism and the Communion Meal? Indeed, was there not some "sanction" in Old Testament precedent for such new views? In Philonic fashion, Paul finds allegories of his new conceptions of Baptism and the Eucharist in the wilderness incidents of the Old Testament (1 Cor. x). "It is very characteristic of the working of the Apostle's mind," Dr. Percy Gardner comments on this (*Religious Experiences of St. Paul*, p. 123), "that although he could not find in Jewish usage any direct justification for his sacramental ideas, yet he is determined to import them in the Jewish Scriptures."

X. THE GNOSIS

We must also take into account another Gnostic feature found in developed Paulinism. The Apostle conceives a "faith-gnosis" or "mystery"—a theosophy which, being contemplated, passes from doctrine to mystic experience (*The Passing and the Permanent in St. Paul*, pp. 192–4). This "faith-gnosis," in fact, turns out to be the Pauline scheme of salvation itself, which rests upon the idea of the worshipper's union or assimilation with Deity, although it includes other elements as well, and would be felt to throw light on the vague doctrine that Jesus had brought about salvation by His death in accordance with the "Servant" prophecy of Isaiah liii. The Christian "mystery" was this: Since Adam, and as a consequence of his transgression, the world has been under the bondage of certain evil principalities and powers, among whom, and typical of the rest, is Death. Jesus, as man, submits to death, and the evil principalities take their due from Him. But this leads to their undoing, for Jesus, more than man, rises from the dead, and the curse is thereby broken! And henceforth those mystically united with Jesus, the conqueror of death, may share His triumph and experience release from the bondage of the evil principalities and powers. Such knowledge, then, is the "faith-gnosis"—the "mystery" doctrine hidden from the foundation of the world. Had these world-rulers of darkness known this "mystery" they would not have crucified the Lord of glory (1 Cor. ii. 8). The knowledge of it by the initiated has effects like those of Baptism and the Communion Meal— it can unite the worshipper with the One he worships.

XI

We can take all these conceptions as suggesting and conveying an idea which is really independent of them, for it is founded upon that experience, characteristic of Mysticism, which gives man the sense of his Communion with God (see p. 60). They are kindred notions, seized upon by Paul because he has found something like them in his own soul, and, taken aright, they are testimony to that independent experience rather than valuable in themselves. We may dismiss them as having little intrinsic importance, and yet retain the experience which led Paul and others to seize upon them as a kind of expression or hint. Their source or their inherent validity is a matter of indifference to us, for they are of the nature of "shadows," suggesting a spiritual reality which exists apart from them. This spiritual reality is that *Paul had found in the spiritual and moral influences proceeding from the life and personality of Jesus of Nazareth a transformation of soul which had made him at one with God.* He had realised a harmony with Him which had given him newness of life, victory over his lower nature, a peace and joy and sense of the eternal goodness. His soul had deepened, and he had discovered the Divine Presence within and a conviction of Eternal Life.

This is the permanent element of Religion: it is the teaching of our Lord Himself. It rests upon simple moral and spiritual laws. It is the experience of human personality at its highest and holiest. Although Paulinism has set such experience in new forms and introduced other elements, strange and questionable sometimes, in the expression of it, we have in this Pauline "system of salvation" through Communion with the Divine what is fundamentally the spiritual and moral teaching of Jesus: "Blessed are the pure in heart, for they shall see God."

XII

A further feature of cosmic consciousness, or religious Mysticism, appears in this Pauline presentation—the significant intuition of the love of God. These theologies of Redemption and Salvation *arise from the fundamental consciousness of the ultimate soundness and goodness of the universe.* This sense is more fundamental and direct than the theological figures and dramas by which men seek to express it. We trace this intuition in the souls of those who gave us the great story of a "God who so loved the world that He gave His only-begotten Son" to save it. A Rationalistic critic may say: "This is only a piece of theosophic doctrine introduced into Christianity, for what do we know of the relationships of the Godhead or of the happenings in the heavenly courts?" He may point to parallels in the Gnostic and Hermetic literature which suggest the literary sources of Pauline and Johannine doctrine, and may say: "How can the Love of God be argued from such fanciful theosophies of an uncritical age?" But we claim that Love of God is not *inferred* from what the Rationalist would call "a mere theosophy"; *rather the "mere theosophy" is an outcome and expression of man's deep intuition of the Love of God.* This created the Pauline Soteriology, and, for that matter, the Gnostic and Hermetic stories as well, and all forms of human hope expressing the seeking and saving Love of God. When man discovers his soul and seeks its depths, he senses the fundamental evangelical truth of the Eternal Goodness, knows that "Love is creation's final law," and expresses this in such ways as he is able, and we must read this significant intuition even under the strangest of these schemes of Redemption and Salvation, and realise the eternal element of cosmic truth underneath the doctrinal form.

XIII

The characteristics of Mysticism are to be seen in other features of Paulinism. In his doctrine of the Church, he expresses the sense of social organic unity. The Church is a "body." We are members one of another. The universalism of Pauline Christianity is a further expression of the mystic love of all mankind from which no race is excluded. A significant monistic strain appears time after time (Rom. viii; 1 Cor. xv. 24 ff.; Col. i. 16, etc.). The mystic's optimism appears again in the confidence in the final reign of right, expressed not only in the crude Parousial expectation of the time, but in the philosophy of a "far-off divine event to which the whole creation moves" (Rom. viii) and in a more general cheerfulness having deep roots in the sense of the Divine Goodness and Overlordship. "Rejoice: again I say—Rejoice."

The Pauline scheme stresses the *inwardness* of faith and inspiration. Christ dwelling in him illumines, stimulates, vivifies, saves. He may speak of Israel's "oracles of God," but the real seat of authority for Paul is not in them, but within his own soul. He receives his faith "not from flesh and blood." Morality also arises from inward sources. The external Law actually allies itself with the evil principalities and powers; a code of commandments, however excellent, cannot take the place of the soul's inward attitude of goodness and love.

Paul never questions immortality—at any rate, for the faithful. It is involved for them in the Resurrection of Christ; in the later Epistles the Apostle finds the ground of

Eternal Life in mystic union with Him. We have noted the sense of immortality characteristic of the mystic's experience of "newness of life."

Paul is a preacher of the new life, which brings with it the sense of immortality. Like the Fourth Evangelist, he teaches that such life begins here and now, and is of such quality that death has no sting for it and the grave no victory over it. His great cosmic convictions and hopes gather in one great utterance: "Nothing can separate us from the Love of God, neither principalities nor powers, nor height nor depth, things present, nor things to come." The saint is master of the universe—all things are his, for he is Christ's and Christ is God's.

Paul's intuitions of Faith are permanent; his theology is largely passing. Did not he himself recognise this, in a supreme moment of insight? Knowledge passes away as clearer light comes, but "now abideth Faith, Hope, Love —these three, and the greatest of these is Love."

CHAPTER XVII

THE IDEA OF MEDIATION

I

THERE are two ways in which men may conceive the function of Christ as a revealer of God. According to the first He stands within the world as a "focus-point," as it were, of the elements in a unified cosmos, a symbol of its profoundest meanings, and a type, in some ways perfectly natural, of the supernatural in the universe.

The other conception of Christ as a Revealer of God has behind it the idea of a divided universe. He is a Mediator, functioning in some way between God and man—a Logos in some fashion linking dissimilar and separated worlds. This second conception involves us in an interesting and important historical quest of the origins and growth of the idea of Mediatorship in this sense and in a consideration of what seems its fundamental and fatal defects.

II. THE WORLD-SOUL

Primitive man was impressed by the difference between a living and a dead body. The living man breathed, moved and resisted dissolution. It seemed, therefore, that there must be something in man, which was naturally conceived as breath (*pneuma, anima,* soul), and as possessing the power of self-movement, constitution and preservation. It gave a unity to the body. In it all things consisted or were held together.

It was natural to find some corresponding existence behind the world as a whole. The universe was a body, constituted and regulated. Aristotle conjectures that THALES believed in a World-Soul. ANAXIMENES (*c.* 495 B.C.) expressly asserts: "Just as our soul, being air, holds us together, so do breath and air compass the whole world." ANAXIMANDER (*c.* 546 B.C.), the "associate" of Thales, was impressed by the spectacle of constitution and order in the universe. Heat seemed to take more than its share in summer and cold in winter, yet they were not allowed to exceed their ordained limits. The idea of cosmic constitution and regulation was developed by Heraclitus. In the midst of flux there is the fixity of law. An equilibrium preserves the world. "The sun will not overstep his measures; if he does, the Erinyes, the handmaids of justice, will find him out" (fr. 27). There must thus be a fiery wisdom "steering all things" (fr. 28), "judging and controlling all things" (fr. 26). Although the use of the term Logos by HERACLITUS probably meant only "the word—the thing he was born to say" (Burnet), and that therefore the term does not bear the latter technical sense of the World-Soul or Cosmic Wisdom, there seems nevertheless the forming of the Logos conception in Heraclitus. There is a World-Soul operating through the universe in the way the individual soul is supposed to act in the individual body.

III

An interesting question with an important relation to Christian theology arises at this point. Is the soul a separate entity, or an aspect of existence? Is the soul a *motion*-unit affecting a *matter*-unit, or a *law*-unit controlling an alien *substance*-unit, or must we think of "soul" as a label for a certain set of natural operations, a name standing for a real distinction in our experience and in the nature of things, but not signifying something detachable, separate, divisible from that which it seems to move and control? We may claim that the soul is just the "idea" representing an aspect of an indivisible nature, and not a separate or separable entity. The danger of thought to be guarded against throughout is that of ontological separation. Matter and Motion and Law are not, of course, to be isolated. If provisionally we take matter as basis, we may say that Motion is the aspect of *Matter moving*; Law is the aspect of *Matter moving with regularity*. We cannot regard Motion as Descartes seemed inclined to, as an outside agent controlling Matter. So we must regard the soul as representing the moving and controlling element in Nature, as an aspect of Nature, inseparable from its unity and wholeness. We must not endow "soul," which is strictly an abstraction, though indicating something real in Nature, with a separate existence set over against and detachable from the body or from the cosmos which it is supposed to animate.

If we are inclined to monadology, we may say that a controlling or hegemonic monad or soul may surrender its leadership of, or co-operation with, the other monads or souls making up the colony of the human body, so that dissolution follows like the demobilisation of an army; but this is a different idea from that of the soul withdrawing from the body, leaving the matter absolutely "dead" matter. There may be a striking contrast between a living and a dead body, but even the "dead" body is full of activity, or it would not display the phenomenon of corruption. When in Plato's dialogue, *Phaedo*, the claim is made by Simmias that the soul means nothing more than "attunement," and that the soul necessarily perishes immediately the "attunement" of the body is destroyed at death, he seems to ignore that there must be something within the parts themselves which has a "soulish" character. We cannot conceive that parts of an utterly dead material nature come together by some accident and produce for a time an alien something —soul, spirit, thought, mind—which, being nothing more than "attunement," presently vanishes through the dissolution of the parts. There must have been inherent in the parts a certain "soulishness" indissoluble from the other features of the part. There could only be "attunement" of something capable of being attuned. We contend, then, that the idea of a "soul" detachable from body or matter is a false notion. Souls or monads may be detached from other souls or monads, but "soul" cannot be separated from dead matter. Either body has a soul, or soul has a body, or souls by monadic resistance produce on other souls the impression of "body" or "matter," which is the Leibnitzian or Lotzian view.

IV

It was natural, however, in the first process of thought to conceive the "soul" as detachable from purely dead matter; thus in Homer the soul is seen separating itself like smoke after death. On the other hand, while it was apparently possible to conceive a soul-less body, man was unable to conceive a bodiless soul. The soul in virtue of its very existence was material, although the matter of which it was composed was attenuated. It might be rarefied air (Anaximenes), or fire, regarded as elemental matter (Heraclitus). Nevertheless *there was a tendency to set in a separate category the soul, or at any rate the World-Soul or Cosmic Wisdom.* It is true that Heraclitan "souls" in the traffic of change might become earth and water, or in the unceasing circulation of the universe a soul could again emerge from the tombs of water or solid matter; but certain Heraclitan fragments suggest that the World-Soul or Wisdom is to be distinguished from the forms of the flux. It is not to be identified with any of the gods, for the latter lie within the universal scheme of change. "Wisdom is apart from all." . . . The wise is one only. It is unwilling and willing to be called by the name of Zeus (fr. 46)—that is, it is the Supreme Power, but is in its nature very unlike the popular conceptions of God, and lies out of the category of the gods, who may descend into the grosser material forms again.

Fire in the conception of Heraclitus has powers of thought and control. But the fiery World-Wisdom is given a permanence denied to ordinary souls. In a sense it stands apart from them, though in some way it is made up of the universal material *phusis*.

V

In the speculations which followed to explain the motion and constitution of the universe, the tendency to postulate some Force or Forces, apart from the inherent nature of the moving and constituted substances themselves, persists. The pluralist, EMPEDOCLES, instead of taking one universal element, assumes four "roots"—Fire, Air, Earth and Water. Between them there is a traffic of mingling and separation, which gives rise to the appearance of particular things which come and pass, as noted by the senses. But in addition to the four "roots" Empedocles finds it necessary to postulate two other elemental existences—Strife and Love—to account for the motion of the "roots" within the universe scheme. These take the place of the fiery Wisdom of Heraclitus. Strife and Love are corporeal elements occupying space. Strife, like the Anaximenian or Pythagorean "air," comes among the four "roots" mingled in combination, increases the interval between them and splits up the combination. Love, on the other hand, brings the elements together, and somehow interpenetrates them as a cohesive substance. But the common defect of all this early speculation appears. *Aspects are materialised. Appearances are made concrete entities.* Instead of the four "roots" being regarded as acting lovingly or striving *from their own nature*, two other members of a corporeal series, Strife and Love, are confusingly added.

In ANAXAGORAS the elemental opposites are never found out of a state of combination. In the hottest thing there is something cold; even in white snow there is something black. "There is a portion of everything in everything" (fr. 11), but there is one important exception—Nous, or Mind.

"Nous is infinite and self-contained, and is mixed with nothing, but is alone—itself by itself" (fr. 12). This feature gives Nous the mastery, and thus it is the source of motion. It becomes the substitute for the Strife and Love of Empedocles. But the difficulty felt in regard to Strife and Love in Empedocles is repeated with the Nous of Anaxagoras. It is regarded as *a substance added to other substances* with the function of combining them, instead of an "idea" in thought, of the "soulish" or mental or "nous-ish" way in which substances behave in their own nature (provisionally taking matter as the basis of existence). The same defect is to be found in the idea of the World-Soul or Logos, the functions of which are similar to those of Strife and Love, or Nous. It is regarded as a separable entity.

VI

The Two Worlds.—The history of the World-Soul enters a new phase in connection with the Platonic doctrine of the Two Worlds. The idea of Mediatorship becomes associated with it. To the questionable notion of the World-Soul as a separate entity is added the further questionable notion of separated worlds which in some way this separate entity of a World-Soul may link together.

SOCRATES, according to Plato, was impressed by the idea that our common judgments seemed to imply two worlds, one the world of sense perceptions, the other a world of thought-forms or norms, or perfections by which we come to judge the things of sense as equal or straight or good. There is a phenomenal and an ideal world, and the latter is real because it is not subject to the changes of the phenomenal world. Socrates conjectures that the things of sense are real only in as far as they "partake" of the reality of the ideal world. This argument of participation is to be distinguished from Plato's own views, for Aristotle does not attribute it to Plato, but "to Socrates in the *Phaedo.*"

This idea of Participation seems to rest upon an analogy from physical nature. The "form" of the thought-world is looked upon as a kind of existence which can be divided up, and enter into the objects of sense-perception, and give them their measure of reality. But are we justified in such an analogy? We might mix gold with other substances of less value, and the value of the new amalgam would be determined by the amount of gold introduced. But we can hardly conceive thought-forms, or norms, as being divided up into this object and that, and imparting thereby to the object a certain degree of reality and value.

Further, we need to examine the worth of the argument for the world of ideas or forms taken over by Plato himself. We call a thing straight because it exhibits certain features geometrically or mathematically peculiar, not because we see its resemblance to an ideal straightness, which has come to us from another sphere. Or, again, certain things exhibit utilitarian features, or make for social health, and we call them good and conceive goodness as a mental idea, descriptive of certain phenomena of correspondence, cohesion or consistency, a matching of our subjective being with its cosmical environment, a harmony between ourselves and the universe at large. But when we make that judgment of goodness, we bring no measuring-rod from another world. Nevertheless these speculations are interesting *as showing the tendency of thought to postulate some permanent and perfect element, to be set over against the changes and approximations of our world of finite experience.* We suggest that the whole general conception arose from the fundamental consciousness of the two aspects of the one world, the aspects of Being and Becoming.

VII

The thought of PLATO leaves a division between the phenomenal world and the eternal world of ideas or forms.

How may they be related? Plato's answer is—through the soul. For the soul is able to act through the phenomenal sphere, and yet it is somehow akin to the real, incorporeal and permanent world of Ideas or Forms. This seems highly artificial. Reality and unreality cannot be reconciled in a third order of being. The mediating term is only a device to cover up the real difficulty.

Plato goes farther and finds, corresponding to the individual soul, a Universe-Soul functioning similarly between the two worlds or orders. The conception of the World-Soul as it appears in the *Timaeus* is meant to be more suggestive than scientific. It is "myth," "something like truth" rather than truth itself. Nevertheless the Platonic figure had immense influence on later religious philosophy and on Christological speculation. The Supreme Deity creates a World-Soul who brings order out of chaos, and fashions the phenomenal forms as far as possible from the archetypal patterns. The "ideas" seem to have become practically "eternal gods" despite the Platonic attempt to distinguish a personal God from "Good," which is a "form," and in a way stands over and against God.

The Platonic scheme of the two worlds is found again in PHILO—a significant figure for the formative stage of Christian theology. There is the reality of a transcendent God, bare of all qualities. But the "ideas" gather into a supreme Idea, the Logos, or "secondary god," who serves as go-between for God and the world. Matter is a strange alien existence. It did not originate with God. It is a lifeless, unmoved, shapeless mass out of which God, by means of the Logos and the divine forces, shaped the actual world. The Logos can be objectively regarded as parallel to the mediating and creative deities or angels of current mythological thought. It may also be realised as an inward experience of communion by the individual soul in its most exalted moments.

VIII

The idea of Mediatorship itself is significant. It tries to preserve the idea of the two worlds, but it is in reality an acknowledgment that thought cannot be content with a severed universe. Unless some bridge could be thrown across the gulf which yawns between the two worlds, human experience would become a detached, lost, and meaningless thing, belonging to nowhere, and without reality and significance. There is a consciousness of an ultimate unity between the apparently divided worlds. Earth is a hopeless, meaningless wilderness unless there can be a Jacob's ladder between the Heaven of Reality and the Earth of Phenomena. But, as a matter of fact, doctrines of mediatorship and emanations are artificial devices to disguise the problems of the direct and immediate relationships of the two terms brought together. Things related to the same thing must be related to one another. Heaven and earth cannot be absolutely dissimilar if a ladder can be fixed between them. In the more or less popular development of Platonic thought this is shown in the difficulty of keeping the world of Ideas purely idealistic. Even with Plato the World-Soul of the *Timaeus* is suspiciously like a secondary god, with a Supreme God rather than a Form of Good behind him; and although Philo regards the mediating entities as "Ideas, or ideal patterns of all things, thoughts of God which possess a real existence and were produced before the creation of the sensible world of which they are types," yet there is free identification of these mediating Platonic "Ideas" with Jewish angels and Greek daimons, and the God behind is the Jahweh of Hebrew Scriptures. If mediatorship brings something heavenly and spiritual to earth, it seems to carry back something earthly and material to high Olympus. The Word becomes flesh, not only upon earth but in heaven. Pure thought wondrously

takes the shape of materialised deity and Ideas become more
or less flesh and blood gods in the skies!

IX

The conception of the divided worlds had its challenge
in ARISTOTLE's principle of inseparability and continuity.
"The soul is the soul of its body, and the body the body of
its soul. We can only distinguish them by logical analysis,
as we distinguish the copper from the sphericity of the
copper globe." But Aristotle seems to fail to apply his
principle to the ideas of God and the Universe. God stands
outside life in His transcendence. He is there to be contemplated. The "appetisation" of the world is drawn by
this immobile spectacle, and the world develops its forms
by means of this contemplation.

In the main, STOIC speculation, however, kept closer to
Aristotle's general principle of continuity. The Stoic Logos
is a seminal Force unfolding in the world's development,
a Divine Spirit diffused through all things. There was a
tendency with the Stoics to follow earlier thinking in
conceiving the soul as a finer sort of matter, affecting and
moving the rest, which, of course, is quite different from the
doctrine of aspects. Matter is drawn apart into separate
forms of soul *and* matter, whereas the pure Aristotelian
principle would suggest the idea of the soul *of* matter.
But the characteristic teaching of the highest Stoicism is
faithful to the Aristotelian principle. SENECA speaks of the
universe and God as interchangeable terms. Neither Reason
nor Law is external to Nature. Law translated into religious
terms is Providence. Spirit is Being in its "spiritual" aspect.
Soul is Being in its "soulish" aspect. Matter is Being in its
"material" aspect. Logos, Reason, God—these are the
rational, spiritual and purposeful aspects of Being. Throughout there is the same Being. The principle of Stoicism sets

itself definitely, on the whole, against ontological separations.

X

The mediating World-Soul can be conceived not only in the relation of bringing the meaning of God into human life, but also as relieving God of some of the responsibility of the apparent flaws of human life. The World-Soul idea lends itself to a doctrine of a Gnostic Demiurge as well as to that of a Divine Logos. The two-worlds philosophy underlay the Gnostic conception of an intermediate creator. The world as it is seemed so full of flaw that the Gnostics found it impossible to believe that a loving God should have ever framed so miserable a product. It must have been the work of intermediate powers, either stupid or actually malicious. This idea was revived by the Cambridge Neo-Platonists of the seventeenth century. CUDWORTH (1617–88) in refuting hylozoic atheism—the idea that matter endowed with life explained everything—came to postulate a doctrine of Plastic Nature: "a substance intermediate between matter and spirit, a power which prosecutes certain ends, but not freely nor intelligently, an instrument by which laws are able to act without the immediate agency of God." He argues that to refer the life and the motion of the universe immediately to God is inconsistent with the slow and gradual development of Nature and with its errors and bungles. But Dr. Robert Flint's comment upon this view is quite convincing: "It is not more difficult to believe the life and motions of the universe as due to the immediate action of God than to the life and motion of the secondary agent, which Cudworth conceived animated Nature and 'drudgingly executed a part of the work of Providence.' An unconscious or 'necessitated plastic power' cannot remove from the creator of it the blame of any 'errors and bungles' which it may commit." Here once more the doctrine of a Mediator disguises a difficulty rather than solves a problem.

XI. The Doctrine of Emanations

We return to consider that school of Neo-Platonists of an earlier date whose influence on Christian theology, through Augustine and others, was so considerable. The problem presented by the teaching of PLOTINUS, the chief of the school, is whether the two parts of his philosophy— his Monism and his doctrine of Emanations—belong to two irreconcilable systems or can be regarded as logically harmonious. The charge of a fundamental dualism which has been brought against both Plato and the Neo-Platonists is challenged by Dean Inge, who asserts that neither Plato nor Plotinus taught a doctrine of separated worlds, and points out that Plotinus definitely sets himself to overthrow the three enemies of true philosophy— materialism, scepticism and *dualism*.

The emphasis upon ultimate unity is undoubtedly characteristic of Plotinus. When Plotinus challenges the Stoics, it is not on the score that they are pantheists, but that their pantheism is materialistic rather than spiritual. They try to explain the higher by the lower rather than the lower by the higher. But not less than they does he assert a philosophic monism.

Nevertheless, the diversity and multiplicity and the grades of value in the world as we see it are to be recognised and in some way related to the One, and instead of pursuing the promising avenue of Correlation—of the truth of which Plotinus shows himself conscious—he chooses to find explanation (or to hint at truths intuitively recognised, which, of course, is a different thing) by a characteristic doctrine of Emanations.

The Primeval Being, the One, the Infinite, Absolute Causality, the only Real Existence, the Good (although, as

Harnack says, this Being is strictly without attributes, for these would imply limitations), first throws out Nous, Pure Intelligence, the perfect image of the One, and the archetype of all existing things. This in turn produces a World-Soul, intermediate between Nous and the phenomenal world. As Nous is to the World-Soul, so is the World-Soul to the universe. Individual souls appearing in men, animals and even "slumbering in inorganic nature" emanate from the World-Soul, and are able to incline towards the rational principle or to turn from it. In the latter case, souls entangled in the mysterious sphere of matter manifest hatred, strife and evil.

XII

As a "myth," the presentation is acceptable, regarded as a pictorial expression of various truths of experience. Man feels that there is within him a spark of the Divine. Certain rational and spiritual courses of life bring him into harmony with the "centre and soul of every sphere." He is aware, too, that certain sympathies and courses of life create a sense of isolation and discord, and he associates these defects with the lusts of the flesh, the "body of this death," the prison of matter. But this scheme of Plotinus as a logical or scientific account of the phenomena expressed is obviously unsatisfactory. (a) The origin and nature of matter is vague and unrelated to the monistic principle. The world begins with pure Spirit; whence, then, does this evil of Matter arise? Has Matter no value as a means of expressing goodness? Is Matter so essentially evil that the sacramental possibility of love and helpfulness being expressed through Matter must be denied? Indeed, in places, Plotinus himself finds the manifestation of goodness and beauty in material nature. (b) The conception of creation is difficult. Even if we pass the peculiar claim made for Emanations, that there is no loss in the producer in the appearance of the product, we have still the problem of the unlikeness of the product, both physical and moral. Good produces evil; the immaterial produces the material; the real issues as the unreal; that which is outside time and space produces that which is in it. (*c*) The "unreality" of the phenomenal world is an especial difficulty. How could the One that is "real" be made up of parts that are "unreal"? If there be "meaning" in the whole, there must be "meaning" in each section. If spirit must manifest itself, prove and test itself in matter, must not that matter be real? How can the real find manifestation and development through a world of dream and phantom?

(*d*) The ghost of a fundamental dualism walks the monistic scheme of Plotinus. We can conceive a correlative dualism in unity. Thus we have the One and the Many, the Infinite and the Finites, Eternity and Time, Being and Becoming. The Absolute of Hegel sums up the universe and gathers its diversity into itself. Each part is needed for the fullness of the Hegelian Absolute. God needs me as surely as I need God. But in Plotinus the Absolute seems to lie beyond the world and to be independent of it (Inge, *Plotinus*, vol. ii, p. 120). The World-Soul is creative rather than comprehensive. It produces rather than is analysed. But it seems difficult to account for the existence or emergence of a world which is not a necessary constituent in the Absolute, latent in the beginning of its cycles and summed up in their culmination, and throughout the process fundamentally a part and parcel of the whole. What can be evolved which was not originally involved? The world of sense and time and space became in Plotinus suspiciously alien, a second principle, a something out of nowhere, bricks made without straw. A fundamental dualism of an isolable as distinguished from a correlative nature asserts itself in spite of the device to cover it up. (*e*) Again, we seem to have a confusion of two orders of thought. In the correlation of Being and Becoming we have two complementary series. The terms of the one cannot be used in the terms of the other. The Infinite and the finites are inseparable, but we can never treat the infinite as an addition to the series of the finites, or regard the One embracing the Many as One among the Many. Sectional time can never be cut away from Eternity, but Eternity can never be set down as a further section of Time. The two series are parallel, inseparably involved but never meeting. But Plotinus in his drama of Emanations breaks this obvious principle. The action lies in the time and space sphere. It is a conception of Becoming. It is Reality under the analytic aspect. Notwithstanding this, Plotinus makes Being, the Infinite or the Eternal, the first figure in the drama of Becoming. He sets the One embracing the Many as One among the Many. He sets the Infinite as the first of the finites. The Absolute which is being analysed intrudes itself as a factor within the analysis. The timeless and spaceless Absolute steps as Creator into the time and space world!

XIII

Plotinus fights hard against the dualism which meets him at every turn. He obviously is seeking throughout to give a monistic supremacy to Spirit, to timeless and spaceless Being, to the Absolute. But unwilling to make bold use of his principle of correlatives, he subordinates Becoming to Being, and finds that this involves him finally in a denial of the reality of Becoming. Becoming is not the analysed content of Being, but a strange intrusion, a shadowy dream world, of which no clear account can be given. Plotinus can conceive an Absolute existing independently of phenomenal nature. If there be but one reality, and that the Absolute, it follows that this separable phenomenon is unreal. It is true that within the sphere of Becoming there are differences and grades of value, but Plotinus goes farther and sets the whole aspect of Becoming as lower or inferior to Being, whereas the whole series of Becoming must be equivalent to, and identical with, Being. If Being is real, Becoming is real. If Becoming be unreal, Being is unreal.

The doctrine of Emanations seems a confession of uneasiness created by the dualism which Plotinus seeks, though in vain, to banish. The descent from perfection and reality must be eased by gradual steps so that we shall not notice the sheer drop. The function of the World-Soul is that of a Mediator, but it is not easy to see why there is logical need of this third term. If the contrast is that of reality and unreality, a third term is of no help. A "real-unreal" is only adding further confusion to the case. If there be some actual relation between the Absolute and the phenomenal world, that relation will be direct, and there is no need of a third term. That is only introducing something else which, so far from explaining, needs to be explained. The correlation number is two and not three. There can be a trinity of aspects or parts, but only a dualism of correlation. The World-Soul seems therefore a disguise rather than a true mediation or explanation.

CHAPTER XVIII

NEW TESTAMENT EXPRESSIONS OF
MEDIATORSHIP

WE have traced the idea of Mediation well past New Testament times to show its forms, nature and defects. We now return to the New Testament perhaps better prepared to realise in its pages the large element of Mediatorship found there and to take its valuation for religious truth. It appears not only in the Hellenistic shape of the Logos, but also in a Jewish form, suggested by Leviticism. Christ is the Propitiation and Sacrifice for human sin. These ideas, separate in origin and nature, have run together, but remain associated rather than amalgamated. They manifest, however, the common feature of Mediatorship, although in different senses—semi-philosophical and priestly.

I

The Alexandrian scheme of the Two Worlds and an associated mediating Logos appears both in the Fourth Gospel and the Epistle to the Hebrews. We have already noticed the conception of a Logos-Christ in Paul. In the Prologue of the Fourth Gospel the Logos is specifically named and identified again with Christ—indeed, in some ways the Logos development as we pass from Paul to the Fourth Gospel tends to obscure the pure mystic tradition which we have recognised in the former as one of the permanent and significant elements of the New Testament. Dr. Rufus Jones thus points out (*Encyclopaedia of Religion and Ethics*, "Mysticism in the New Testament") that "although the influence of the Johannine writings on the mysticism of the Church has been far greater than that of any other New Testament writer, yet the term 'mystic' does not as properly belong to St. John as to St. Paul. John is primarily a theologian occupied and absorbed with interpreting the eternal significance of the Incarnation. These writings predominantly turn our gaze not to the immense resources of the soul's inner experience, not to the native testimony of the heart's kinship with God, but to the historical person who was the Logos of God, in whom the glory of God is revealed, and from whom we may receive eternal life. We do not find primarily in John an interpretation of experience but rather a theological interpretation of Christ." The Prologue identifies Christ with the Logos that was in the beginning with God and was God; all things were made by Him; He was the Light and Life of men, and the Logos became flesh and dwelt among us. The Platonic-Philonic scheme of the Two Worlds emerges. "There are for the author," continues Dr. Rufus Jones, "two worlds—the world that is 'above,' the world that is true or real, and the world that is of darkness, shadow and evil. Christ is eternally of God! In Him is life of the real and eternal order. He is Truth as it is in its pure effulgence. His Incarnation exhibits in 'this world' of shadow the intrinsic nature of the world 'above'—the world of spirit and light and life and truth— the 'God-nature' which nothing from 'below' could ever truly reveal or even adumbrate. It is thus wholly through Christ's mediation that men like us—empirical natural beings—can partake of life. All that we can have we 'receive.' Spiritual life, the life of God, is not in us or of us. It is from 'above' and is appropriated by 'faith,' by 'knowing' Him and by a sacramental eating of His flesh as the soul's bread, and by drinking His blood as the soul's life-substance." Schweitzer, hotly denying Hellenistic influence of a "Mystery" nature upon Paul, finds in the Fourth Gospel the transformation of Christianity into an exalted "Mystery" Religion.

II

From this Johannine presentation of the Incarnation the Christological speculations have started out, and their problems are chiefly due to the difficulties of the mediating Logos philosophy involved. Behind them lies the fatal scheme of the Two Worlds between which Christ serves as a Mediator. The forms have come to be those of humanity and divinity, and between them there is a great gulf fixed. The difference is not that of aspects—there is ontological separation and a divided universe. It is true that Sabellianism stressed the idea of aspects of the Godhead, but it still left an abyss between God and human nature. God had "aspects," but humanity was not one of them. God streamed through a human body in the case of Christ without being united with it. God was a unity, but Christ was not. There was not real unity of human and divine in Jesus; there was nothing but the juxtaposition of alien natures. Arius, influenced by polytheistic mediatorship, found Jesus a "second God," existing before creation, but Himself originally created. Jesus became an artificial, confused figure, who was neither genuinely human nor divine, because Arius tried to make Him both, while still keeping human and divine as absolutely exclusive ideas. Among the other theologians, Athanasius, without being absolutely clear and consistent, showed the truest instincts. He rightly denounced the polytheistic speculations of Arius. He felt out after the right solution of an organic conception of being and refused to admit the ontological cleft, although even he seems to be struggling with distinctions and separations imposed upon him by his predecessors in thought and the language of the New Testament itself. If we go far enough back we come to the fatal ontological cleft of the Two Worlds. Our Christological confusions have largely their origin in a sundered universe and in the idea of mediation between realms conceived as without direct and immediate relationship. If humanity and divinity, God and man, be mutually exclusive, how can there be any real unity of nature in Christ, however the proportions of the two elements in His person be varied by the Christologians?

III. The Paraclete

The Fourth Gospel introduces another mediating figure— the Paraclete. In the First Johannine Epistle (ii. 1) the term is applied to Christ as Advocate with the Father, but in the Gospel (xiv. 16, 25; xv. 26; xvi. 7) it is used of the Holy Spirit—"another Comforter"—to be sent after Christ's departure. He is the Spirit of Truth, guiding men to all the truth, and known inwardly to the souls of the disciples. "He abideth with you and shall be in you." The world cannot receive Him nor know Him. He will teach them and help them to remember and interpret the teachings of Christ. He is spoken of as separate from Christ. He bears witness of Him. He cannot come till Christ departs. He is sent by Christ, or as a consequence of Christ's petition to the Father, and is sent by the Father in Christ's name. And yet in some sense he is identical with Christ. It is Christ who comes in the advent of the Paraclete, and the Paraclete's functions merge into those of Christ's own. The term was doubtless borrowed from the vocabulary of contemporary Alexandrian thought. Philo tells us that God in determining to create the cosmos used no assistant or advocate (parakletos). In describing the vestments of the high priest, as symbolical of the various parts of the cosmos, Philo finds that the breastplate represents "the Logos which holds together and administers the universe," and proceeds to say that "it was necessary for him who was consecrated to the Father of the cosmos to use as a paraclete a son most perfect in virtue, with a view to the amnesty of sins and the supply of most abundant blessings." Thus the Paraclete seems to be conceived as a further assistant to the Logos, and distinct from the Logos. We seem to move in the region of thinking from which the Neo-Platonic idea of Emanations was born. There is also the idea of reconciliation with God after sin, in the conception of the Paraclete in Philo, as in the Johannine Epistle. In other passages the Paraclete in Philo appears as conscience in the soul of a man prompting the offender to beg forgiveness, and Israel, returning to God, possesses three "paracletes of reconciliation with the Father." These are, "God's equity and kindness; the holiness of the founders of the nation; and their own 'improvement.'" The term seems a loose personification of mediatorial agencies operating in human personality. The Paraclete's functions are those of the Spirit in Romans viii. The figure, however, lacks clear definition both in Philo and in the Johannine writings. It seems to signify one of those personified hypostases of the divine working found in Alexandrian thought, which pass so readily into the shapes of heavenly subordinates attendant upon the Supreme, and yet return as readily into reconciling and uplifting moods of the human soul.

IV

We cannot be blind to the elements of experience in all these forms and figures. We have the testimony to the soul's communion with God, and the joy, peace, strength, illumination and new life flowing therefrom. The doctrine of the work of the Logos and Paraclete is largely the outcome of mystic experience. In the identification of Jesus with the Logos there is the significance that it was through Jesus of Nazareth that the souls of men were found and the inherent possibilities of fellowship with the Father discovered. By that same message and influence the power of sin was broken in men's hearts—and to this experience the conceptions of Propitiation and Salvation through Christ are witness. One must sympathetically notice the claim of C. C. J. Webb, in his *God and Personality* (p. 167), that the doctrine of a Mediator "is a contribution of permanent value to the understanding of the spiritual world. . . . Religious experience in its most complete form presupposes a twofold relation to God to which the phraseology of a Mediator gives a more satisfactory expression than any other we can find." But in using this language we must guard ourselves from attaching a scientific or precise philosophic significance to it. Mediatorship is the conveying of truth in Plato's sense of "myth"—it suggests truth rather than states it.

V

The Book of the Revelation in its theological details belongs to the second stage of New Testament development, but in its spirit and emphasis it largely reverts to the earlier more Jewish and apocalyptic phase. The Logos doctrine is present. The name of Christ is the Logos of God (xix. 13). Christ is the "beginning of the creation of God" (iii. 14), the "Son of God" (ii. 18), who speaks of God as His Father (ii. 27, iii. 5, 21). He exhibits the characteristic double Logos relation to God, (a) as equal, for, like God, He is "the first and the last" (i. 8, xi. 6). He is "the living one" (i. 18); unlike the angels, He can be worshipped, and God and Christ apparently carry only a singular verb (xi. 15, xxii. 3); and yet (b) He is clearly subordinate to the Father (ii. 27, iii. 2, 12, 21).

The doctrine of Christ as a cosmic sacrifice finds emphasis. He loved us and loosed us from our sins by His blood (i. 5). By His death He purchased unto God with His blood men of every tribe and tongue and people and nation (v. 9). Twenty-nine times He is spoken of as the Lamb, and redemption is "through the blood of the Lamb." The process is not clearly defined, but the Pauline conception of breaking the rule of the evil principalities and powers by Christ's death and resurrection is suggested by i. 18: "I was dead; and, behold, I am alive for evermore, and have the keys of Death and Hades"—the last of the evil powers to be destroyed (xx. 14).

For the rest, the figure of Christ finds Parousial interpretation. His mediatorship is of the Second Coming type. He is to beat down Rome and the kings in alliance with her (xxx. 11–21, xvii. 12–14). The method is that of the heavenly sword (i. 16, ii. 12, 16, xix. 15). Christ is Warrior and King, Lion of the tribe of Judah (v. 5) and conqueror of the heathen world (ii. 36, xii. 5, xix. 15). The contest is set between Christ and anti-Christ; the dragon even seeks to prevent the birth of the Messiah (xii. 1 ff.), probably a form of a widespread ancient myth (Peake, *The Person of Christ in the Revelation of St. John,* Mansfield College Essays). Various other angelic agencies are involved in the overthrowing of the dragon. Michael casts him from heaven (xii. 7, 9); an angel chains him in the abyss (xx. 1, 3), and an angel holds the key of the abyss (ix. 1, xx. 1). But these angelic powers are subordinate to Christ. They are not to be worshipped as He is (xix. 10, xxii. 8, 9). On the contrary, they join in the worship of Him (v. 13).

The religious values of the book lie in the element of trust in the power of the Divine overlordship; anti-Christ is great, but Christ is greater; the stress on pure morals and worship and heroic faith, and the characteristic New Testament witness to Christ as Saviour and Lord. The weaknesses of apocalyptic hope are evident; there is the mistaken historical perspective, and the action of the world drama lies beyond all human agency, but there is a moral appeal to a fidelity which in the issue of apocalyptic events receives its sure and glorious reward.

VI

In the Johannine Epistle Mediatorship, as we have seen, takes the form of propitiation. Jesus Christ is a Paraclete, an Advocate with the Father. He is the propitiation for human sins (ii. 1, 2). He was manifested to take sins away and in Him was no sin (iii. 5). He was to destroy the works of the devil (iii. 8). God showed His love to us by sending His Son to be the propitiation for our sins (v. 10). This doctrine finds fuller expression and emphasis in the Epistle to the Hebrews. The mediating Logos passes into the figure of a unique High Priest offering a sacrifice which makes the new life of the higher world possible. Leviticism finds an Alexandrian dress, and Philonic allegorisation makes the somewhat strange combination possible.

The idea of the Two Worlds reappears. There is an ideal heavenly world, and the present world of imperfect copies, and the superiority of Christianity over Judaism—nay, the former's absolute finality—is explained by its place in the perfect world of ideal and archetype. Judaism belongs to the lower world; its work is only a shadowy copy of the upper world of realities. Christianity introduces men to this higher world through a supreme Mediator, Jesus Christ. He has the Logos features, for through Him "God made the worlds." He is "the effulgence of God's glory, and the very image of His substance, and upholds all things by the world of His power" (i. 23). In the beginning the Son laid the foundation of the earth, and the heavens were the work of His hands (verse 10). The Logos of God is living, active, sharper than any two-edged sword, scrutinising the thoughts and conceptions of the heart, and no created thing is hidden from Him (iv. 12, 13). For Him and through Him are all things (ii. 20).

Following the Pauline and Gnostic tradition, Jesus has undergone an earth-phase for man's salvation. He assumes

R

human flesh in order to break the tyranny of the evil spirits—
"that through death He might bring to nought him that
had the power of death, that is, the devil, and might deliver
all them who through fear of death were all their lifetime
subject to bondage" (ii. 14, 15). But apparently the deliverance is not effected by the Mystery methods of assimilation
of the worshipper with a deity who dies and rises, as Pauline
language suggests. "While with Paul the resurrection is
as important in Christ's work as the death, in Hebrews it
has no theological importance at all. . . . With Paul
everything is included in union with the crucified and risen
Lord and participation in His experiences. This is the very
heart of the Pauline theology, but not a trace of it is to be
found in Hebrews" (Peake's *Hebrews*, Cent. Bible, p. 32).
The mediating figure of Hebrews is the High Priest of the
heavenly order, who offers himself as sacrifice, once for all,
and thus allows men to enter into the inner presence behind
the veil (vi. 19). The mode of Christian salvation is suggested,
not by the priests of the Gentile *thiasi*, with their rites of
assimilation, but by the High Priest of Israel on the Day
of Atonement.

But the spiritually significant features of the Epistle are
found (1) in the fact that Jesus is still the centre of the
conception; every New Testament writer finds Him, in
one way or another, the One who has brought new life and
freedom to men; the theories of the process change as we
pass from writer to writer, but the significant spiritual
witness remains, and must be accounted for. (2) The nature
of the new covenant established in Christianity. The inwardness of true religion is realized. Jeremiah's dream comes
true—"I will put my laws into their mind, and on their
heart also will I write them." (3) In addition to isolated
gems of spiritual thought, serving strange and unappealing
Alexandrian arguments, we have the magnificent idea of
the "Faith-Urge" of the eleventh chapter; the saints
generation after generation are pressed forward to serve

purposes beyond their sight and exceeding the possibilities of their own achievement. They fail to complete, but they contribute, and in the eternal purpose of God others carry forward the work! They witness how we run our race and how we help to complete their labours—and the thought is an inspiration to run well.

VII

We can conceive a Mediatorship which can stimulate direct relations between God and man, inherent in human personality, to awaken the possibilities of "fellowship with the Divine," but this is different from the conception of the Fourth Evangelist and the writer of the Epistle to the Hebrews, which has behind it the idea of two separated worlds, and needing a mediator who must bridge the gulf by his nature or effect a contact through a priestly act. The idea of the fissure is not only full of intellectual difficulty of how half the cosmos can be unreal, or of how a third order of being can link the strictly unlinkable, but the way is also opened to a host of "go-betweens"—not only of Christ, but Virgin and Saints, and the idea of a Church with priestly functions, standing between earth and heaven, and granting or forbidding access. All sacerdotal claims rest upon a two-department view of the universe. The *ex opere operato* view of the Sacraments belongs to this same circle of thought. These are contacts with another world and order through priestly operation. They constitute an ecclesiastical parallel to the High Priestly action presented in the scheme of the Epistle to the Hebrews. The issue between the non-priestly and the priestly Churches is largely that between a universe, unified and organic, the soul of which is God, and an ontologically divided universe, between the two parts of which the Church somehow forms a bridge.

VIII

The term Mediator may be applied to our Lord as indicating His function of revealing in highest moral and spiritual terms the nature of God, and in leading men by His message, influence and example to a moral and spiritual harmony with God, a possibility inherent in human personality. He taught men to realise their direct relationships with the Father. He led them to repentance, to a change in their souls which allowed them to become, directly and immediately, one with God. This is a mediation which is intelligible by the operations of common moral and social law. This leads us also to our interpretation of Salvation, Atonement and the redemption of the world by Jesus Christ.

SALVATION AND ATONEMENT

God to the early worshipper was a Spirit Chieftain, capable of being displeased and angry, and manifesting this displeasure and anger by allowing calamity to fall upon his people. In human relations it was often possible to placate a displeased and angry chieftain by some gift or propitiation. He might be won over by someone interceding for the offender. Thus the ideas of propitiation and the mediations of priests came into existence in respect to the relations of man and God. The propitiation was variously regarded; sometimes it was completely unethical in its nature; sometimes a ritual propitiatory act was considered necessary over and above moral repentance. During and after the Exile, prayer, fasting, and especially the sufferings of the righteous, were regarded as substitutes for the older material sacrifices (2 Macc. vii. 38; 4 Macc. vi. 29, etc.). This idea appears in the famous Servant Passage (Isa. liii. 10).

Curiously and significantly, however, the doctrine of propitiation receives no clear support from the teaching of Jesus as given in the Synoptic Gospels. Repentance and new life are the conditions of the restoration of the Divine favour. Our Lord does not seem to have ever taught that reconciliation depended upon His own death as propitiation, although He did teach that spiritual ministration and the service of love involved suffering and sacrifice, so that the death of the Son of Man (and this may include more than Jesus, see p. 190) might be figuratively regarded as a ransom for many (Mk. x. 45). The teaching of the Acts of the Apostles agrees with that of the Synoptics. Jesus in the early preaching is described as a Saviour, but in the sense that He gives "repentance to Israel and remission of sins," even as the Baptist had done (Mk. i. 4)—that is, *by bringing about a change in the hearts of men, and in accordance with prophetic teaching, such as is found in the eighth-century prophets, pardon follows repentance.*

If elsewhere in the New Testament the propitiatory theory of the death of Jesus is to be found, we must remember the deep hold upon the Hebrew mind of the Levitical doctrines of propitiatory sacrifice; we must take account of the influence of Isaiah liii and the Maccabean passages declaring the propitiatory value of the sufferings and death of the righteous; and we must realize the relief which such a doctrine would afford the early Christians in view of the Jewish prejudice concerning the ignominious death of Jesus upon the Cross—"Cursed is every one that hangeth upon a tree." One conceives that at first the idea of the suffering Servant of God, whose death should be an offering for sin, would be taken somewhat mechanically as an identification prophecy, but sooner or later Christian thinkers would attempt to understand it and relate it to a general philosophy of life—and such attempts we have noticed (pp. 229, 258).

But in view of the very grave objections, moral and intellectual, which are naturally felt in regard to these theories of the saving and mediatorial work of Christ, one seeks to state a doctrine of Atonement which will avoid these difficulties and yet retain the vital thought of Jesus as Saviour of men. In the first place, *the idea of Atonement in its root meaning of making "at-one" with God does not necessarily involve propitiation.* That is a detail from human analogy which seems to do violence to the nature of God as "our Father," as we have come to conceive Him in and through Jesus Christ. We realise that in the parable of the Prodigal Son the character of the father is infinitely greater and nobler than that of the elder brother, who "was angry and would not go in. Therefore came his father out and entreated him." We cannot attribute the inferior temper to God, as the doctrine of propitiation would require. Nor must we regard the Atonement in the light of Levitical ritual sacrifices which had their roots in magic religion and in a false notion of sin as a material which could be transferred from place to place and from person to person by appropriate incantation. *Sin is a state of mind and must be cured by a transformation of attitude, a change of spirit, a transformation of affection and motive.*

We then seek to understand the meaning of salvation as a process of mental transformation, a "cleansing by the washing of water by the word." "And pray," comments Dr. Jowett, "in what other way can the mental habits of a life be changed? If you want to purify a man's mind, to give him a new mental attire, you can only do it by the washing ministry of new ideas. Give a man a new set and circle of ideas and you give that man a new life; and the clean sweet thought of Jesus pouring into a mind washes it like the passing of a tide over the littered sands of the seashore." Jesus saved men from their lower natures, and brought about the changed life to which every writing of the New Testament bears witness, because His teaching of word, deed and personality possessed the power of spiritual and moral transformation. This evangel did not consist merely in ethical teaching. There were those too morally broken to accept at once the evangel of a lofty code of ethical law. Christ's methods of redemption with these, the outcasts, the publicans and sinners, were those of personal sympathy, stress upon the love and mercy of God and a recognition of a higher nature even in the worst. The personality of Jesus is a precious element in the saving appeal of His message. The spirit of His life, the reason and manner of His dying, intensify this appeal. In this thought the Cross truly enters into the saving powers of Jesus, for even as the blood of the martyrs proved the life-seed of the Church, so Jesus, loving to the end and at the utmost cost, has set His seal upon the gospel of love for men. But the whole salvation must be interpreted in the light of mental and moral law, and not in terms of ritual Leviticism.

IX

We may look upon the sufferings and death of Jesus as involved in the sacrificial law of progress. The alternative to the conception of a static, formless, meaningless God is that of an active Divine Spirit, manifesting itself and showing its nature by *encountering and overcoming a cosmic opposition.* If it were as easy to rise as to fall, virtue would be unintelligible. Nature is so planned that it demands a purchase price for all noble achievement. The upward thrust of life ever brings suffering. "Every good has its birth of pain," and, because of this, moral life gains a meaning which it would not otherwise have. *Could we have realised the courage, virtue, the divine in Jesus had there been no pain and sacrifice to measure the holy passion and steady determination of His soul?* We know His love because there was a price of love to be paid. The Cross standing against the darkened sky of the first Good Friday was a symbol of the limitation whereby consecrated love and courage gain their moral values. Thus a doctrine of the Cross can be conceived which makes the death of Jesus neither sacrifice to devil nor propitiation to God. Nor is it a "satisfaction" to God's majesty or to His justice. The death of an innocent Jesus because other people have sinned hardly satisfies our sense of justice.

One remembers the old story of the village carpenter who had killed a man and was sentenced by the judge to death. His fellow-villagers asked for his pardon, for he was the only carpenter in the village, and if he were executed who would do their woodwork for them? The judge insisted that it was necessary for justice to be satisfied. The villagers realised the force of what he said, and went away. Before long, however, they returned, bringing with them a weaver. "We know that justice must be done," said they, "but let this weaver be executed instead of the carpenter, for we have two weavers in the village, and can spare one to satisfy justice." The story is worth considering in relation to the popular "satisfaction of justice" theory of the Atonement.

But our suggestion is akin to the "satisfaction" theories, although what is "satisfied" is not God's majesty or justice, but the whole scheme of manifestation by means of which He expresses in necessary conditions of limitation what He is.

Further, *in virtue of race solidarity, sacrifice has a vicarious element, to be distinguished, however, from a penal or forensic element.* If a man sins, he involves others in the consequences. He pulls back the upward movement of the race, and greater must be the sacrifices of others in order to uplift the hampered world. In this sense the sins of Christ's generation brought Him to the Cross. He hung there, a victim of the cowardice, the ignorance and hypocrisy of those who brought about His death. But there is a gracious converse. The consequences of the life and actions of a noble soul go out beyond himself. The personal conquest of Jesus lifted up a multitude of other men with Him. The world was raised to higher conceptions of life and duty. By His teaching and inspiration men were delivered from the tyrannies of their lower nature. By His stripes we are healed.

The truth in the "moral" theory of the Atonement follows : "In the Garden secretly and on the Cross on high, He taught His brethren and inspired to suffer and to die." Then, further, if the moral influence of Christ's life and death be conceived as having its culmination in a fellowship with the Divine—and the ethical factor must enter into any full and healthy process of Mysticism—we have the "moral" theory of the Atonement passing into the mystic "salvation by faith into Christ."

In this view of the Atonement we retain the facts of the reality of a salvation from sin, the seeking and saving love of God in Jesus, the vicarious sacrifice, the glory of the Cross which towers over the wrecks of time, but we save the conception of the Father from moral outrage, and we find the Atonement still proceeding in the upward struggles of the common life. In men in whom the spirit of Jesus dwells, the eternal Christ still walks the *Via Dolorosa*, still carries the Cross and wears the crown of thorns, and, lifted up, continually draws men unto Himself.

CHAPTER XIX

THE INCARNATION

I

OUR line of study has raised the specific question of how we may regard the person of Jesus in the light of these considerations. In many ways our conclusions may seem to mar those values of Incarnation which have meant so much to the consciousness of the Christian Church during its history that we have come to regard them as central and vital. It may indeed seem that our main thesis that the Love of God is sensed as a cosmic intuition (p. 231) renders superfluous any revelation of the Love of God through the historical life and work of Jesus; on the other hand, the mystic intuitions belonging to the world of Being must have their parallel facts in the processes of that world of Becoming in which we normally think, feel and act. We may *feel* the Love of God as a spiritual intuition as Augustine did (p. 82), but we want also to *trace* as we can the operations of that Love in our world of finite experience. The doctrine of Incarnation belongs essentially to the mode of Becoming, and has its specific values as such. Jesus reveals in the sectional process what the mystic feels is true of the whole. But we need to realise what is and what is not involved in such a doctrine of Incarnation, or of a Revelation of God through the historical Jesus.

Our thought has led us to disregard certain features of the Gospel biography which have traditionally been claimed as signs of the Incarnation; our analysis of the thought of the New Testament, and our conclusions as to the nature of its doctrinal development, and our rejection of some of the older theories of Atonement may seem to challenge the whole conception of the Christian doctrine of Incarnation. But this is more apparent than real. The conception of the nature of God outlined in an earlier chapter (Chap. V) provides for the acceptance of the great evangelical truth: No man hath seen the Father at any time, but Jesus, full of grace and truth, hath revealed Him.

II

Commonly the Incarnation is conceived in the parabolic form of Milton's *Paradise Lost*. In a heavenly court, remote from the world, stands God, His Son and the angels. The omniscient Lord takes pity on the ignorant, feeble, blundering world, and therefore sends His Son, with all the credentials of miracle, to bring to the world a revelation of celestial truth which the world could not otherwise discover, and to accomplish a death with certain mysterious values, delivering men from their impotence and guilt. As a parable, this may hold most valuable truth; as a statement of literal facts, it bristles with obvious difficulties. It implies a false separation between God and the world which lives and moves and has its being in Him. The scheme has a polytheistic background. The conception is theosophical rather than philosophical. But we must seek truths behind the parable. To gain these, we must conceive God in His aspect of Becoming. He is the Soul of the Universe, expressing Himself in its unfolding life, and seen and judged in the highest, holiest and best which the universe manifests. "The world is the vesture for that great Unnamed," cries Carlyle. Or we have Tennyson's dream: "The sun, the moon, the stars, the seas, the hills and the plains—are not these, O soul, the vision of Him who reigns?" Does not Walt Whitman see God in the faces of men and women, and "in all great ideas, the race's aspiration, all heroisms, deeds of rapt enthusiasts?" For the physical wonder and greatness of God we look to starry heavens and to the miracles of commonplace nature. But for the revealing of the moral personality of God we must look to the region of the universe where alone moral values can be expressed. Strictly physical nature is amoral. Even an isolated God freed from the limitations of the human struggle would be amoral. The moral character of God must be revealed in the finite conditions of human life, and only humanity can show the divinity of the character in God. There is no character without test; no virtue without opposition; no courage in a world free of difficulty and fear; no mercy and pity without need; no love without contact with other personalities and a field for the practical functioning of love; no moral victory where there is no battle. In order that God should have meaning and character in the world of Becoming He must be right in the heart of the world's struggle, hemmed round by human limitations, bearing the Eternal Cross. If by endowment of omnipotence and omniscience Jesus should be lifted out of the real human category, He would thereby be made incapable of expressing the moral Divine. This is the all-important fact about the Incarnation. The moral nature of the Soul behind the universe could only be known through a genuine life of conquest over limitations, and through grace, virtue and character, shown under the conditions of the common human lot. The creation of God, gods and demigods detached from such a scheme and principle of expression can only complicate and confuse the world-system, and go beyond all data of experience.

III

Have we, then, in the historical Jesus such a one as would have for the world this value of the Incarnation and Revelation of God? We have seen that much of the theologian's Christ has been created by first-century speculations about

Jesus—ideas of the Messiah, of the apocalyptic Son of Man, of the semi-philosophic Logos and the like. The New Testament theologians and writers were children of their own day, inheriting a mass of ideas and conceptions which were local and temporary, and quite naturally they expressed their sense of wonder and reverence for Jesus in these familiar terms of their day. There is no religious compulsion laid upon us to accept or defend these forms into which some of the early Christian speculation shaped itself. But we realise their deeper significance; *in their various ways they point impressively to the figure of Jesus, and compel us to inquire into the secret of His power and the significance of His life and work.* That impression was due to no mere thaumaturgic power; the "sons of the Pharisees" possessed psychic abilities, but they did not draw men's souls as did Jesus. Other men made Messianic claims, but wrought no such transformation of human life as that effected by our Lord. Messianic claims and apocalyptic expectations were subsidiary, accidental and passing, and yet Jesus retained His hold over the personalities of men. His influence survived the collapse of many ill-based hopes of this kind.

We can understand the appeal which Jesus made to the men of the first generation of Christians from the appeal which He still makes to the men of our own time, apart from and even despite the accretions of early speculation and the artificial interpretations of the Church. Iconoclasts have been hard at work through the ages, and have repeatedly destroyed forms of religious belief, yet the figure of Jesus remains eternally fresh and commanding. Renan finds Luke's Gospel "the most beautiful book in the world." Shelley denounces Christianity as he knows it in ecclesiastical forms and in the practice of Churchmen; for priests and clergy he has no redeeming word, yet despite this hard and largely unjustified judgment upon the Church, he speaks rapturously of Jesus as "standing in the forefront of those true heroes who have died in the glorious martyrdom for liberty, and have braved torture, contempt and poverty in the cause of suffering humanity." Such illustrations as these might be multiplied almost indefinitely. Amid the rise and fall of theological systems, Jesus retains His appeal and hold upon the hearts of men.

It is in this fact of the moral and spiritual supremacy of Jesus, His appeal and influence, that we seek the significance of all the Christocentric speculations of New Testament thought. The power which is realised to-day through the spectacle of the life of Jesus, and the knowledge of His teaching, operated nineteen hundred years ago. Our earliest witness to Christ in the New Testament is the Apostle Paul. Curiously, "of the person and life of Jesus, Paul tells us almost nothing," says Paul Wernle, "but in one sense Paul gives us more than the most exact and copious letters could give. We learn from him that Jesus was able, in spite of His death upon the Cross, to stretch forth such power through and beyond His death that a man like Paul felt himself mastered by Him, redeemed, beatified, so that his own life and the whole world was cloven by Him into two parts—without Jesus, with Jesus. This is a fact which, explain it as we will, simply as a mere fact, fills us with astonishment and with an irresistible sense of the greatness of Jesus" (*Sources of our Knowledge of the Life of Jesus*, p. 4). This is true of all the other writers of the New Testament—they have different ways of expressing their tribute, but they all *trace back to Jesus of Nazareth the transforming power which has led to newness of life, and all their various Christological theories and speculations find their significance in such gracious experience. This explains, we believe, the wonder-stories of the Infancy, the setting of Jesus in the centre of the apocalyptic hopes, the Pauline drama of salvation, sin-propitiation and cosmic theosophies. It is the reason of the greatest names of the Jewish and Gentile worlds— Messiah, Logos, Wisdom, Paraclete—being bestowed upon this Jesus of Nazareth.* His was a spiritual and moral supremacy and influence not possessed by any other contemporary.

Men beheld His grace and truth as of the only-begotten of the Father.

IV

Along these lines we have a new approach to the essential values of the Incarnation. We are unhampered by ancient speculations; at the same time, the fact of the moral and spiritual supremacy of Jesus to which they point, invites and compels speculation of our own. We must ask what is the cosmic significance of this fact and the light it throws upon the nature of that God in whom we live and move and have our being. We are conscious of a convincing and appealing historical figure, conspicuously noble and lovable, great enough to break with the harsh and narrow conventions of His time, One who ate with publicans and sinners and had ever a word of sympathy with the poor and outcast, a strong soul militant for the Kingdom of God, perfectly wholesome, natural, unconventional, independent, impatient with all forms of meanness, selfishness and hypocrisy, a Teacher appealing to all that is greatest in the soul, a Martyr willing to lay down His life that the Kingdom might come—does not such a One express in human circumstances of limitation that great spirit which must lie behind the whole universe and its processes ? Could God be inferior in spirit and character to this Prince of Glory? This figure of Jesus, full of grace and truth, is the starting-point for a fresh theological interpretation which we believe restores the genuine religious values of the Christological traditions of the Church.

The New Testament homage to Jesus found expression in contemporary categories which showed how men, conscious of the Divine in their own souls, saw God in Jesus. We may find accidental factors in the use of these categories, but the underlying instinct of seeing God in Jesus was not mistaken. The world follows a true instinct in deifying the best it knows. This is the only way of finding in finite life any tangible expression of God. God is the greatest, most precious, most impressive fact which we have found in the world—and more. In our human ignorance, we cannot tell how much more that plus may mean; that is the transcendent element; but God, at any rate, is revealed in the best which we know. We read Him from that. Men in a lower stage of culture worshipped the greatest physical objects and made gods of physical power. Divinity seemed embodied in thunder and wind and earth and sky. That same instinct led men, developed in the world's evolution, to find the expression and symbol of God in human personality at its highest. Man cannot see the soul of the universe as a concrete thing apart from the universe; man can only see it through the universe, realising it where the universe has shown its highest, noblest and greatest. Thus men rightly saw the soul of the universe morally expressed in Jesus, the Dreamer of the Kingdom, the Man of Sorrows, the Friend of publicans and sinners, the One going about doing good; the courageous, the sympathetic, the merciful, the loving; the agonised figure of the Garden; the One who laid down His life that others might have life and have it more abundantly. We see as much of the heart of God who is "Spirit," in personality at its highest, and Jesus has become for us in this way the expression and revelation of the Father, the Over-Soul "in whom we live and move and have our being."

V

Thus we arrive at a value of Jesus quite independent of the miracle element in the Gospels. It rests simply upon the character and moral greatness of Jesus. "Miracles" may or may not have happened. Their significance is entirely neutral to the Incarnation values as we have here conceived them. Nor have we any problem of the "localisation" of

God. We are not asked to suppose that for some thirty years the life and power of the universe was in some way concentrated in a single human body. Nor are we thrown into the difficulties of polytheism. We think in terms of an organic universe in which the highest in the part approximates to the soul of the whole, and expresses it. We can hold perfectly naturally the two statements "I and the Father are one"; "My Father is greater than I." We can accept the human elements in the portraiture of Jesus without questioning His Incarnation values. We do not require or expect omniscience in this prophet of Nazareth, who is described in Luke's Gospel as "growing in wisdom and stature" as a child. We believe that in some respects He may have shared the intellectual limitations of His own day. At any rate, He spoke its language and used its thought-forms. He did not anticipate the encyclopaedias. His references to Old Testament authorships need form no deadlock with the scientific conclusions of modern Biblical criticism. Nor was His revelation in the form of a theosophy of otherwise undiscoverable celestial truths. His revelation of truths as distinguished from His revelation of personality is to be sought in the expression of spiritual and moral intuitions inherent in developed human consciousness. But what Jesus primarily revealed was divine character, not intellectual truths about God, but God Himself in understandable human terms of love, mercy, courage and sacrifice. It is for man to work out as he is able his speculations concerning the facts of life; across the ages that quest for fuller light and knowledge ever proceeds, unlimited by any finalities of dogmas, creeds and systems. Here in Jesus is something more important still—the manifestation of the soul of the universe in moral and spiritual greatness of living. He brought no Athanasian Creed, but men saw God in Him, and found in Him something which set them speculating throughout the ages, and, greater still, discovering the divine life within themselves.

S

VI

Neither does this view of the Incarnation involve the divorce of Jesus from the human race. It might be possible, we grant, to set Christ so physically and mentally different from us as to constitute practically a new type, and yet have sufficient points of contact, of mental and moral affinities with us to preserve some vital degree of human solidarity. But the religious gain in this would be slight, if any. It would only be in the polytheistic interest. We should find signs of a new race of demigods in creation, still finite, limited and distinguishable from the Infinite and Eternal. On the other hand, there would be a distinct religious loss in raising a separation of this kind between our Lord and the human race. The meaning of His character would have become vague and unintelligible. We could not understand Him by understanding ourselves. The significance of His moral exemplarship would become uncertain. We should probably lose much of His inspiration. "There is no Saviour," says Mark Rutherford, "like the one who has been placed in circumstances like our own, and has prevailed. Salvation is the spectacle of a victory by another over foes like our own." Most of us must have felt that in the strange, semi-human, semi-divine creature of much popular theology there is an unreality constituting an obstacle between Him and our human hearts. One recalls the Hindu story of the three gods who sought to impersonate the human lover of a certain maiden. They put on human forms, and presented themselves as her wooers. The four men stood before her. But she saw that the eyes of three of them were bright, for they shed no tears. Their feet did not touch the ground and mingle with the common dust. But the girl's heart went forth to her true lover, whose feet touched the dust and whose eyes were dulled with human weeping. There is a similar appeal in Jesus, our Brother and Comrade, whose

feet have trod earth's pathway rough, whose lips have drawn
human breath, who was truly tempted and tried, faced the
same kind of world which we face, and overcame it.

VII

We have noted the philosophical difficulties of the conception of the Two Worlds and Mediatorship between them, which
lies behind the traditional view. But with the idea of an
organic universe, with its two aspects of Being and Becoming,
which we have sought to present throughout, we can look
not only upon the human life of Jesus, but realise something
of its cosmic and divine significance. We can see through
His life to the great Reality which He not only symbolises
but expresses. We find Him as the great Life and Power
of God coming into manifestation. Behind the historical
figure is the Good Will of the Universe, the Divine Energy,
the Spirit and Character of God. We look at a growing,
evolving world, where there is the highest expression of
its process, where the cosmic building shows its most
finished parts, and realise something of the meaning of the
whole. Because there is Love, Mercy, Compassion in Jesus
of Nazareth, we know that such a spirit rules the universe.
We could trust Jesus of Nazareth for our destinies of life and
death were He on the Throne; we could feel ourselves and
ours safe if that kindly, compassionate soul of Galilee were
behind this world and all worlds, "life, death and the great
forever." If we look not merely *at* but *through* Jesus, we have
what we want. "Jesus we know, and He *is* on the Throne!"
They that have seen Him have seen the Father.

VIII

With this realisation in Jesus of the moral values of that
Spirit of Life and Good behind the universe, we may justify

that valuable mystic conception of the Eternal Christ, known inwardly to the pure in heart, and giving a sense of inspiration, enlightenment, joy, peace and eternal life. Christendom, following Paul, has found in its doctrine of Communion with Christ the essential truth of the religious consciousness and life—the union of the soul with the Over-Soul, the individual feeling his part in the Infinite and Eternal, the section finding its harmony with the whole. It is a spiritual experience which other men may have described in other ways, for Mysticism is a phenomenon found in many faiths, but its association with Christ in our Christian language and tradition has given it a rich ethical content and appeal. It has kept the meaning of the historical Jesus living and progressive; it has kept Mysticism from shallow, unethical sensuousness. And in the light of our interpretation of the Incarnation a deep religious justification can be found for it. For is not the God whom men saw in Jesus the very God known to the seeking soul and the pure in heart—that Spirit with whom spirit can meet? "Closer is He than breathing, and nearer than hands and feet."

IX

Our general study leaves us with two or three practical conclusions: (*a*) We have realised that Christianity even in the New Testament period made amalgams with the thought of its age, which while in some respects conveying the message of Christianity, in other ways obscured and confused it. Modern methods of Bible study have allowed a healthy and necessary "regress" to the eternal and reconciling root-principles which lie in human life and personality. We have been enabled to separate the eternal truth from the temporary form, and to relieve those who seek the fellowship of faith from an alien burden of unscientific first-century thought and even elements of semi-paganism. (*b*) We believe that the search for the root-principles of faith beneath the letter of Scripture should be a factor of reconciliation between some of the sections of a divided Christendom. Our unhappy schisms exist largely because we understand neither what is living in our neighbour's faith nor in our own. We must find the basis of a larger fellowship, not in the highest common factor of our detailed doctrines, but in the underlying intuitions and experiences from which all creeds and theologies have issued, and in which they have found all the spiritual vitality which they have ever possessed. (c) Further, since Religion arises from life and experience, and not from particularist, miraculous revelation, we realise the important truth that Christianity belongs to a family of religions. Our claim for it is that in its highest and purest form it more fully expresses the religious intuitions and satisfies the religious needs of mankind than other faiths. (d) The essence of Christianity is not in abnormality, miracle, unlikeness, but in the fulfilment and completion of all the sound and healthy elements of human life. The supernatural must not be confounded with the unnatural. Reason and Faith will have no quarrel. Science is not an alternative or rival to religion, but a special application of the religious spirit, namely the love and quest of Truth. (e) Religion arises from its own region of feeling and intuition, and is primarily a matter of spiritual experience, attitude and will rather than of arguments and intellectual propositions. We need, therefore, to reconsider the old insistence upon intellectual formulae as tests of faith. The proper function of Reason in Religion is that of simplifying and interpreting the phenomena of Religion and giving useful practical application to its fundamental urgings. Its work is that of discovering the relations of Religion to other knowledge, but hardly acting as examining door-keeper for the Temple of Faith. (f) Our study should send us back to the quest of personal religion, to the first-hand experiences of those intuitions and that spiritual life which are primary and fundamental in faith. Modern religion will lay stress upon intellectual honesty, welcome new light and know that truth will never perish for the reverent in spirit, the sincere in mind and the pure in heart, but it must primarily lead men to seek the breathing of the breath of God upon their souls, to lay hold on the Eternal Christ, and to find the peace of God which passes all understanding. According to our generation, training and temperament, we may find different approaches to this vital experience of spiritual reality. We falsely limit the grace of God by insisting that religion will make its appeal to all men in identical fashion and with the same intellectual presentation.

> Some seek a Father in the heavens above:
> Some ask a human image to adore:
> Some crave a spirit vast as life and love;
> Within Thy mansions we have all—and more!
>
> G. MATHESON

INDEX

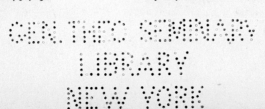

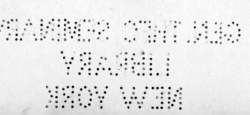